THE GREAT ANDAMANESE AND THE ONGES

Cultural Dynamism and Impact of Change

MAP WITH EXPLANATIONS: SETTLEMENT POSITIONS OF THE TWO ETHNIC GROUPS – THE GREAT ANDAMANESE AND THE ONGES

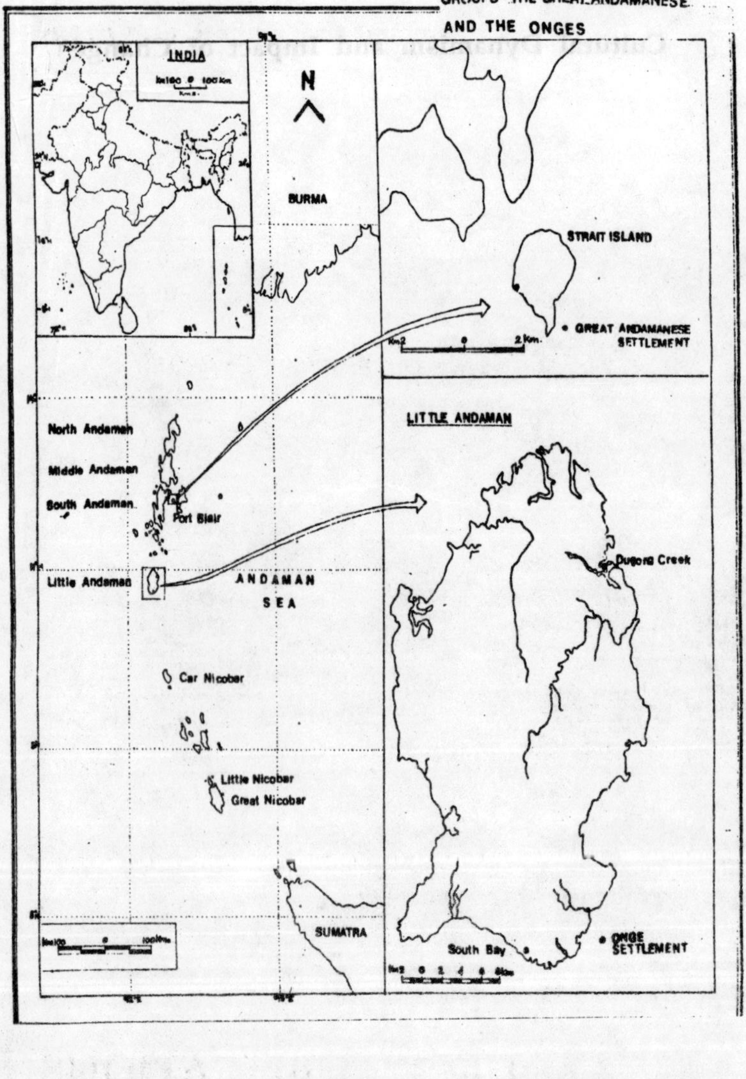

THE GREAT ANDAMANESE AND THE ONGES

Cultural Dynamism and Impact of Change

Swapan Kumar Biswas

ABHIJEET PUBLICATIONS
DELHI 110094

ABHIJEET PUBLICATIONS
2/46 Tukhmeerpur Extension
Delhi 110094
Phones: 011-22960492, 65698474
e-mail: abhijeetpublication@gmail.com
abhijeet_singh1@indiatimes.com

THE GREAT ANDAMANESE AND THE ONGES

First Published 2008

ISBN 978-81-89886-65-3

PRINTED IN INDIA

Published by J.K. Singh for Abhijeet Publications, Delhi 110094, Lasertypeset by Gaurav Graphics, Delhi and Printed as Himanshu Printers, Delhi.

Foreword

India is a vast country characterized by ecological, ethnic, economic, social, political and religious diversities. This country in the remote past, was ruled by feudal lords and kings in different areas. But for its vast landmass, limitless natural resources and very large human resources, countless treasures of the feudal lords and kings and also for many other reasons, this country attracted the attention and could raise the interest of the foreign powers. As a result India faced a number of invasions by the foreign powers like the Pathan, Mughal and others. Finally came the British who kept under its subjugation the whole of India for centuries. But the Indians fought relentlessly to get rid of the British control and earn freedom. Ultimately the colonial rulers thought of handing over the power to the Indian national leaders.

The midnight of August 14, 1947 is remarkable to every Indian as on this hour a new era began in India, and the people of India started tasting the essence of freedom after several centuries and embracing a very new phase of life. Ultimately on this day India won freedom. On that hour every Indian eagerly listened to what the first Prime Minister of Independent India spoke:

Pandit Nehru and his cabinet colleagues shouldered a great responsibility to honour the pledge and give all Indians freedom, rights and facilities through a constitution of free India. The Constituent Assembly which was already formed, met for the first time on December 09, 1946.

The honourable members of the Constituent Assembly started their exercise to present a new Constitution to the people of India. On January 26, 1950, the Constitution became effective. During the pre-independence period the colonial rulers did not undertake any significant development work for the tribal people. Rather they kept them isolated and beyond the reach of the general mass of Indian population, of course, for obvious reasons. They had bitter experience of the tribal insurrections during different periods of time. They never wanted the tribal people to get involved in the freedom movement. But in the free India our political leaders and constitution makers could not turn their face away from those downtrodden people. Realizing the deplorable condition of over 400 Scheduled Tribes resided in different parts of India and led a very miserable life for centuries past, the makers of Indian Constitution kept a number of provisions in the Constitution for the development of 400 and odd tribal groups with a considerable number of population (8.20% of the total population of India according to 2001 Census) by providing different facilities and safeguarding their rights and interests. The tribal people are enjoying all these Constitutional facilities since the promulgation of Constitution on January 26, 1950 and have been able to uplift their condition to some extent. But unfortunately the condition of all these Scheduled Tribes are not same. The socio-economic condition and educational status of the Scheduled Tribes are in general, pitiable, but the same for some are worse. The latter tribes with their 'extremely underdeveloped stage' as Shri U.N. Debar puts it, have been given the status of Primitive Tribes. There are 75 Primitive Tribes therein giving special emphasis on the impact of the State sponsored development schemes which have brought distinct changed in their life. While implementing the development programmes the administration of this Union Territory faced and is still facing some peculiar problems. While highlighting the same, the author has also pointed out the defects of the planned programmes which have created obstacles in implementing the programmes properly and fruitfully ; and people for whom these programmes are meant, have failed to reap the exact and total benefit from these development programmes. Further the processes of modernizations are driving them to nowhere. Their identity is at stake.

This book by Dr. Biswas is undoubtedly a very important document not only for the researchers and academicians who are interested to study the tribes of Andaman and Nicobar Islands, but also for the planners and administrators who have shouldered the responsibility of planning and implementing the development programmes properly for the benefit of our tribal people of India in general, and tribal people of Andaman and Nicobar Islands in particular. I firmly believe that the readers will welcome this important and interesting book by Dr. Biswas, as he has been able to present a true, vivid and lively picture of the contemporary life style of the tribal people of Andaman Islands.

Dr. M.K. RAHA
Former Joint Director
Anthropological Survey of India
Government of India

in India of which five live in Andaman and Nicobar Islands. These five Primitive Tribes are the Great Andamanese, Onge, Jarawa, Sentinalese and the Sompen. While the former four are found to inhabit in Andaman Islands, the latter one live in Great Nicobar.

Besides, the Nicobarese are Scheduled Tribe but not a Primitive Tribe. Out of the six Scheduled Tribes of Andaman and Nicobar Islands four who are found in Andaman Islands, are Negroid and the other two are Mongoloid. The population of the four negroid tribes (the Great Andamanese, Onge, Jarawa and the Sentinalese) are rapidly declining. Their very existence is at stake for varied reasons.

No doubt the Governments are trying hard for the speedy development of the Scheduled Tribes, particularly the Primitive Tribes, by giving special emphasis for their economic and educational upliftment, yet for various reasons, the rate of development is not always significant and upto the mark. The recent planned development programmes, contact with outsiders and also for some other reasons, a number of changes has taken place in the life of these Primitive Tribes. The Primitive tribes of Andaman Islands are also not out of reach of the forces. Some distinct changes have taken place in their life and activities.

The book by Dr. S.K. Biswas reveals multi-faced changes in the life of two Primitive Tribes of Andaman Islands—the Great Andamanese and the Onge, the two very important Primitive Tribes of Andaman Group of Islands who are on the verge of extinction. Dr. Biswas undertook intensive study among these two Primitive Tribal groups for a considerable time, collected very important data on the life and activities of these two tribes, assessed the impact of the development programmes on their socio-cultural life and keenly observed the nature and extent of changes in their life-style. The book has covered social, economic and political life of the Great Andamanese and the Onge and changes

Acknowledgements

First of all I express my sincerest thanks to my respected teacher and guide Prof. (Dr.) Sobhanlal Mookerjea, but for whose constant guidance and encouragement this work could never be finished.

I like to thank the Library Staff of Rabindra Bharati University, Calcutta, National Library, Calcutta, Indian Statistical Institute, Calcutta, State Central Library, Port Blair, Mr. Chinmay Chatterjee, Mr. Anil Das, Mr. Shakir Ahmed, Mr. Ramananda Biswas, Mr. Samir Biswas for helping me in their capacity as Library Assistants of the Anthropological Survey of India, Calcutta and Port Blair.

I also express my thanks to Mr. Sudhendu Chanda, Mr. Palash Chandra Coomar, Mrs. Ratna Ghosh, Mr. T.N. Ghosh, Mr. T.N. Pandit, Mr. S.A. Awaradi, my elder brothers Mr. Subrata Biswas and Mr. Debabrata Biswas for their kind suggestions, advice and moral support in my research works as well as publishing of this Book.

Moreover I shall ever remain grateful to my friends Mr. Bishnupada Mazumder, Mr. Prabir Biswas and Dr. Dhananjay Dhara, who gave me shelter in my odd times at Calcutta.

Thanks are also due to Mr. Tambolai, Mr. Kota, Mr. Nabekutti, Mr. Nao 'Raja' and senior members in the

Onge and Great Andamanese commnities, Late Dr. Amit Dutta, Mr. Sudhansu Biswas, Mr. B.K.Thakur, Miss Anjali Roy, Mr. Habil Lakra, Mr. Kanchan Toppo, Mr. Jagannath Pillai, Mr. John Thomas, Mr. Balvir Singh, Mr. Ramesh, Mr. Sajal Sengupta and Mrs. Nau. They helped me in various ways between 1988 abnd 1990 for my field study and made me communicate freely with the people of the two ethnic groups; the Great Andamanese and the Onges.

I am also indebted to Mr. Sujit Ghosh and Mr. T.P.N. Dasan who sincerely helped me in preparing the manuscript and tables through typing.

I also place on record my gratitude and thanks to Dr. M.K. Raha, for writing a Foreword for the book.

Last but not least, I must thank Dr. P.C. Coomar, Deputy Director, Census Operation of India, Sikkim and Mr. Tarun Coomar for providing those attractive photographs of Island Tribes.

I also share my thankful and loving feelings to my wife Mrs. Hema Biswas, HOD, Economics, JNRM, Port Blair who had inspired me to publish this Book.

S.K. Biswas

Contents

Present Information on Tribes of Andaman and Nicobar Islands

An expert committee on tribes has sent an alarm that tribal groups of Andaman and Nicobar Islands are under threat from a large influx of people and burgeoning construction, which have put their traditional lifestyle and the fragile ecology under stress. The entire chain of islands is known as that land of endogenous people. The author since his childhood was keen to know about the people, who occasionally visited his native place. A teenage girl along with her Grandfather (Raja of Great Andamanese) with a small country boat used to go out for hunting turtles and often anchored at the seashore of author's place. Their physical feature, complexion, language, behaviour attracted the local people and the author too. Later when he was a teacher posted at Havelock, had come across the same tribal community, who used to visit Havelock and being cheated during their bartering of coconuts by the local people. Younger groups were mostly addicted to liquor as a result of which they were easily exploited. The Great Andamanese and the Onges are the victim of so-called civilised society. All the way the author was interested to know these ethnic groups from meaningful terms.

There are in all six Scheduled Tribes in Andaman and Nicobar Islands viz., Great Andamanese, Onges, Jarawas, Sentinelese, Shompen, and Nicobarese. The tribes other than Nicobarese are classified as Primitive tribes. The welfare and development of the Nicobarese are undertaken by various departments of Administration under Tribal Sub-Plan while that of the Primitive Tribes is looked after by an autonomous body known as Andaman Adim Janjati Vikas Samiti (AAJVS), which is headed by the Lt. Governor, ANI. Which meet periodically and lay down policies and programmes for the protection, welfare and development of the Primitive Tribes. The Tribal Welfare Department provides cent per cent grant-in-aid to AAJVS out of its Annual Plan. The Great Andamanese are settled at Strait Island and their total population is 55, which includes two non tribal ladies and one non-tribal lady who has married to Andamanese tribe. Thirteen Andamanese Children are studying in Vivekanand Kendriya Vidyayalaya Port Blair. The total expenses of which is borne by the Government through AAJVS. Eighteen are engaged in various government departments.

The Jarawas tribals with the estimated population of 328 inhabit the western coasts of South and Middle Andaman Islands. Jarawas policy famed by the government of India and notified in December 2004, being implemented strictly to ensure protection and welfare of Jarawas. In order to ensure a rich resource of forest based traditional food like wild pigs, turtles, honey, fish etc. Jarawas Tribal reserve has been increased from 847 sq. km. to 1028 sq. km. (*The Daily Telegraph*, IP&T department, Andaman, 15th August, 2007). The protective activities like patrolling the Andaman Trunk Road and preventing poachers are being undertaken. Exclusive words as P.H.C. Tushnabad, Kadamtala, and G.B. Pant Hospital, Port Blair for Jarawas and other primitive tribes have been provided and such words are declared as tribal reserves to prevent curious non-tribals from interacting with them. A buffer zone of 5 km radius has been notified around the Jarawa reserve, to ensure that they do not become unwiling targets of large scale tourism or commercial activities.

The Sentinalese is a hostile Negrito tribe and remains in isolation, inhabiting an exclusive island named North Sentinal Island. They are hunter-gatherers, whose population is estimated to be 39 as per 2001 census. The Administration seeks the assistance from the Indian Coast Guard in maritime surveillance around the North Sentinal Island to ensure that no outsiders attempt to enter into the tribal reserve, thereby preventing the exploitation of the resources by the people other than the Sentinalese.

Onges: Before their settlement at Dugong Creek and South Bay of Little Andaman, by the AAJVS almost all portion of Little Andaman were occupied by the Onges. Their movement to hunt and fish with their indigenous canoes between Little Andaman and Rutland was quite regular but with their resettlement with introduction of monthly free ration by the Administration made their such moves rare. Some are engaged in the wage labour and some have been appointed in the Administration sectors. Apparently the friendship with outsiders of the Onges has proved to be too expensive for them. The total population of the Onges is 96 as per census 2001.

The Shompen is a semi-nomadic tribe inhabiting the vast area of Great Nicobar Island and thei population is estimated 398 as per 2001 census. The Administration is providing necessary medical coverage, ration articles etc. at their places totally free of cost.

Nicobari are the most advanced and populous tribes in Andaman and Nicobar Islands. As per census 2001, the total populations of Nicobari was 29469. Most of the houses of Nicobari were destroyed due to Tsunami hit the Island, on 26 December, 2004. The entire Nicobar group of islands, was worst affected by this natural calamity, which claimed thousands of lives and crores of rupee worth of properties washed. Out of 3513 dead (official record, unofficially more than 10,000) and missing person, 2955 were from Nicobar Islands. Majority of them were

Nicobari Tribals. Number of death and causalities increased due to the fact that the Nicobari mostly live in coastal areas. It also affected their traditional economy and sources of income. About 10,000 families lost their houses. About 24,000 people were evacuated to Port Blair in various relief camps. The Union Government had sanctioned crores of rupees for construction of 10,000 permanent shelters of affected families. All possible efforts have been undertaken to restore the normal traditional lives of the tribals of archipelago as soon as possible.

1

Introduction

Choice of Theoretical Construct

The study of Indian tribes has inspired many researchers for a long time. This is due to some important causes. In the first phase, India being the classic homeland of various tribes, castes, sub-castes and other forms of ethnic groups, offers a very good Laboratory for empirical observations. As the theories of statistics and their practical applications through modern process of collection and systematisation of data have been undergoing advancement on an unprecedented scale, the application of empirical analysis to the study of such large numbers of ethnic groups is highly fascinating.

Secondly, the concept of acculturation through the media of harmony, integration and assimilation is the accepted approach to the study of what is now known as 'Sociology of culture'[1]. Cultural pluralism is a major factor of the world today.

In India, the process of cultural assimilation has been undergoing through the ages. India is a unity in diversity and the variety of ethnic groups in India is due to the fact that there are large number of people who are divided from each other on the basis of caste, religion, language, rites and rituals. It is exactly for these reasons that the country adopted a federal type of Constitution balancing national unity with local autonomy in 1950.

Though the Indian sub-continent is culturally plural, unfortunately the process of cultural harmony has not been smooth and produced the desired effect of cultural unity. Different vested interests have utilized the ethnic differences, economic, linguistic, religious and cultural, to organise violent movements in different parts of India through terrorism and "ultra-leftist" methods. The agitation in Punjab, Assam, agitations like the Jharkhand or the Gorkhaland movements are well-known illustrations as to why cultural harmony and unity, integration and assimilation have not been successful in modern India.

During the Indian freedom movement, the Indian National Congress, through its great nationalist leaders, tried to lay emphasis on a broad, humanitarian, universal concept of nationalism. This philosophy of liberal nationalism was preached by great philosophers and thinkers like Swami Vivekananda, Rabindra Nath Tagore, Jawaharlal Nehru, Mahatma Gandhi, Sree Aurobindo and Subhas Chandra Bose.

After independence, however, the unequal development of various areas of India created a sense of deprivation and discontentment among the people of those areas. This economic factor has often been responsible for the growth of regionalism which has created problems like Jharkhand movement and the Gorkhaland agitation.

A large section of India consists of tribes. India, as great social and cultural anthropologists like D.N. Majumder, H.C. Chakladar, Nirmal Kumar Bose, Risley and Redcliffe Brown point out, offers a unique case where more than six hundred tribes and sub-tribes, big and small, have been found to exist in different parts of the country. Still now, no thorough cultural mapping of these ethnic groups has been produced either at the Government level or through private initiative. This has made tribal studies highly imperative for Indian sociologists. How the tribes and sub-tribes behave in the particular surrounding, how they interact, tribe against another tribe, tribe against sub-tribe, tribe against caste, caste against sub-caste, these are very important sections where tribal studies are becoming more and more relevant and timely.

The Government of India, after independence, has been following a policy of peaceful integration and acculturation of the different tribes with other ethnic groups. This has broadly been the tribal policy of the Government of India on the basis of the advice which Verrier Elwin, the great anthropologist and the official advisor to the Government of India provided to Prime Minister Nehru during the fifties of the Twentieth Century.

However, neither the different states nor the Union Government could build up a co-ordinated tribal welfare programme for India. But some progress towards this direction has undoubtedly been made.

One of the important aspects of tribal studies is the study of the process of social change. In this respect, there are two major theories—the linear theory and the cyclical theory. The main supporters of the Linear theory are Pareto, Comte, Herbert Spencer and Karl Marx himself.

The cyclical theory is mainly supported by Arnold Joseph Toynbee, the noted historian and cultural anthropologist.[2]

According to the linear theory, social change, at the different levels, including the tribal level, is due to a particular factor. Comte said that society progresses from the lower stage to the higher. The highest stage he called the "Positive Stage". At the earlier stage, knowledge is mostly based on faith and belief. As reason develops, the higher stage arrives. The highest stage is a stage of maximum perfection. However, Comte's Linear theory presupposes the supremacy of a perfect authority to enforce the level of Knowledge at the Positive Stage. Hence, critics of Comte like John Stuart Mill pointed out that Comte's theory is against cultural autonomy in a plural society.[3]

Pareto's theory of social change is also Known as the elitism theory. This is because, this great Italian sociologist and economist, declared that governments come and go out but the elitism leadership remains intact. That means he presupposed that elitism is a universal phenomenon and that the change of government and other forms of social, political and economic changes, can be explained as the broad continuation of elitist leadership in some form or other. Obviously, Pareto's Linear theory cannot be applicable to study the process of change in ethnic groups like tribes and other aboriginals. This is because such ethnic groups, due to various limitations, are extremely backward and have been victims of different types of exploitations by various vested interests within their own tribal periphery. It may even be said that in many cases, powerful elitist leaders, as agents of the vested interests, have been exploiting them for their own selfish gains.

The biological theory of Herbert Spencer is an attempt to explain the linear theory of social change in the context of the theory of evolution associated with the name of Charles Darwin. Spencer and Darwin were great Victorians. Like Darwin, Spencer declared that social evolution is an inevitable biological process operated by nature. Darwin said that "survival of the fittest" is the law of nature through what he calls "natural selection". If any species can adapt itself to changing circumstances, it can survive. Man is the most intelligent animal compared to other creatures in the world. So he has survived against huge primitive, sometimes aggressive creatures like the Dodos and Dinosaurs. Extending this theory to the conflict between ethnic groups, Spencer argued that the survival of mankind depends on the strength of one group collectively or one person individually against the others.

L.T. Hobhouse, the great British Liberal thinker and sociologist, has rightly criticised the biological theory of social evolution of Darwin and Spencer.[4] He said that if, the Spencerian theory of social evolution is accepted, then only strong musclemen alone could survive and the weaklings cannot. But it may be that such weaklings may contribute to knowledge and human civilization by their individual talents and qualities. So it is the duty of the society to protect such weak people, apart from the humanitarian question involved.

Spencer, in this context, suggested that the law of "Equal Freedom" should be applicable to the evolution of human relationships. He said, as a political individualist, taking the help of the biological theories of Darwin, that all individuals should be made equally free and should be allowed to compete with each other freely without any interference from the state or the government, or the society. This is exactly the substance of Spencer's philosophy of biological individualism under the name of laissez-faire. In fact, Spencer's theory of state-interference, or more specifically, the theory of non-interference by the state is built upon such principles.[5]

Hobhouse also criticised this point strongly.[6] He said that the so-called weaklings of the society should be encouraged by the society to develop their talents and qualities. Hence it is the social and cultural duty of the state to help them in this direction. Thus, if the biological theory of evolution of Spencer is accepted, then there is no meaning to help the backward ethnic groups of a country like India on the supposition that such people, being backward, would not be able to take part in the race of life and survive as the fittest human beings against those who are superior or forward communities.

About the cyclical theory of social change, Toynbee argued that the test of the strength of a civilization lies in the way it can cross-fertilise with other cultures through the process of cultural give and take.[7] Toynbee thought that civilizations die and are often re-born. This is because change of civilization, through social, economic, political or cultural changes, is a historical process. He illustrated his point with the classic proverb that "History repeats itself". This repetition is due to the fact that man cannot learn from the lessons of history. He is selfish and greedy and often becomes involved with the unnecessary forms of conflict.

Toynbee's theory on civilizations is highly applicable to the social and cultural anthropologists. They point out that development of weak and backward classes of the society like the handicapped ethnic groups can help the cross-fertilisation of one civilization by cultural integration or acculturation. In this context, Toynbee praised the Hindu civilization warmly, because in his opinion, the Hindu civilization, based on the Aryan culture in India, has been cross-fertilised by the process of cultural give-and-take which is the characteristic of Indian history. The view of Indian culture as a unity in diversity, is supported by great Indian nationalists and savants like Rabindra Nath Tagore, Jawaharlal Nehru, Mahatma Gandhi, Netaji Subhas Chandra Bose etc.[8]

The theory of Toynbee, is opposed to the most publicised linear, theory of social change which is supported by Marx. Both Toynbee and Marx took note of conflict as an important factor of social change. But Toynbee believed in the policy of integration of cultural differences. Hence, in this view, class-integration, and not class-conflict is the final decisive social process through which changes in society are found.

On the contrary, Marx put the greatest emphasis on the class-conflict as developed in his theory of class struggle. He thought that class-conflict is a historical phenomenon, because since the earliest times, society is divided into the haves and have-nots. This class-struggle assumed different phases in the primitive communism, in feudalism, characterised by the slave-owning society and the institution of private property. However, according to Marx, class-struggle becomes the sharpst under Capitalism. The bourgeoisie become very much powerful, taking advantage of the benefits of large-scale production under mechanical processes due to the Industrial Revolution. Finally, the bourgeoisie are thrown out by the largest number of the people in the capitalist society, namely, the proletariat who revolt against the exploitation of the bourgeoisie. The historical Socialist Revolution ultimately leads to the abolition of the class and the state. The state is abolished because it flourished under the patronage of the bourgeoisie. So, the fall of the bourgeoisie inevitably leads to the fall of the state and the abolition of class-differences. A classless society is born which is named "Dictatorship of the Proletariat".

There are many socialists and social scientists in the world who, directly or indirectly, support the Marxist linear theory of social change. But for the purpose of the present thesis, social change has been understood as a multi-casual phenomenon, not a uni-casual one. This view has been accepted by the researcher for some special reasons. First, social, political and economic policy of the Government of India is based on a policy of Mixed Economy, balancing

Private Enterprise and state intervention, the Nehruvian type of socialism which is based on peaceful evolutionary and democratic socialism favouring a Welfare State rather than a violent revolution. The Gandhian philosophy which Nehru praised and adopted in India through the Panchayati Raj and rural democracy at the grass-roots level, now functions in the villages of India. While study the progress of the two important ethnic groups of the Andaman and Nicobar Islands, namely, the Great Andamanese and the Onges, the policy-structure of the Government of India from 1947 has therefore been considered.

Secondly, the researcher has noted that the growth of socialist ideas has not yet crept in the Andaman and Nicobar Islands. Traces of primitive communism as such have not yet been found by the researcher in the areas where he moved and carried out his data-collection. Even traces of feudalism have not yet been found in these Islands in a strong and organised manner. So when the Indian Republic was proclaimed in 1950, the tribes and the backward castes and classes were suddenly in front of a type of government which believes in total socio-economic development which cannot exactly been classified in the Marxist typology as feudal or capitalist or socialist. So the researcher studied Modernity and Tradition in these Islands in a non-Marxist context. The same perspective of research with the same research focus and even the same research methodology, the researcher believes, could be applicable to the study of Modernity and Tradition as the manifestations of social change of other ethnic groups of India, tribal, caste-based, or other linguistic, religious or cultural ethnic groups.

Choice of the Concept: Modernity and Modernisation

The focus on Modernisation or Modernity has been very popular in many modern researches on the theory of social change and analysis of the practical sides through the external manifestations of this change. Modernisation is not only a composite concept but is also taken as an ideology. The compositeness of this concept may be understood when it is found to comprehend its kinship concepts like

'Development', 'growth', 'evolution' and 'progress'. Hence Modernisation covers almost the entire field of sociology.

According to Yogendra Singh, the impact of Modernisation is supposed to be almost equivalent to the ideological perspective from which the concept of Modernisation is studied. The struggle between Marxism and Capitalism is not only due to ideological differences but also on the differences of the two viewpoints for analysing Modernisation.[9]

Most of the important sociologists like Raymond Aron, Alien Tou-raine, Talcott Parsons, Ralph Dahrendorf and Daniel Bell, think that Modernisation is a post-industrial concept. On the other hand, the Marxist concept of Modernisation is mainly based on primacy of variables of the social structure. Such variables are mainly governed by economic forces, affecting the raw materials, the capital funds, the productive forces. Marx and Engels think that scientific socialism reaches the culmination through various structural changes. Each stage in the process of social change negates and replaces the other, that is, the next stage which is structurally and functionally different from the previous stage.

According to the Marxist theory, Modernisation highlights the, materialistic interpretation of history through the process of dialectics. Thus, the Marxist concept of Modernisation is also a part of the concept of Dialectical Materialism. That means Marx and Engels accepted the primacy of the conflict theory when they thought that the process of social change is mainly a process of economic change through the eternal manifestation of class-struggle between the bourgeois and the proletariat. These two classes have opposite class interests. Hence, according to the Marxists, class-antagonism is the major determinant of social change[10].

Lenin elaborated the Marxist concept of change through class-struggle further[11]. He said that the state is the major weapon through which the bourgeoisie try to exploit the proletariat. This process of exploitation, he declared, reaches the climax when Capitalism and Imperialism are combined. Thus, he said that in all mature capitalist regimes where the liberal bourgeois democracy operates, the proletariat, who are in a majority, first throw out the bourgeois state by the socialist revolution. Only when, according to the Marxists, the classless society through the Dictatorship of the Proletariat is established, can the class conflicts or the process of dialectical materialism is stopped. As there is no class-conflict, there is not any inequality or exploitation in the post-revolutionary socialist community.

Yogendra Singh thinks that "this schematic formulation of Marxist theory of social system, its relationship with the processes of Modernization and its basic ideology is indeed incomplete because the treatment is heuristic and abstract. A closer scrutiny of this treatment would also reveal the fact that modernization as a concept is quite redundant in Marxist sociology, at least it begs for its justification. It could well be equated with the notion of a Communist Society. It is here that specific historical and concrete structures that are involved in the stages of societal evolution, their modes of production, the bases of their self-contradiction and their eventual replacement, provide the backdrop for a fuller and comprehensive treatment of modernisation.

On this critical issue, however, Marxist sociology tends to lack a systematic unified perspective." In the words of Singh, "The sequence and character of the stages of social evolution and their respective modes of production, the social processes representing the unfolding of contradictions and their outcome, their universalism or historical specificity, these and several other issues in Marxist sociology are subject to intense debate and divergent interpretations"[12].

Marxist sociology talks about plurality of paradigms. But the trouble is that while even the modern structuralist sociologists like Talcott Parsons support the pluralist paradigmatic process of sociology, they do not necessarily admit that such analysis should be segmentary or a phase by phase process of analysis as is characteristic of Marxist sociology. Marx followed this type of segmentary paradigmatic analysis in his typology of Capitalism and typology of Utopian Socialism, finally declaring Scientific Socialism as the only form of revolutionary socialism[13].

Yogendra Singh has his own argument on this point. He says "Whereas much of the emphasis on paradigmatic pluralism in this (Marxist) sociology is based on a segmentary rather than systemic understanding of Marxism, there is ground for innovative interpretation and application of its methods and categories in the framework of its essential paradigmatic. This could be discerned at a level of abstraction and generality somewhat detached from specific substantive structures or culture patterns in concrete historical settings. The unity of the Marxist sociological paradigm is essentially that of its ideology. At the substantive level, societies as they are placed into historically specific settings, it is but natural that the exact forms of encapsulations of their concrete structures would differ from society to society, it may well be class structure in one society, caste in another and race and ethnicity in yet another, or it may well be a combination of several of these structural categories into adaptive new series of encapsulations generating contradictions in society."[14]

The capitalist ideology of Modernisation, though following a typological process similar to that of Marxism, is based on fundamentally different suppositions. The capitalist process of analysis presupposes an abstract rational individual as the primary unit of society. The social system, according to the capitalist ideologues, is pulled towards stability or equilibrium on the basis of the rationality of a particular type of situation which finally resolves the different motivations of different individuals. Although, sociologists supporting the capitalist system like Werner Sombart admit that human motivations may often come into conflict, they assume that they are finally systematised by the social system through the conflicting process of Social Statics and Social Dynamics[15].

At this point, the multi-paradigmatic capitalist and Marxist sociology differ with each other. Both suppose the realist hypothesis that social change is multi-causal and, therefore, multi-paradigmatic. But Marxist sociology assumes only the conflict theory as the valid hypothesis explaining social change. Capitalist sociology, on the contrary, accepts the duality of the Conflict Theory as well as the Theory of Cooperation as the valid hypothesis for sociological analysis.

Yogendra Singh, therefore, concludes his discussion on the debate between Modernity and Tradition recording the

Third World position. He says,[16] "Modernization in the Third World nations is not only a means of economic and social development but also a process for the projection of their cultural self-consciousness and national identity. The ideology of modernization which appeals to these nations is sharpened by the sense of history, the background of colonialism and the constant threat of neocolonialism. The Capitalist ideology of modernization being devoid of the base in history, and being doubly vitiated by the role capitalism plays in the expansion of the 'metropolis' and the exploitation of the 'colonies', does not appeal to the intelligentsia and elite of these nations and is highly suspect. The Marxist ideology has comparatively greater appeal, but only in its reformulated and innovative form, a form which conforms with the national cultural ethos. Hence, Marxism as a modernization ideology in most Third World nations provides a canopy under which along with some of its essential principles, a lot of local, cultural, symbolic and emotional urges could be sheltered for self-assertion of national identity." Singh admits that the problematic of Modernisation in the Third World countries like India is ideological, in the sense that it becomes a value-based term covering different processes of economic growth, application of science and technology, formulation of a system of economic planning commonsurate with a system of economic planning. The preference which India in particular has shown is on the liberal, democratic planning with a view to building up India as a progressive, liberal, democratic, social service state or what is known as a 'Welfare State'. Like Robson and Titmuss, Singh thinks that a model for Modernisation might be built up independent of the two opposite models—the Marxist and the liberal democratic.[17]

However, this so-called independent model for Modernisation, according to the present researcher, is another name for the liberal democratic, capitalist model for Modernisation. This is because such a model is based on values like liberal, parliamentary democracy, individualistic constitutionalism, mass-participation or populism and socialist egalitarianism.[18]

S.N. Eisenstadt, the foremost exponent of the concept of Modernity, thinks that the concept of Modernisation, as a concept of Development, has followed classical sociology in the sense that the West, that is Europe, went through a steady phase of Modernisation from the times of Christianity[19]. The most important of the three phenomena, which greatly changed the tradition-bound society into a relatively modern society, were the Renaissance, the French Revolution of 1789 and the Industrial Revolution in England during the last part of the 18th century. These three phenomena, were not isolated, but they became pervasive, because their affects, social, political, religious and cultural spread over almost the whole of Europe. Thus, the Renaissance of Italy became a European affair, almost revolutionary, in its impact. Humanist sociology became a prominent feature of the Renaissance. With Martin Luther's Protestantism and other forms of anti-establishment trends, the Renaissance brought its distinct sociology of peaceful, organised protest of the people[20].

The social philosophy of Auguste Comte was the natural outcome of the French Revolution. Comte believed that society becomes more and more modern, after crossing the stages of superstition, finally reaching the most rational phase of knowledge and outlook as epitomized by the stage of Positivism. Hence, whenever, society tends to change from superstition to reason, Comte would think that it is progressing and thus reaching the stage of Modernity.

The Industrial Revolution, with its emphasis on applications of science and technology to production developed its own sociology. Capitalism, according to leading social and political thinkers like Towney, Sambert and Schumpeter, was the natural outcome of the industrial society based on Capitalism. The capitalism system involved many socio-economic changes like application of machine to production, reducing time, labour and cost of production. Durkheim and Max Weber developed their concepts of sociology in the context of the socio-economic innovations of the capitalist system[21].

Eisenstadt, after surveying the history of Sociology of Modernisation, concludes that Modernisation is not any particular concept of a particular period. It is a part and parcel of the history of civilization proving the tendency of the individual to move from a particular condition and status to a better standard of living and culture. Hence, according to Eisenstadt, the main characteristic of man is that he is not only a social animal, as Aristotle pointed out, but he is a progressive and rational being also. He always tends to follow the culture of self-improvement and self-development. If a particular group of people like the Indian tribes, cannot follow the eternal cultural pattern of man for self-improvement and self-development, it is because there are certain great impediments due to environmental, that is, ecological limitations. If these limitations can be removed by a better planning and orderly, systematic process of change by a democratic, liberal, well-intentioned government, the handicapped people can become better as a modern group. Here the government and its policies would act as the modernising agents. This field-study on the Great Andamanese and the Onges has been based on these positive assumptions of the concept of Modernisation which experts like Eisenstadt have projected.

It must be understood that Modernisation is not a very smooth and easy process. Eisenstadt, himself, talks about "the Dynamics of Tradition" in this connection[22]. By this he means that through charisma of leadership and the rationality of the time function, a conservative trend is accepted by a group of people so as to construct a social and cultural reality. In India, for example[23], the caste system has not only isolated a particular caste from the higher sections within the caste-hierarchy, but also from the large number of tribesmen in India. Hence, caste in India has laid to a rigid system of social stratification where the social structure has developed an in-built tradition of resistance to change. Such division of the society cannot be considered as a system of pseudo-reality, because a long process of Tradition has generated a type of acceptance of the reality so much that it has become a part of the collective unconscious which Sigmund Freud pointed out long ago[24].

In fact, Eisenstadt himself speaks about Modernity as "a new type of great tradition"[25]. In the case of India, he thinks that the race for Modernity can be seen as a parallel course as it is found in the PRC (People's Republic of China). In both cases, he says, considering the massive area of society and the large number of population who have been clinging to the almost Totemic process of Tradition and superstition, the process of Modernisation is bound to be "gradual". What Eisenstadt might also have said is that this process of "hastening slowly" in the case of Modernisation is not a process confined to PRC and India today but has become almost a Third World Strategy. Even within the limitations of the massive nature of the problem in PRC, India as well as other Third World countries, Eisenstadt admits that the adaptability of the people undergoing the stages of Modernisation from the restrictions of a Tradition-bound society, is quite commendable[26].

In another context, Eisenstadt points out that the most important difficulties which beset the agents of Modernisation in countries like India is the problem of demolishing the structural monolith of customs, practices, beliefs and superstitions[27]. That means tradition has been deeply rooted in such societies as that of India and the problem is highly complicated by the structural diversity in the society. Hence arises, according to Eisenstadt, the need for orientations of protest, systemic transformation of the social structure, orientations of the elitists to make them perform the role of modernising agents, so that the growth in Modernisation can be sustained.

Eisenstadt thinks that the sustained growth in Modernisation can be ensured if the Modernisation process is developed on certain phases of development. In this connection, he points out that the rigidity or flexibility of the social structure, the ideological transformation and cohesion of elites are some of the features on which growth in Modernisation depends[28].

Choice of Methodology

The field survey of the researcher covers a period of over two and a half years from 1988 to 1990. During this period, he visited three selected spots several times in a year, where the Great Andamanese and the Onges live. The period of his stay at the spots varied from one month to three months at a time. Since the area is protected under the "Aboriginal Protection Act of 1956", as an area of primitive tribals, the researcher got "tribal pass" from the issuing authorities of the Andaman and Nicobar Administration.

Strait Island is a tiny, isolated island, which is the permanent place of the Great Andamanese. The researcher visited their island from the Neil Island, is the homeland of the researcher, a distance of 40 k.m. which one covers by ferry boats. The Onges live in Dugong Creek and South Bay are two isolated and remote corners of the Little Andaman Island. On an average distance of these two places is 36 k.m. from Hut Bay, the headquarters of Little Andaman. The researcher covered this distance by foot or country boats. Little Andaman is a big, isolated island, a distance of over 100 k.m. from Port Blair, the headquarters of the Andaman and Nicobar Islands, which one cover by ships. At the initial stage of the field survey, the researcher faced language difficulty in the case of the old Onge men and women. The youngsters and present leaders of the Onge community, however, know Hindi well as a link language. Moreover, most of the old individuals are naturally very conservative. Thus they mostly tried to avoid to speak and did not like to open their hearts to the researcher. After frequent visits, he won their confidence. The language difficulty for communicating with the respondents against the questions was overcome with the help of the field staff of the Welfare Agencies and their community leaders. Where the researcher was unable to obtain answers to the questions, he used the observation method to collect the relevant information. He faced no such language barrier from the Great Andamanese. Fortunately, he has got some advantages as he was brought up in the Andaman island since childhood and inhabited in this Union Territory since then. That is why he had some extra advantage in freely mixing-up with the people of these two ethnic groups. From his childhood, he was attracted to their uncommon physical features, language, way of living and habits. These certainly created some curiosity for him. Moreover, he thinks that though the tribals seem to be docile, honest and simple, they are reluctant to speak out. This is perhaps due to their past painful experience of exploitation by strangers from outside. Often the non-tribals look down upon them and mention them as "uncivilized". Therefore, the researcher faced some problems to collect first hand knowledge from them at the initial stage of his survey.

For the present study, the researcher has adopted the method of field survey as also the case study method. The data of the study have been collected both through primary and secondary sources. The primary data have been collected from the field survey through direct questionnaire basis involving adults of the two tribal communities surveyed—the Great Andamanese and the Onges. The questions related to the various aspects of problems of Modernisation. Since most of the tribals are illiterate and ignorant, the researcher has taken the easiest method to obtain maximum first hand knowledge from the individuals. Most of the questions were made on "yes!" or "no!" basis, also given the option to answer the questions expressing their specific opinions.

The secondary data have been collected with the help of both published and unpublished government documents and those of private researchers. Moreover, information from some case studies was also collected from the staff of the Welfare Agencies who are directly and indirectly related to the tribesmen. To acquire better knowledge about the past and present life and culture of the tribals, some questions were framed for old and young individuals separately to construct the hypotheses and distinguish between the opinions of the two generations, specially, to mark the changing positions of the women in their societies.

The question may arise as to why the researcher has chosen these two ethnic groups for the field-study. The reasons are stated below.

First, at present the population of these two ethnic groups is few in number, but once they were the second most populous group amongst the ethnic groups of these islands.

Secondly, they are the original inhabitants of these islands, living in this Archipelago from time immemorial.

Thirdly, they belong to the primitive negrito stock which is considered as a rare human species. They still hold some original paloelithic socio-cultural identities in them.

Fourthly, now they are about to be extinct. As soon as they have come into contact with the outsiders, their number of population has been dwindling very sharply due to their infection with venereal diseases, change of environment and also due to the atrocities of the "civilized" persons.

Earlier Research Work Undertaken by Others

There are many administrators and scholars who carried out researches on the Great Andamanese and the Onges along with other inhabitants of these islands during British rule. In 1869, the ethnographic study on these communities started and it came to cover geography, languages, ethnography and pre-history of the tribes in the context of the colonial interest of the Britishers. The Well-known works of this category are : F.J. Mouat, *Adventures and Researches among the Andaman Islanders* (1863), M.V. Portman, *History of Our Relations with Andamanese* (1889), E.H. Man, *Aboriginal Inhabitants of the Andaman Islanders* (1932), *The Nicobar Islands and Their People* (1933). Their works suffer from some limitations as the researchers did not get cooperation from the hostile tribesmen during the field-study. In fact, almost all the earlier accounts were made by the administrators or travellers. Before A.R. Radcliffe-Brown's *Andaman Islanders* (1922), no scientific and descriptive work was published on these people. Brown, as a trained German anthropologist, performed an outstanding study on the Great Andamanese. Previous works were of a general nature abounding in interesting descriptions of the tribesmen[29].

However, it was only after independence that serious research began to be undertaken by the Indian as well as foreign anthropologist scholars. Their works were, to some extent, limited to cultural, linguistic, social, physical or genetic sides of the field of anthropology. The scholars referred to are Lidio Cipriani (1953), Pranab Ganguli (1953-57), E.G. Buchi (1955), R.C. Nigam (1962), R.S. Mann (1984), B.K. Basu (1987) and D.K. Chakraborty (1987)[30]

In the broad perspective of modernisation and changing socio economic orders, the basic objective of this study has been to observe the problems of the two ethnic groups—the Great Andamanese and the Onges. The researcher, to some extent has tried to draw some conclusions on the basis of new hypotheses in connection with their present social, economic, political and cultural changes along with the impact on health, education, behaviour and environmental conditions due to state planning. Since independence, both the central and the local government have been undertaking several Modernisation programmes for these two ethnic groups. The intention of this study is to find out the main hinderances to the process of Modernisation. The main endeavour of the researcher has been to highlight the problems qualitatively, not quantitatively so that conclusions may be drawn. That is why he has taken these two small ethnic groups as a unit or model for hypothesis and field-study. What types of problems the Administration faced during the time of implementation of welfare measures for these two communities have been studied. The object of the researcher is to find out the main defects of the process and objectives of implementation of these plans and programmes. The researcher has sought to study the reactions of the people of these two communities in relation to the plans and programmes for mordernization introduced by the Government for these two ethnic groups. Based on the originality of the field study, focus has been made on the broad spectrum of social and cultural anthropology relating to the Great Andamanese and the Onges, the central theme being mordernising.

Main Research Focus: The Land and The People: Socio-Ecology

Among the Union Territories, the Andaman and Nicobar constitute the single largest Union Territory in the Indian Republic. This territory was declared a Union Territory on November 1, 1956 under the jurisdiction of the Indian Union. According to the 1981 census, 226 Islands have been divided into two districts namely, the Andaman group of Islands and the Nicobar group of Islands for administrative convenience. The Andaman group of Islands consists of a chain of Islands said to be 204 in number and the Nicobar group of Islands consists of a chain of 22 Islands. Out of these 226 Islands, only 33 Islands are inhabited by the people in which 20 and 13 Islands are located in the Andaman district and the Nicobar district respectively[31].

Nomenclature of the Islands

The position as well as the nomenclature of the Andaman and Nicobar Islands are extremely obsecure. Many scholars have tried to find some reasonable answers and put their opinions regarding the nomenclature of these Islands. From the writings of Clude Ptolemy (2nd Century A.D.), the position and existence of the people of these two groups of Islands are known for the first time. He referred to these Islands in his map, where he indicated the Islands of Buzacata to be the place of the present Andaman Islands. He reported that these Islands produced high quality of shells and the naked inhabitants of these Islands were called *Agmatea*. Chinese Buddhist monks—Fa Hien (6th Century A.D.) and I-T'sing(7th Century A.D.) also mentioned in their travelling descriptions about the land and people of both Andaman and Nicobar Islands. In the 9th century, in the notes of Eus on the Arab countries some references about the Andaman Islands, India and Ceylon could be found. The present Andamanese were then called the *Angamanians*. From the writings of other Travellers like Marco Polo (1286 A.D.), Friar Oderic (1322 A.D.) and Nicolo Conti (1430 A.D.), it was known that the people of these Islands were very ugly and behaved like brutes who were supposed to be cannibals. Nevertheless, these Islands were enriched with natural resources and was named *"Islands of Gold"*. Some more details about the Andamanese could be found in the writings of Marco Polo, where he described *"Angamanian"* as a very long Island. The people were without any 'King' and were no better than wild beasts. According to Marco Polo, the men of these Islands had heads like those of dogs, and teeth and eyes likewise and they were most cruel cannibals[32].

Some scholars think that the name *"Andaman"* is a corrupt form of the name *"Hanuman"* or *"Monkey People"*, referred to in the Sanskrit *epic* the *Ramayana*. Malayans were the first people who spread some knowledge about Andamans into different parts of the world. They used the word *"Handuman"* which seems to be a corrupt form of the word, *"Hanuman"*[33].

The Nicobar group of Islands on the other hand, is an ancient place along the international sea route for trade from Colombo to Malaysia, Indonesia and Sumatra. The voyagers referred to these islands as the *"Land of the naked"*. In the Indian tongue, this term took the form of *"Nakkavar"*, later it was referred to as "Andaman and Nicobar" in the Gazetteer (1909). In this connection the vital point is that the medieval Arabic name *"Lankha-i balus"* is more likely to be either a mistranscription or misapprehension of either *"Nakabar or Nakkavar"*. Mathur (1967) claimed that the hero of the *epic, Ramayana,* God Rama, was supposed to have passed through these islands during his period of exile. Foreign travellers and traders have referred to the position and existence of the Andaman Islands and have referred to similar descriptions on the Nicobar Islands along with its inhabitants. Clude Ptolemy (2nd Century A.D.) along with two Chinese travellers known as Fa Hien (6th Century A.D.), I-T'sing (7th Century A.D.) mentioned in their travelling experience about the position of the Nicobars. The Chinese referred to these Islands as *Lo-Jan-Kuo* (Land of naked people), a name found in the writing of I-T'sing, who was a Chinese Buddhist monk. In A.D. 607, Yong-ti, the Emperor of China, sent an envoy to Siam who reached the Nicobar then spoken of as the country of *Rakshasas,* meaning demons.

He reported that the inhabitants were very ugly, having red hair, black bodies, teeth like those of beasts and claws like those of hawks[34]. Apart from these above evidences, in the 13th Century, Marco Polo, and in the early 14th century, Friar Oderic mentioned about these islands in their valuable travelling records. Some Indian scholars like S.K. Gupta (1951) and K.K. Mathur (1967), claimed that in 1059 A.D. these islands were the part of the overseas kingdom of the Chola King of Tanjore.

Geographical Location

The Andaman and Nicobar Islands are the largest Union Territory in India, having an area of 8249 sq. km., in which the Andaman group of Islands covers 6408 sq. km. and

Nicobar group of islands having 1841 sq. km. These islands exist in the midst of the Bay of Bengal, a distance of 944 k.m. from the mouth of the river Hooghly, 192 k.m. from Cape Negrais in Burma, about 145 k.m. from the northern extremity of Sumatra and about 1120 k.m. from Chennai. The Nicobar group of Islands lies to the southernmost tip of Andaman group of Islands. The Andaman group of Islands is separated from the Nicobar group of Islands by the 10 degree channel.

The extreme length and width of the Andaman group of Islands are 350 k.m. and 51 k.m. respectively, while the Nicobar group of Islands has the maximum length and width of 260 k.m. and 58 k.m. respectively[35].

The Andaman group of Islands lies between 10° to 30° North Latitude; and between 92° to 94° East Longitude[36]. The Nicobar group of Islands is situated in the South East of the Bay of Bengal between 6° to 10° latitude and between 92° to 94° longitude. Landfall Island is the northernmost island in the Andaman group of Islands. The Andaman group of Islands is divided into three divisions, namely North Andaman, Middle Andaman and South Andaman. Besides this, there are innumerable small islands like Ritchie's Archipelago, the Sentinel Islands and Little Andaman Islands with outlaying volcanic islands, the Barren and Norcondum are in the Andaman sea. The Southernmost island of these two groups of islands is Great Nicobar. And the extreme southern point of Great Nicobar (including in India) is previously known as Pygmalian Point and now it is renamed as Indira Point. This point is about 151 k.m. from Pulo Brass off Achin Head of Sumatra.

The Andaman group of islands is generally hilly and undulating. The main hill range runs from North to South. The important peaks are Saddle Peak (2400 feet), in the North Andaman, Mount Harriet (1678 feet), in the South Andaman. The Mount Thulier (2105 feet) and Empress Peak (1420 feet) are the highest peaks existing in Great Nicobar and in Kamorta respectively in the Nicobar group of Islands. The important rivers in the Andaman and Nicobar Islands are Kalpong river in the North Andaman and Galatheo and

Alexandra in the Great Nicobar.

The Andaman and Nicobar Islands form a part of the continuous ridge which runs from the Cape Negrais of Burma through the Preparis and Coco Islands to the Andamans and continues further to the Nicobar and Sumatra. The whole ridge has a geological affinity with the Arakan Yoma Range of Burma and Sumatra and Java. This ridge is separated from the Nicobar group of Islands and from other continuous islands by a strait of say 400 fathoms deep and 120 k.m. wide. The available flora and fauna indicate that these islands must have formerly been attached to the mainland or once part of a continental land mass during the geological era of Mid-Tertiary (about 25 million years ago).

Climate

The climate of these islands is tropical, particularly the islands which lie near the equatorial region in the south. Naturally, the climate of the Nicobar group of Islands is tropical, hot and wet throughout the year. It is the sea breeza and heavy rainfall which keep the temperature pleasant.

The Islands have broadly four major seasons[38].

(1) Cool season (December to February) when the maximum mean temperature is 94° F and minimum temperature is 72° F.

(2) The hot season which lasts from March to mid-May and the maximum mean temperature is 100° F and the minimum mean temperature is 76° F.

(3) The monsoon season when Southwest Monsoon lasts from May to Mid-October, bringing the maximum rainfall. During this period, the maximum mean temperature is 93° F and the minimum is 70° F.

(4) The post-Southwest monsoon period, popularly known as the cyclonic season which starts from Mid-October to November. The maximum mean temperature and minimum mean temperature vary in between 93° F and 70° F[39].

The Average rainfall is 323.4 centimetre (98.20"). The temperature varies throughout the year between 90° F and 100° F.

Humidity

The monsoon influences the humidity of the Island atmosphere. During the South-West monsoon, the average humidity is 90%. The lowest humidity occurs between December and February, when its varies from 72% to 75%. The annual variation of the humidity is thus about 15%[40].

Soil

The soil of Andaman and Nicobar groups of Islands is immature and not very thick (about 4"). Three types of soil are found in Andamans.

(1) The hilly region soil is low organic, rich in clay and yellow in colour, the texture is clayey.

(2) In the valley region, the soil is rich in silica and blackish in colour.

(3) Coastal region soil is highly saline in character giving rise to halophytic types of vegetation. The texture of the soil is coarse[41]. The Nicobar group of Island's coastal plain soil is sandy but the soil of the central part of the Islands is similar to the Andaman Islands. The soil is suitable for plantation of red oil palm, rubber, spices, betel-nuts, cocoanuts, cotton, fruits and bananas. The soil of the plain land in the Andaman group of Islands and Great Nicobar in the Nicobar group of Islands is suitable for paddy and vegetable production.

Flora and Fauna

The natural vegetation of the Andaman and Nicobar groups of Islands is unique in India, showing affinities to the vegetation to Assam and Burma in the north, Thailand and Malaysia in the east and Sumatra and Java towards the south. The very interesting feature of this flora is the availability of over two thousand species of vascular plants in these Islands. Three main types of forests are found in the Andaman group of Islands.

(1) Evergreen forest, which is concentrated in the regions of moist valleys of the fresh water streams and also on the high-hills. Principal trees available in these

forests are Garjan (*Dipter ocarpus*), Black Chuglam (*myristicamani*), Lalchini (*Calophyllum spectabile*), Toungpeing (*Arto-carpus-chaplasha*), White Dhup (*Canarium euphyllum*).

(2) The Deciduous forest, which exists in the lower and more gentle slopes of the hills. The trees found in the forests are: Padak (*Pterocarpus dalbergiodes*), Koko (*Albizzia Lebbok*), Papita (*Stereulia companulata*), White Chuglam (*Terminalia bialata*), Didu (*Bombax Chaplasha*), Pyinma (*Layerstramia hypoleuca*) etc. Beside these well-known trees, there are several other trees found in these two forests. These are Badam (*Terminalia procera*), Lal Dhup (*Parishiainsignis*), Marblewood(*Diospyros marmorata)*, Sea Mohwa (*Mimusops Litteralis*) etc.

(3) The mangrove forest, which is widespread over almost all the coastal region along with the estuaries of many creeks in the belt. The important species found in these mangrove forests are *Bruguiera gynorhiza*, Rhizophers Conjugate and Mucronata[42].

The Islands of Nicobar are covered with dense forest except Car Nicobar in the Nicobar group of Islands. Some valuable commercial timber is also found in these forests. These are available in the Andaman forests. Thousands of varieties of trees are reported to be found in these forests but these are not important from the revenue points of view. Apart from the commercial and non-commercial trees, various kinds of canes, bamboos and medicinal plants are also found which are commercially useful.

Fauna

Both forest and sea of the islands are enriched with various varieties of common and rare species. Plenty of wild boars and deer are found in these forests. The endimic species are: Norcandum Hornbill, Nicobar Mega-pode, Andaman Teal, Nicobar Pigeon, Andaman Cat Snake, Nicobar Legless Lizard, Wild goats along with Iguana, Huge Pythons; various types of venomous and non-venomous snakes are also found in these islands. Monkeys are found only in Katchal and Great Nicobar Islands.

The Andaman and Nicobar sea is full of marine species and sea weeds. There are various and huge types of sea-fishes and sea-creatures like sardines, promfrets, shark and prawns, turtle, lobsters, crabs, dugong, crocodiles, tuna, turbo, octopus, swordfish, dolphins etc. Edible fishes are also available in the coastal areas, creeks and open sea.

People of the Islands

The Union Territory of Andaman and Nicobar Islands is populous, inhabited by different ethnic groups both tribals and non-tribals. Among these ethnic groups, the six Scheduled Tribes, namely, the Great Andamanese, Onges, Jarawas, Sentinlese, Nicobarese and the Shompens are constituted as the "original inhabitants" of these islands, and others are considered as the immigrant groups. The most interesting feature of these islands is that the tribals of Andaman group of Islands are racially negritoes, while the tribals of Nicobar group of Islands are mongoloid in race. According to their stages of civilization or nature of socio-cultural background, the aborigines of Andamans along with the Shompens of Great Nicobar Islands are called "primitive tribes".

Apart from these six tribal groups, there are several groups having different ethnic background, who came and settled in different periods of time in the Andaman and Nicobar Islands. However, it is a matter of controversy to the anthropologists, ethnologists and social scientists about the origin of these four negrito ethnic groups of Andamans. Likewise, their migration story is mysterious and confusing. The same negrito people are also found in some parts of South East Asia, for example—Semang and Sakai of Malaya, the Veddas of Ceylon and the Tapiro of New Guinea. According to Cappieri (1974), the Andamanese, Semangs of Malaya Peninsula, Aetas of Philippines, some primitive Indian ethnic groups and some Pygmies of New Guinea are very ancient races. He tentatively assumed that the Andamanese form a branch of the negrito group which is a sub-race of Oceanic Negrito[43]. Other scholars like Dobson (1874), reported that the present Andamanese are the descendants of a group of shipwrecked Portuguese negro slaves[44]. But this story is controversial on the consideration of Cipriani. Cipriani (1951), thinks that the Negrito people of Andamans have a great diversity, physically and culturally, distinguishing them from the people of Africa. He proves that the Kitchen middens date back to millenniums, that is, long before the arrival of the Portuguese anywhere in Asia[45]. Sarkar (1953), points out that one possible solution about the existence of Andamanese descendants is the assumption that the migration effected through the continuous land bridge[46]. Temple (1901), mentioned in his report that the stature and pigment are similar both among the Semangs and the four negrito groups of Andamans. The bows and arrows used by the Semangs are identical with those used by the Onges, all of whom lead a typical nomadic life. Hunting and collecting activities are the same as those of the negritos of Andamans and of Semangs and Aetas[47]. Von Eickstedt, a German anthropologist, also mentioned that the Onge, Jarawa and the remaining Andamanese represented two different layers of primitive negrito races. He further stated that among the Onges of Little Andaman prevailed a somatic influence of Arabs and people of other alien origin, whereas, the Great Andamanese possessed a considerable mixture of Burmese and other species[48].

Similarly, the Indian school of thinkers made an attempt to trace the origin of Andaman negritos in the Hindu Mythology. Gupta (1951), said that according to the *Ramayana*, the Andamanese are *Kiratas*. "These *Kiratas*", he declared, "have been described in our epic literature as shiny black, with a copper coloured head of hair *(Tamra-murdhaja*), bulging eyes and strong teeth. The description of this tribe, recorded several thousand years ago, holds good to-day. All these tribes have copper coloured, curly short hair growing as it were in separate insulated tufts". He further observed "The aborigines of Andamans are the same people who, in the dim past, inhabited marshes of Bengal, the uplands of Santhal Pargana or the dense forests of Burma and Malaya. They are of that race of hunters and fishers who practically ruled this part of the world, away from the ravages of the *Purusada* (Cannibalistic) Rakshasas. The local tribes had either drifted away to these islands in their frail craft or saved themselves somehow during the cataclysm[49]".

According to Andamanese mythology, the islanders are the creatures of *"Puluga"* (Supreme Being). They also carry the idea that "Puluga" made the world and a man named "Tama" and a woman named "Chlinaelewadi" who gave them dialect and sustenance in life. Their union produced the present survivors of the Andamanese. Another story recalled that a pregnant lady was created by "Puluga" and she was landed at Kyd Island, where she gave birth to several male and female children, who subsequently became the forefathers of the present race[50].

The Nicobarese believe that they had been living in the Archipelago of Nicobar from time immemorial. They are Mongoloid, having a similarity with the people of South East Asia. According to Barbe (1846), the Nicobarese and the people of the sea-shore of Sumatra belong to the same race. Bonnington (1932), referred to them as a branch of Mon race. Temple (1901), pointed out that they are immigrants to the land thay now occupy. They migrated before the Christian era from greater India, the land now occupied by the Burmese, the Talainy (Mons), Shans and Malayans[51]. Whitehead (1924), reconsidered them as an offshoot of the Mongoloid race[52]. Temple (1901) further commented that the Nicobarese seemed to be the descendants of the Indo-chinese race as distinguished from the Tibeto-Burmese and Malayan tribes. But the Nicobarese have their own folklores about their origins. The popular mythology is that a pregnant Burmese princess, exiled by her father, due to her unnatural connection with a dog. Later, she landed upon the shores of the Nicobars and gave birth to a son. She married her son and the result of their union was the birth of the Nicobarese. That is why the Nicobarese believe in the canine origin of their race[53]. Therefore, they are supposed to be descendants of this incestuous or Oedipal union. The elderly people of Car-Nicobar claimed that they were a group of exiles from Tenasserim coast of Burma, who had to leave that land in the wake of a violent revolution[54]. Man (1886), thought that the Shompen of Great Nicobar were the original stock of the Nicobarese. Kloss (1903) remarks that the Shompen are the admixture of the Andamanese. The Andamanese who came here and were unable to return, mingled with the

Shompen. He also mentions the second possible theory according to which some Dravidian mariners came to the eastern Archipelago for trade and got stranded. They later mingled with the local (Shompen) people. According to the Census of 1931, the Shompen appeared to be totally different from other Nicobarese and the male possessed the distinct features. Coastal tribes exhibited all the characteristics of a mixed Malayan race[55].

Apart from these aborigines of the Union Territory, several non-tribal and tribal ethnic groups migrated and they were brought by the then British administration as well as by the Government of India, after independence. British authorities during the time of penal settlements brought thousands of political and criminal prisoners for imprisonment in these isolated islands. The descendants of these convicts are known as local born or "Andaman Indian". The people who originally belonged to different communities and inhabited in different corners of India, are now moulded into a homogeneous group of people having a strong tie of affinity. They now represent themselves as a single ethnic group irrespective of racial affinities like religion, caste, language and culture. They were settled in and around the Port Blair Archipelago before and after Indian independence. During 1907-1927, the Mophillas, a Muslim community from Malabar region, now Kerala, were brought by the British authorities as convicts due to the Mopla Rebellion in the Malabar coast. In 1929, a group of Bhatus were brought by the then British Government to this island as convicts due to their criminal habits. The Moplas and Bhatus, after their imprisonment was over, permanently settled in these islands. Also in 1925, some Karen families were brought from Burma for working as labourers in the Forest Department. Presently, they were settled in the Middle Andaman. Many Burmese convicts were also transported from Rangoon between 1907 and 1923 by the Britishers in Andamans for confinement in the jail. After attainment of Indian independence, many Burmese repatriated to Burma, their homeland, and the rest were accepted as the settlers in Port Blair town and neighbours of the Archipelago.

After independence, the Government of India undertook a rehabilitation scheme to settle the Bengalee refugees from East Pakistan (now Bangladesh) and Tamil refugees from Sri-Lanka and Keralites from Kerala, to these islands. As a result, thousands of people came to these islands after 1947. A good number of tribal people of Ranchi district of Bihar came here as labourers and settled in different islands of the Union Territory.

Since independence, people from the different parts of the country have been coming. They belonged to various ethnic groups. These people are still coming for business purposes, for official and private jobs. Though the Nicobargroup of Islands have been declared as a reserved area for tribal benefits, the Great Nicobar island has opened for settlement of ex-militarymen of India from the mainland. So far as ethnic situation of this island territory is concerned, it may be called a MINIATURE OF INDIA.

Demographic Profile

The total population of the Andaman and Nicobar Islands, according to the Census of 1981 was 188741 having 107261 males and 81480 females. Out of this population, 22361(12%) were Scheduled Tribes. Out of the total tribal population only 344 (1.55%) of them were living in Andaman district and the rest 22017 (98.45%) tribals were in the Nicobar district. People of all major Indian languages are found in these two districts. According to the Census of 1981, 44147 (24%) people were Bengali-speaking, which was followed by 32446 (18%) Hindi-speaking people. The fourth populous group was the Nicobari-speaking, having 21424 (12%) individuals[56].

According to the 1981 Census, the density of population of the Andaman and Nicobar Islands was 23 persons per sq. km., which was 14 persons per sq. km. in 1971. Out of the total 188741 population, 97321 (51.51%) were literate in which 62983 (58.72%) were males and 34338 (42.56%) were females.

Table 1
Population Statistics Since 1901 Census of Andaman and Nicobar Islands

Census Year	*Population of Andaman Islands*	*Population of Nicobar Islands*	*Total Population of the Union Territory*	*% of decadal variation*
1901	18138	6511	24649	
1911	17641	8818	26459	+ 7.34
1921	17814	9272	27086	+ 2.37
1931	19223	10240	29463	+ 8.78.
1941	21316	12452	33768	+14.61
1951	18962	12009	30971	(-) 8.29
1961	48985	14563	63548	+105.19
1971	93468	21665	115133	+81.17
1981	158287	30454	188741	+63.91
1991	241453	39208	280661	+48.70
2001	314239	42026	356265	+26.94

*Census reports of the Andaman and Nicobar Islands 2001.

Table 1 shows that the overall population (all ethnic groups, both non-tribals and tribals) of the Andaman and Nicobar groups of Islands has increased to a great extent during the last few decades (1901-2001) except during 1941-1951. But the growth of the population of the primitive tribal groups have decreased very sharply, while the Nicobarese tribals population has increased very remarkably since 1901. Details are given in the Table 2 and Table 3 separately indicate declining demographic profile of the primitive tribals of these islands in general and the Great Andamanese and the Onges in particular. In 1858, the number of population of the Great Andamanese was estimated around 5000. No enumeration was done on the Onges before 1903. Since 1901, the actual enumeration has been started on the Great Andamanese and the Onges along with the other tribals of the Union Territory. We found from the Census of 1901, that the total population of the Great Andamanese was 625 and of the Onges was 672. Census of 1931, specially mentioned the "pure-bred" and "half-bred" among the Great Andamanese with sex-wise data given separately. In this census, it is revealed that the total number of pure-bred was 74 (27 males and 47 females) and half-bred came to 16 (11 males and 5 females). According to Census of 1931, we came to know that half-bred is a child whose mother is a Great Andamanese but his/her biological father is a non-tribal[57].

Table 2

Demographic Growth Trends of the Andaman and Nicobar Tribals Since 1901[1]

Census Year	*Great Andamanese*	*Onges*	*Jarawas*	*Sentinelese*	*Shompen*	*Nicobarese*
1901	625	672	585	-	342	6501
1911	455	631	114	117	375	8818
1921	209	346	114	117	375	9272
1931	90	250	70	50	200	10240
1941	-	-	-	-		-
1951	23	150	50	-	20	12009
1961	19	129	(500)*	(50)*	71	14563
1971	24	112	(N.F)+	(N.F.)+	92	17874
1981	42	97	31	(N.F.)+	223	21956
1990[2]	30	100	-	-	-	
2001	55	96	328	39	398	29469

1 Census reports of the Andaman and Nicobar Islands.

2 Field Survey conducted by the researcher on the Spot during 1988-90.

+NF Not found

Table 3

The declining population trends of the Great Andamanese and the Onges since 1901

Census Year	*Great Andamanese with % of decadal variation*	*Onges with % of decadal variation*
1901	625 (-)	672 (-)
1911	455 (-27.04)	631 (-6.10)
1921	209 (-54.16)	346 (-45.10)
1931	90 (-56.93)	250 (-27.74)
1941	(-) (-)	(-) (-)

1951	23 (-74.44)	150(-40)
1961	19 (-19.39)	129 (-14)
1971	24 (+26.31)	112 (-13.17)
1981	42 (+75)	97 (-13.40)
1990	30 (-28.57)	100 (+3.10)
200	55 (+83.55)	96 (-4.16)

1 Census reports of the Andaman and Nicobar Islands.

2 Field Survey conducted by the researcher on the spot during 1988-90.

Table 3 indicates that except in the 1971 and 1981 Census, the population of the Great Andamanese and except 1990 Census, the population of the Onges has been decreased.

From the history and empirical evidence, various causes of the dwindling of the population of the Great Andamanese and the Onges are known. One of the major causes of the decline of population was that a considerable number of persons were killed at the gunpoint by the British administrators on various encounters. At the initial stage, the Great Andamanese tried to resist the strangers with their bows and arrows. Several skirmishes resulted to the killing of thousands of the Andamanese by the British rulers indiscriminately to establish their colonial rule. Particularly, the people of the reproductive age-group sharply disappeared during these encounters. Further, their dwindling process was accelerated with the induction of various new diseases. Due to indiscriminate sexual unions of the convicts and the naval staff with the aboriginal women, venereal diseases spread like wildfire. The causes of diminution of population due to the infectious and contagious diseases were the results of contact of the tribals with the new civilization. Epidemics like pneumonia (1868), syphilis (1876), measles (1877) and influenza (1892) together with over-exposure to the sun and wind in open spaces, the excessive use of tobacco and over clothing have been the chief means which destroyed them[58]. The Onges of Little Andaman were the objects of prey by British rulers and they died also in several encounters at the British gunpoint, diseases and over-clothing.

Forest and Forest Based Industries

The administrative report on Andaman and Nicobar Islands, published in 1985, revealed that the total forest area of Andaman and Nicobar Islands was 7163 sq. km. Out of which, 3048 sq. km. have been demarcated as reserved forest area and 17 sq. km. as protected area. The rest of 4098 sq. km. of forest area is demarcated as proposed reserved forest[59]. Island forest is still now enriched with various varieties of commercial timber such as Garjan, Black Chuglam, White Chuglam, Padak, Papita, Koko, Marblewood, Badam, White dhup etc. used for manufacturing plywood, luxurious furniture, house decorating materials, match sticks and boxes.

A few wood-based big and small industries are functioning both under public as well as under private sectors. The Andaman and Nicobar Forest Department has opened two big saw mills named Chattam Saw Mill at Port Blair and Betapur Saw Mill at Middle Andaman. Under private enterprise, there are several big industries producing plywood, match sticks and boxes at Bamboo-flat, Bakultala, Hut Bay and Long Island. There are five large scale industries and 373 small-scale industries functioning since 1985. The Andaman, and specially, the Nicobar group of Islands are rich in cocoanut plantations. Cocoanut is the main economy of the Nicobarese.

Marine resources have good prospects in the Island's commercial craft industries. Cottage industries in the private sector enterprises utilise sea-shell for producing ornaments and house decoration articles. These sea-shell articles have a great demand to the foreigners as well as the Indian tourists.

Infrastructure

The Island Territory is far off from India, the mainland, being surrounded by the Bay of Bengal. So sea and air routes are the only means of communications to reach these distant islands. From 1858 ship services are the only means of communication which was used by the British authorities for transporting political and criminal convicts from Calcutta to Port Blair and carrying defence articles and foodstuffs. After the attainment of Indian independence, the islands have been further connected with air services from Calcutta and Madras to Port Blair. Recently, the air services and shipping facilities have been improved for faster communication by increasing its number of trips from Mainland to Port Blair and vice~versa. For Inter-Island communication, the Andaman and Nicobar Administration uses ferry boats for carrying passengers and-consumer goods.

For land communication, the local administration operates its own state bus services along with some private bus services. In 1985, the Andaman Trunk Road, a length of 250 k.m. from Port Blair to Mayabander was opened for bus services. For emergency relief services, the navy helicopters are also available to bring patients and other persons in distress from distant islands. Under the modern infrastructure facilities, every island is further connected with S.T.D. telephone link from Port Blair to other islands and vice versa. For local calls, every big island has connected with telephone lines. A low power transmission radio station is functioning at Port Blair. Recently, all big islands have been provided with short distance TV transmitting centres which also include the Onge, the Great Andamanese and the Shompen settlements.

From the statistical information of the Union Territory, it is found that in 1989, the postal department has opened 90 Post Offices, sub-post offices and branch post offices for covering every remote island under postal facilities. For speedy and emergency news, the Police wireless and civil wireless have jointly opened 35 telegram offices to each and every island. To maintain law and order, the Andaman and Nicobar Police Department has opened 12 police stations, 12 outpost and 3 fire stations. For medical services to the islanders, the Health Department is running 10 hospitals, 17 dispensaries, 12 primary Health centres and 63 Sub-centres providing free medicines and clinical treatment. One Sessions Court and two other branch courts have been set up to settle civil and criminal disputes. Banking services are functioning quite well with one branch of bank in each island. Many research institutions have opened their offices in these islands for conducting research work for the all-round development of islanders[60]. Indian Military, Navy, Air Force and Coast Guard have posted their one battalions at Port Blair for defence purposes and for patrolling the sea-route along the Indian Ocean round the clock.

REFERENCES

1. Northrop, F.S.C. "On Plurality of Culture", in *American Sociological Review,* Vol. 4(I), (1939), pp. 36-41.
2. Toynbee, Arnold Joseph, *Civilization on Trial,* Oxford University Press, New York, (1948), pp. 78-81.
3. Mookerjea, Sobhanlal, *The Political Philosophy of John Stuart Mill,* S. Gupta and Brothers, Calcutta, (1966), Chapter VII.
4. Hobhouse, L.T., *Social Evolution and Political Theory,* Columbia University Press, New York, (1928), Chapters I-III.
5. Spencer, Herbert, *Man versus the State, Principles of Social Static.* Ritchie also follows Spencer in this connection Vide Ritchie's *Darwinism and Politics,* Williams and Norgate, London, (1885), pp. 113-117.
6. Hobhouse, L.T., *Social Evolution and Political Theory,* Columbia University Press, New York, (1928), Chapters I-III.
7. Toynbee, Arnold Joseph, *Civilizations on Trial,* Oxford University Press, New York, (1948); pp. 263-268.
8. Mookerjea, Sobhanlal, "Synthesis: The Keynote To Tagorean Culture," *Visvabharati Quarterly,* September-December, (1961), pp. 17-21.
9. Singh, Yogendra, *Essays on Modernization in India,* Manohar Book Service, New Delhi, (1978), pp. 1-2.
10. Marx, Karl and F. Engels, *Communist Manifesto,* (ed.) by D. Razianoff also V.I. Lenin, *State and Revolution,* Burman Publishing House, Calcutta, (1944), pp. 77-81 (First Indian Edition).
11. Lenin, V.I., *State and Revolution*, Burman Publishing House, Calcutta, (1944), pp. 4-6.
12. Singh, Yogendra, *Essays on Modernization in India,* Manohar Book Service, New Delhi, (1978), pp. 5-6.
13. Appteker, Herbert, *The nature of Democracy, Freedom and Revolution,* National Book Agency, Calcutta, (1974), pp. 112-115.
14. Singh, Yogendra, *Essays on Modernization in India,* Manohar Book Service, New Delhi, (1978), pp. 5-6.

15. Sorokin, Pitirim Aleksandrovich, *Social and Cultural Dynamics: A Study of Change in Major Ssystems of Art, Truth, Ethnics, Law and Social Relationships (abridged in one volume)*, Peter Owner Ltd., (1959), pp. 605-621.
16. Singh, Yogendra, *Essays on Modernization in India*, Manohar Book Service, New Delhi, (1978), pp. 10-11.
17. Robson, W.A., *Welfare State and Welfare Society : Illusion and Reality*, George Alien and Unwin Ltd., London, (1976), p. 184.

    Titmuss Richard Morris, *Essays on the Welfare Stage*, George Alien and Unwin Ltd., London, (1958), p. 232.

    Also Singh, *op. cit*, p. 12.
18. *Ibid.*, p. 59.
19. Eisenstadt, S.N., *Tradition, Change and Modernity*, John Wiley and Sons, New York, (1973), p. 5.
20. *Ibid.*, p. 8.
21. Aron, Raymond, *Main Currents in Sociological Thought*; Penguin Books, Harmondsworth, (1969), pp. 185-211.
22. Eisenstadt, S.N., *Tradition, Change and Modernity*, John Wiley & Sons, New York, (1973); pp. 24-31.
23. Srinivas, M.N., *Caste in Modern India and Other Essays*, Asia Publishing House, Calcutta, (1962), p. 102.
24. Freud, Sigmund, *The Origins of Religion: Totem and Taboo, Mosses and Monotheism and Other Works*, Penguin Books, London, (1985), Vol. 1, Chapter I.
25. Eisenstadt, S.N., *Tradition, Change and Modernity*, John Wiley & Sons, New York, (1973), pp. 203-211.
26. *Ibid*, pp. 280-307.
27. Eisenstadt, S.N., *Modernisation: Protest and Change*, Prentice, Hall of India Pvt. Ltd., New Delhi, (1969), Chapter III.
28. *Ibid.*, Chapters IV-VII.
29. Singh, K.S. (ed.), "A Note on the series" quoted from the book, *The Great Andamanese* by D.K. Chakraborty, Seagull Books, Calcutta, (1990) (Introduction Chapter).
30. Chakraborty, D.K., *The Great Andamanese*, Seagull Books, Calcutta,(1990), pp. 1-6.
31. Census of India 1981, *Andaman and Nicobar Islands*, Director of Census Operation, New Delhi, (1985), Series-24.
32. Sen, P.K., *Land and People of Andamans*, The Post Graduate Book Mart, Calcutta, (1962), pp. 4-5.

33. Census of India 1931, *Andaman and Nicobar Islands,* Central Publications, Delhi, India, (1932), pp. 4-5.
34. *Ibid,* p. 64.
35. Census of India 1961, *Andaman and Nicobar Islands,* Manager of Publications, Delhi, (1965), p. 1.
36. Sen, P.K., *Land and peoples of Andamans,* The Post Graduate Book Mart, Calcutta, (1962), p.l.
37. Justin Austice, *The Nicobarese,* Seagull Books, Calcutta, (1990),p.l.
38. Sen, P.K., *Land and Peoples of Andaman,* The Post Graduate Book Mart, Calcutta, (1962), pp.26-35.
39. Andaman and Nicobar Administration, *Basic Statistics, 1989,* Statistical Bureau, Port Blair, (1989), p.l.
40. *Ibid.*, pp. 47-52.
41. Sen, P.K., *Land and Peoples of Andaman,* The Post Graduate Book Mart, Calcutta, (1962), pp. 44-45.
42. Chengapa, B.S., "Andaman Forests and their development", in *Census of India 1951. Andaman and Nicobar Islands,* (ed.) by A.K. Ghosh, Manager of Publications, Delhi (1955), Appendix C.
43. Cappieri, Mario, *The Andamanese: Cultural Elements—Elements of Demogenetics, Physical Anthropology and Raciology* (ed.) by Henry Field, Field Research Projects, Miami, (1974), p. 57.
44. Dobson, G.E., "On the Andamans and the Andamanese," in *Journal of the Anthropological Institute of Great Britain and Ireland,* (1874), vol. 4, pp. 457-467.
45. Cipriani, Lidio, "The origin of the Andamanese", *Census of India, 1951, Andaman and Nicobar Islands,* (ed.) by A.K. Ghosh, Manager of Publications, Delhi, (1955), Appendix E.
46. Sarkar, S.S., "The Origin and Migration of the Negritos in the Andaman Islands", in *Man in India,* (1953), Vol.33(2), p.274.
47. Temple, R.C., *The Census of India 1901, Andaman and Nicobar Islands,* Government Printings, Calcutta, India, (1903), pp. 1-5.
48. Census of India 1931, *Andaman and Nicobar Islands,* Central Publications, Delhi, India, (1932), p. 10.
49. Gupta, S.K., "The Andaman and the Nicobar Islands" in *Census of India 1951, Andaman and Nicobar Islands,* (ed.) by A.K. Ghosh, Manager of Publication, Delhi, (1955), Appendix A.

50. Man, E.H., *The Aboriginal Inhabitants of Andaman*, Royal Anthropological Institute, London, (1902), pp. 88-97.

51. Temple, R.C., *The Census of India 1901, Andaman and Nicobar Islands*, Government Printings, Calcutta, India, (1903), pp. 176-181.

52. Whitehead, G., *In the Nicobar Islands*, Seelay Service and Co., London, (1924), pp. 7-15.

53. Mathur, L.P., *History of the Andaman and Nicobar Islands*, Sterling Publishers, New Delhi, (1968), pp.228-229.

54. Shyamchaudhuri, N.K., *Territorial Arrangement, Traditions and Village Organisation in Car-Nicobar Island*, An.S.I., Calcutta, (1957), p.20.

55. Chengapa, B.S., "On the Shompen of Great Nicobar", in *Census of India 1951; Andaman and Nicobar Islands*, (ed.) by A.K. Ghosh, Manager of Publications, Delhi, (1955), Appendix F.

56. Census of India 2001, *Andaman and Nicobar Islands*, Director of Census Operation, New Delhi.

57. Census of India 1931, *Andaman and Nicobar Islands*, Central Publications, Delhi, India, (1932), p.22.

58. Government of India, *Andaman and Nicobar Gazetter, 1909.* Calcutta, India.

59. Andaman and Nicobar Administration, *Basic Statistics 1985*, Statistical Bureau, Port Blair,(1985), pp. 47-48.

60. Andaman and Nicobar Administration, *Basic Statistics 1989*, Statistical Bureau, Port Blair (1989), pp. 1-7.

2

Welfare Measures Taken by the Government for the Great Andamanese and the Onges

The fathers of the Indian Constitution, while taking note of the centuries of old injustice perpetrated against many ethnic groups, adopted a two-pronged strategy of tribal development. It seeks to protect them against exploitation and assist them in their economic development. Protection is requisite to development, particularly during the transition period, until they come up to the general level or the modernising stage and join the mainstream of the nation. For the upliftment of the tribals, the Indian Constitution has provided special protection under the following articles:-

Article 15 (4) "Nothing in this article or in clause (2) of article 29 shall prevent the State from making any special provision for the advancement of any socially and educationally backward class of citizens or for the Scheduled Castes and Scheduled Tribes".

Article 16 (4) "Nothing in this article shall prevent the state from making any provision for the reservation of appointments or parts in favour of any backward class of citizens which, in the opinion of the State, is not adequately represented in the service under the State".

Article 19 (5) "Nothing in sub-clauses (d), (e), and (f) of

the said clause shall effect the operation of any existing law in so far as it imposes, or prevent the state from making any law imposing, reasonable restrictions on the exercise of any of the rights conferred by the said sub-clauses either in the interests of the general public or for the protection of the interest of any Scheduled Tribes."

Article 46 "The state shall promote with special care the educational and economic interests of the weaker section of the people, and, in the particular, of the Scheduled Castes and Scheduled Tribes, and shall protect them from social injustice and all forms of exploitation".

Article 330 (1) "Seats shall be reserved in the House of People for

(a) the Scheduled Castes.

(b) the Scheduled Tribes (Except the Scheduled Tribes in the Tribal areas of Assam and in Nagaland); and

(c) the Scheduled Tribes in the autonomous districts of Assam".

Article 330 (2) "The number of seats reserved in any State (or Union Territory) for Scheduled Castes or the Scheduled Tribes under clause (1) shall bear, as nearly as may be, the same proportion to the total number of seats allotted to that State (or Union Territory) in the House of the people as the population of the Scheduled Castes in the State (or Union territory) or the Scheduled Tribes in the State (or Union territory) or part of the State (or Union territory), as the case may be in respect of which seats are so reserved, bears to the total population of the State (or Union territory)".

Article 332 (1) "Seats shall be reserved for the Scheduled Castes and the Scheduled Tribes, (except in Scheduled Tribes in the tribal areas of Assam and in Nagaland) in the Legislative Assembly of every state.

(2) Seats shall be reserved also for the autonomous districts in the Legislative Assembly of the state of Assam.

(3) The number of seats reserved for the Scheduled Castes or the Scheduled Tribes in the Legislative Assembly of any state under clause (1) shall bear, as nearly as may be the same proportion to the total number of seats in the Assembly

as the population of the Scheduled Castes in the State, as the case may be, in respect of which seats are so reserved, bears to the total population of the state".

Article 335 "The claims of the members of the Scheduled Castes and Scheduled Tribes shall be taken into consideration, consistently with the maintenance of efficiency of administration, in the making of appointments to services and posts in connection with the affairs of the Union or of a State".

The provisions in the Fifth and Sixth Schedules laydown the special powers of the Governors of those States to enact special regulations, check transfer of land from tribals to non-tribals, control money-lending, debt bondage, etc. to safeguard the interest of the tribes. Moreover, the Governor could by order direct any act or any part of the act not to be operative in Scheduled areas when those are not conductive to the interests of the tribes. The tribal areas in Assam no doubt enjoin special privileges including restrictions on the extent of the Civil Procedure Code, 1908.

Similarly, provisions have been made for the economic development of tribal communities under Articles 275 (1) "first provison, in the Indian Constitution lay down the purpose and conditions on which grants-in-aid shall be paid out of the consolidated fund of India for the tribal welfare activities. The purpose as stipulated therein is promoting the welfare of the Scheduled Tribes in the State or raising the level of administration of the Scheduled areas therein to that of the rest of the areas of that state", and,

Article 339 (1) "The President may at any time and shall, at the expiration of ten years from the commencement of this Constitution, by order appoint a Commission to report on the administration of the Scheduled Areas and the welfare of the Scheduled Tribes in the States.

(2) The executive power of the Union shall extend to the giving of directions to (a State) as to the drawing up and execution of schemes specified in the direction to be essential for the welfare of the Scheduled Tribes in the State[1]." These provisions assign special responsibility to the Government not only for drawing up of special, scheme of development

but also for providing them financial assistance.

Various planned efforts have been made since independence for economic development and modernisation of the tribal people. The first attempt was made in 1954 when 43 special multi-purpose development projects were undertaken to supplement the Community Development programmes which aimed at comprehensive development of rural areas[2]. Though after the independence, Our Constituent Assembly appointed a Committee under the chairmanship of Late A.B. Thakkar, well known as Thakkar Bapa to consider and contemplate adequate safeguards for the tribal people. The findings and recommendation of this Committee found expression in various provisions in our Constitution[3].

The situation was reviewed in 1956 by the Elwin Committee which recommended a cautions approach in the introduction of multiplicity of schemes in tribal areas. A special commission called the Dhebar Commission was set up for the developmental programmes for Scheduled Areas and Scheduled Tribes in April, 1960, under chairmanship of U.N. Dhebar along-with 10 other distinguished members. Commission submitted its report in 1961.

Dhebar Commission's Report 1960-61[4]

The main task of the Dhebar Commission was to investigate the situation and problems of the Scheduled Tribes of India at that time. The Report was made with intensive care, collecting valuable data from all possible angles of the life and culture of the scheduled tribes of India. The Commission tried to sort out the problems of the Indian tribes, and recommended some measures for their upliftment. The reports contain some important recommendations for Indian tribes including of Andaman and Nicobar Islands.

It was observed by the Dhebar Commission that the Indian tribes were mainly forest dwellers. Many of them practice shifting cultivation, rearing cattle and are engaged plantation and horticulture. But their agricultural output is low due to some drawbacks. For improving of the cash crops and horticulture, the tribals as whole need sufficient technical assistance, irrigation facilities and soil conservation. The Commission recommended that first of all, the holders of land should be granted full rights over the trees and their fruits. Arrangements should be made to supply plants, seedlings, manure and fertilizers. Transport and marketing facilities should also be provided to them.

Among the tribals the commission observed some groups have chosen cattle rearing as their livelihood, but their performance is poor. As such the commission suggested few steps for improving their domestic animals husbandry. These are:

(i) Establishment of special unit for development of animal husbandry to guide and direct the tribals like rearing goats, sheep, horses and development of poultry and piggery and cows and arrangement for breeding, feeding for these domestic animals.

(ii) Training on a mass scale for spreading the knowledge about improvement of the livestock and its economic utilization and development of credit and marketing facilities.

The Indian tribes are very expert in indigenous craft work. For improvement of Village and Cottage Industries, the Commission recommended following measures:

(i) To utilize and develop the creative faculties of the tribal people and to provide gainful employment.

(ii) To offer them an avenge for converting their raw materials into processed articles and thus taking their economy a step further.

Unless cooperative movement is well organised among the tribals exploitation and injustice in respect of the tribes could not be eliminated. So, the Commission suggested that:

(i) Every village should be served by a Cooperative Society with at least one member from each tribal family as a member and the Society should embrace all the avenues of economic development such as agriculture, animal husbandry, forest and handicraft, consumer goods as a part of an integrated programme of economic development.

(ii) The sale and marketing of the produce and supply

of the tribal people's requirements at reasonable prices should receive special attention through Co-operatives.

According to the Commission, education is an important modernising medium for the tribes of India. So it should be developed in tribal areas. Illiteracy and ignorance are the twin problems for the Indian tribals. The report pointed out that as parts of the state education policy free midday meals, free clothing, supply of free books, and stationery to all tribal children in areas where education has not made sufficient headway might be included.

The report indicated that one of the most important problems in connection with the health of the tribal people is their addiction to narcotics and intoxicating liquor. The report contained some suggestions for checking this propensity as follows: Smuggling of liquor must be stopped with a strong hand. Traffic in it should be made penal offence with serve punishment. Health education is very necessary for the tribal areas. Programme in phased manner should be undertaken for supply of clean water to all tribal villegers.

Rehabilitation and housing are two other major problems which the displaced tribals have been facing. The Commission pointed out that the most important aspect of housing is the need for a planned approach, bearing in mind the needs of the tribals, their choice, sanitation and finance. No colonization scheme should be undertaken unless it is possible to provide employment to the people of 'the locality. Before and during the construction of the colony, full advantage should be taken of the tribals' own advice.

Regarding the problem of communication in the tribal areas, the Commission reported that development of communication will provide greater opportunities for the tribals to develop their consciousness of and eagerness for national integration. Roads should be expanded; posts, telegraphs and telephones should be extended; if possible, cannels of air communication should be increased.

The Commission made an attention on bettering the lot of Scheduled Tribes of Andaman and Nicobar Islands. It is true that the Dhebar report did not go into the details about the Great Andamanese and the Onges and other primitive tribals. Of the tribesmen, Nicobarese of the Nicobar group of Islands were taken into consideration. In the Second Five Year Plan of the Andaman and Nicobar Islands, the Commission found sufficient amount of funds were allocated for the implementation of development programmes under various sections in the areas inhabited by the Scheduled Tribes living there. The plan outlay was Rs. 603.135 lakhs including a special provision of Rs. 1 lakh for the amelioration of the Scheduled Tribes. There had been considerable shortfall, according to the Commission, in the implementation of the programme. The report stated that during the Third Five Year Plan for the Onges, economic development programmes included a cocoanut plantation scheme with a fund of Rs. 1.60 lakhs.

About the health conditions of the Andaman tribes, the Commission reported that the tribals there suffer mostly from malaria, sand-fly fever and worms. In the Second Five Year Plan, there was a scheme for the establishment of a medical-cum-anthropological unit in the Little Andamans. Provision was made in the Third Five Year Plan for increasing the number of sea-going vessels. With such measures, the administration hope that it would be possible to provide better medicine facilities more frequently to the Islanders. In the Little Andaman, however, there was no facility of water supply. The Commission suggested that provisions be made for better water supply. The huts of the Onges were also very bad and unhygienic which needs repair. The Commission suggested that a provision of Rs 5 thousands might be made for this purpose. Also there was no proper communication system between the headquarters and the areas inhabited by the Onges, the Jarawas, the Sentinelese and the Shompens. The Commission suggested that unless this problem is solved, these tribals would continue to remain as prisoners of isolation in perpetual darkness.

After independence, the district administration of Andaman and Nicobar islands was vested with the special responsibility of protection and welfare of the aboriginal tribes of these islands. Under the protection of Aboriginal Tribes Regulation Act of 1956 these areas (including the whole of Andaman & Nicobar islands 2-9 listed) were notified as Tribal Reserve as per the Notification No. APART/3(1)/1 of April 2, 1957[5]. These are the laws which govern islands for legal protection of the tribals. By the protection of Aboriginal Tribes Regulation, 35% of the areas has been reserved for the aborigines[6]. Since then nobody would be allowed to settle and hold business in the scheduled areas without prior permission of the administration.

Before 1969, no concrete programmes were sorted out for the welfare and rehabilitation of the aboriginal ethnic groups of the Andamans. Neither economic nor hygienic steps were taken for the both ethnic groups, the Great Andamanese and the Onges. This was because of our advanture of inducting people from India mainland into this territory under the rehabilitation programme of Government of India since the middle of 1949. In the rush of the rehabilitation activities the administration failed to take note of the primitive negritoes who had been abiding in the island for millenniums[7].

According to Kochar, (1969), in 1966 the number of the Great Andamanese was 34. They were uprooted from their primitive surroundings living in and around the Port Blair and South Andaman division. Four person lived in the house of a Burmese in Memeotara hamlets in South Andaman. Six persons lived in Port Blair town itself. There are three persons in Laltikri outpost in Baratang Island and three in Long Island. These include seven persons with known marital links with Burmese[8]. Thus from 1949 to 1969, means for twenty years, no welfare measures were undertaken by the administration for the Great Andamanese. They were exploited physically, mentally and financially by the outsiders, specially by the Burmese.

Before 1949, the Andaman Forest Department, in the departmental interest for the first time, took all of the Great Andamanese to Bluff Island and settled them there. Because, at that time all the adult males could be employed as Forest Guards and Bush Police constable to defend non tribals from hostile attack of the Jarawa. Before the settlement of the Great Andamanese in 1969, all the 23 survival individuals lived in and around the Port Blair Town. They used to live in an abandoned Japanese bunker in most unhygienic conditions. Most of the adults were addicted to opium. During 1969-70 the surviving Great Andamanese were taken to Strait Island and were settled there under the immediate care of a social worker of the "Bharatiya Adimjati Sevak Sangh" with funds made available under the sector "Welfare of the Bakward Classes" of the Five Year Plan of this Union Territory[9].

In 1967, for the first time the Little Andaman has been opened for the outsiders. Since 1969, hundreds of mainlanders refugees of erstwhile East Pakistan (now Bangladesh) were admitted there settlement. Many families were also admitted from Sri Lanka, Kerala and Nicobar Islands for settlement. With the settlement of outsiders, the administration have undertaken minor welfare programmes for the 112 Onges. Under the charge of the Education Department, they are being given snacks and sweets. At the time the Onges were living at scattered places in the coastal area. They maintained their traditional nomadic character. Occasionally, they visited the outsiders at their settlement and took snacks and sweets. At that time they took part in barter trade with commodities like honey, resin and the sea-shell in exchange of tobacco, food and sweets. However, some unscrupulous government servants and mainlanders misbehaved with them and the barter trade suffered much[10].

Till 1969, there was no clear programmes for the welfare measures of the Great Andamanese and the Onge tribals. Social Workers were posted in March, 1970 at Strait Island and at Hut Bay, Little Andaman Island. They were originally belonging to the Bharatiya Adimjati Sevak Sangh. "Bharatiya Adimjati Sevak Sangh" as a welfare organisation was founded by revered Thakkar Bapa in the year 1948. It was registered under Societies Registration Act, XXI of 1860. Dr Rajendra Prasad, the first President of Indian Republic was its first president.

The basic aim of the Bharatiya Adimjati Sevak Sangh is to work for the "adimjatis" (primitive and aboriginal tribes) in India, socially economically, culturally and educationally with a view to enable them to take their legistimate place in the national life of the country as equal citizens. For the attainment of this basic aim, it has been started multifarious activities like establishment of centres for the alround amelioration of the conditions of the tribal communities; start centres for training of workers for social and other allied aspects of work; organise and encourage research in anthropological study of the problems of tribal communities and arrange seminars and conferences and publish books, brochures, magazines and maintain a museum; open and maintain libraries[11].

On the above persuance the "Sangh" was extended its welfare service to the primitive tribes of Andaman and Nicobar Islands in March, 1970. The "Sangh" was established its full cooperation for the overall development through its social workers. Two Social Workers were posted at the Onge and Great Andamanese settlements for accelerating the welfare activities for them. But their works have apparently not been upto the expectation of the administration. They failed to communicate with the Onges and the Great Andamanese. The behaviour of the Social Worker of the Onges was rough. He forced the Onges to live in a conjusted place and restricted their movement. So, if they moved from the settlement they never come back[12].

In 1969, a team visited the island. It was lead by Shri Sundaram, Director General (Backward Class Welfare, Government of India) and also included Dr. Surajit C. Sinha, (the well known anthropologist). The welfare team mainly paid attention to the situation of Negrito tribes of the Andaman. The team offered some suggestions. These included some urgent measures to be taken before, rehabiliting these tribes, measures like production of food resources both in the sea and in the forest, adequate medical facilities, provision of water and shelter. In short, an infrastructure for the both ethnic groups should be built up. For remaining the health hazards of the two tribes, the Indian Council of Medical Research deputed in February, 1969, a team of medical experts from the Nutrition Research Laboratories to study to cause of decline in the population of the two communities[13].

In mid-seventies, there was a new wave for the welfare of tribal communities in India following a workshop on primitive tribes organised by the Ministry of Home Affairs, Government of India in 1975. Accordingly, the Andaman and Nicobar Administration also launched certain programmes for the welfare of primitive ethnic groups of these islands. An Advisory Committee for Primitive Groups in Andaman and Nicobar Islands was founded by the Ministry of Home Affairs. Almost simultaneously, in 1976, a voluntary organisation called "The Andaman Adim Janjati Vikas Samiti" (AAJVS) also known as "Samiti" was created and Registered at Port Blair with the following objectives[14]:

(i) To protect health and prevent extinction of the primitive tribal groups namely Great Andamanese, Onges, Shompens, Jarawas and Sentinelese inhabiting Andaman and Nicobar Islands.

(ii) To promote the economic and social development of the said primitive tribal communities.

(iii) To take a comprehensive view of the problems of these tribal groups and to develop and promote programmes in pursuance of the national policy of their development, and

(iv) To develop measures for co-ordination of governmental institutional and voluntary action for protection of their economic and social environment essential to their survival and growth.

In the Fifth Five Year Plan of the territory a new sector called "Welfare of Backward Classes" was created. Under this section, the following was an essential tasks of the authorities to the tribesmen before implemented any welfare programmes. Therefore, Samiti in its General Body meeting decided that restriction must be imposed on the Great Andamanese, so that they could come out of the Strait Island only on passes issued by the Deputy Commissioner, Andaman through the Social Workers of the settlement for specific purpose. Similarly entry into the Onges reserve specially in the Dugong Creek settlement by anybody had been completely banned. Only those of the Government officials having direct bearing on the developmental work at Dugong Creek would be allowed to go there[15].

For better administration and welfare of the Great Andamanese and the Onges, several new steps were taken at the administrative level. The "Samiti" in its meeting decided that one representative each from the Great Andamanese and the Onges must be nominated in the Chief Commissioner Advisory Committee since 1976. The same individuals also be represented in the Samitis General Body and Sub-Committee. Moreover, the same nominated Great Andamanese individuals also given the scope to represent in the Home Ministery's Advisory Committee from amongst the primitive tribals of these Islands. The main intention of the administration behind their nomination in the various committees was to give them scope to come forward and uphold their own community problems before the administration and hold discussion for its solution.

The tribal situation was further reviewed on the eve of the Fifth Five Year Plan by a Task Force on "Development of Tribal Area" constituted by the Planning Commission. The Task Force recommended that to ensure balanced socio-economic development of the tribal areas in Andaman and Nicobar Islands, a policy of integrated development would be necessary for the Fifth and subsequent Plans. Therefore, a Tribal Sub-Plan strategy was evolved in 1974-75.. This strategy emphasised area development with a focus on improving the quality of life of the tribal community Its immediate objectives were elimination of exploitation in all forms, speeding up the processes of social and economic developments. The Tribal Sub-Plan approach was supplied to certain identified areas in 17 States and 2 Union Territories of India including Andaman and Nicobar Islands[16].

The tribal people in these islands is, therefore able to take advantage of various socio-economic programmes of the Government. But the primitive tribal communities of these islands were not in a position to take advantage of any sophisticated plan schemes for their benefit like the tribal people in West Bengal, Bihar, Orissa, Nagaland, Mizoram and other such tribal areas in the mainland of India. The Administration had, however, not ignored the primitive tribal communities, namely, Great Andamanese, Onges, Jarawas Sentenelese and Shompens. It had rather taken special care of these primitive groups of people both under State Plan and under Special Central Assistance of the Union Governments. Since Sixth Plan Period, the Administration had formulated a separate Five Year Sub-Plan for the betterment of the lot of these primitive tribes exclusively. The Administration had asked for separate Central Assistance and had formulated thirteen scheme for their welfare under sectoral Sub-Plan. The main intention in having a separate Tribal Sub-Plan for this territory was to enable the Administration to properly implement and monitor the various programmes which had been drawn up for the benefit of the tribal population of this territory[17].

Under this welfare scheme, the administration was planned during the Fifth Five Year Plan to construct a half-mile pitch- road, community hall, with radio-listening set, piggery shed, barbed wire fencing for their kitchen gardens, pucca wells, fishing dinghi with fishing net etc. at Strait Island, a home for the short stay at Port Blair, medical facilities, food, clothings and presents to the Great Andamanese in all 25 lakh of rupees. Indeed, it was surprising that it came to a little more than Rs. 1 lakh per person in five years, Rs.20,000 per year and about Rs. 1700/- per head per month. Though an outlay of Rs.25 lakh had been planned in Fifth Five Year Plan, the scheme at initial stage was to provide a settlement of Dugong Creek for Onges. A hut with a kitchen should be provided for each family. The settlement would be provided with medical facilities and water supply, approach road, community hall with radio, chairs and tables for welfare of the Onges[18].

Welfare Measures Taken Under Andaman Adim Janjati Vikas Samiti

Shelter

The Onges were settled at Dugong Creek and South Bay in Little Andaman during 1976-77. In 1978-79, the target included construction of 30 huts for the Onges and for establishment of support staff. A scheme was taken up in 1979-80 for the improvements of huts at Dugong Creek. But in 1976, a resolution was passed by the Andaman Adim Janjati Vikas Samiti in its General Body meeting that only building materials would be made available to the Onges for constructing their own houses. They might use indigenous methods according to their liking.

An "Adibasera" for stay by the Great Andamanese whenever they come to Port Blair had been constructed. This had helped to attract the Great Andamanese to this place of dwelling instead of going to spend the nights in the old wretched bunkers[19]. A Guest House had been built for the Onges at Hut Bay for their short period staying purpose. Whenever they come to Hut Bay for their own purposes, they can stay here for sometime or for somedays. In the Onges settlement 26 semi-pucca independent houses at Dugong Creek and 6 similar at South Bay were constructed. 26 houses at Dugong Creek were modified with A.C. Sheet roofs and plank floors for which an expenditure of Rs. 4.26 lakh was incurred. Besides this, 26 Onge huts, the staff quarters and community hall etc. were constructed. In the same way, 8 houses with a community hall were also constructed for the Great Andamanese. For the maintenance of community hall and the Adibasera, Rs. 0.10 lakh was proposed for the Sixth Five Year Plan period[20].

During the Seventh Five Year Plan period the following welfare measures were taken under the Tribal-Sub Plan. Maintenance, additions or alterations of transit house, staff quarters and non-residential buildings at Dugong Creek and at Strait Island. Maintenance of primitive guest house at Port Blair. Construction of 9 Onge model huts at Dugong Creek for South Bay Onge families who are proposed to be shifted from South Bay to Dugong Creek and one staff quarters for Plantation-in-charge. Proposed to construct two building in each year for which an expenditure of Rs. 9.35 lakhs was incurred[21].

Food and Other Subsistences

Under the rehabilitation and welfare schemes, modern food items were supplied since 1974 by the administration to the Great Andamanese and the Onges free of cost. Every adult male and female of both the ethnic groups have been receiving a certain quantity of foodstuffs. Children get half of this quota. Essential items like rice, wheat, flour, sugar, pulse, vegetables oil, ground nut oil, tea, milk powder, salt, spices, tobacco, bath soap, washing soap and candle are also supplied. Except the milk powder and soap, children upto the age of 8 are given all articles (except tobacco) at half of an adult. In addition, every adult women would get a pair of petticoats and jackets and every adult man a pair of half pants and bush-shirts per year. The dole system was introduced to change their traditional subsistence pattern by supplying modern articles. Apart from supply of free ration, the unemployed adult Great Andamanese are being paid cash allowance at the rate of Rs.75/- per month. A cash allowance of Rs.200/- per month is paid to the head of the Great Andamanese. Proposed outlay for the two Five Year Plan periods 1980-85, 1985-90 was Rs.1.35 lakh for the Great Andamanese. Supply of free food, clothing, monthly ration and gifts for the benefit of Great Andamanese and Onges an outlay for the yeurs of 1980-85 was Rs.7.03 lakh and Rs.24.900 lakh was outlay for Seventh Five Year Plan was sanctioned[22].

Cultivation of Horticulture

In 1961, about 25 acres- of land was earmarked for growing coconut and orchards at Dugong Creek. This plan was intended to encourage the communities for horticulture. At the same time 7 acres of land were reserved for plantation of coconuts and orchards in 1969 for the Great Andamanese at Strait Island. In addition, two acres of land were provided with barbed wire enclosures for gardening purposes in the 1975-76 plan year. To make the Great Andamanese self-relient, the Samiti, at its Executive Council meeting held on 28th March, 1977, resolved to plant coconuts seedling and other fruit bearing trees in another stretch of land on the island at an approximate of Rs.5000/-. The scheme had been formulated and approved for implementation. The coconut plantation at Dugong Creek settlement, at South Bay settlement and at Strait Island were raised with a plan that the Great Andamanese and the Onges would become self-supporting communities in due courses. It was expected they would utilize the coconuts as an item of their food as well as the cash crops i.e. nuts would be sold to purchase their other requirements in their future life.

The cocoanut plantation of the Onges at Dugong Creek was damaged very badly by the cyclonic storm of December, 1976. The Executive Council of the Samiti, at its extra ordinary meeting held on 28th March, 1977, resolved to plant 500 coconuts seedling on a plot of land in the settlement area at a cost of Rs. 10,680. The council also resolved to raise another cocoanut plantation and grow other fruit bearing trees in the South Bay settlement at an approximate cost of Rs. 25,000/-. This was done with the courtesy of the Agriculture and the Rehabilitation Departments respectively. During 1980-85, the Sixth Five Year Plan, Rs. 1.96 lakh were allotted for maintaining the existing coconut plantation-cum-orchards-cum-kitchen garden in and around the Onge settlement at Dugong Creek. With this endview, the Samiti proposed to raise and maintain coconut plantation-cum-kitchen gardens on an area of eight hectors in South Bay area, during the Sixth Five Year Plan period with an outlay of Rs. 1.04 lakh. Under the same plan an outlay of Rs. 1.25 lakh was earmarked for clearance of 5 acres of land, for planting seedlings and for paying wages of labourers and fencing around the 5 hectors of plantation for protection from pigs and deer and purchases seedling and their planting so as to make economic of Great Andamanese agriculture oriented[23].

In the Seventh Five Year Plan an outlay of Rs.3.850 lakh for maintenance and improvements and for raising of citrus and fruit plantation in an area of 5 acres of land at Dugong Creek, providing of barbed wire fencing. Additionally an outlay of Rs. 0.525 lakh was fixed up for maintenance of existing coconut-cum-orchard plantation at Strait Island and raising of citrus and fruit plantation in an area of 5 acres land at Strait Island. Supply of agricultural implements seedling and plants for raising the above plantation at Dugong Creek and at Strait Island[24]. At present a total area of 80 acres at Dugong Creek and 20 acres at South Bay had been reserved for the horticulture schemes for the Onges.

Poultry Unit

In the Seventh Five Year Plan, a new process of cultivation had been introduced by the Samiti as one of welfare measures and as a self-economy drive for the tribals. The Samiti was proposed to provide with poultry units of 10 each to each Onge family at Dugong Creek and South Bay and each Great Andamanese family at Strait Island. For this welfare measure, a total Rs.0.50 lakh was allotted during this plan period[25].

Bee Keeping Culture

The Great Andamanese and the Onges are very much fond of honey and they collect it from the jungle for their personal consumption and sale. Indeed, honey is one of the important and favourite item of their food and they often find it difficult to collect honey from the jungle for use. Under the horticulture scheme it was proposed to keep 60 bee-colonies along with bee-hives among the tribesmen and provide them with the necessary technical know-how by training them in the modern methods of extraction of honey. It was also proposed to provide them with marketing facilities for the sale of surplus honey so as to supplement their income. In this regard, the total outlay during the Sixth Five Year Plan was Rs. 0.09 lakh for the cost including transportation charges covering sixty bee-colonies and the bee-hives for the Onges and the Great Andamanese. The above scheme was proposed to intensify during Seventh Plan with provision of one bee-colony for each family annually. For these extension programmes the total outlay of Rs. 1.05 lakh was sanctioned during the same plan period[26].

Multi-purpose Co-operative Society Ltd.

A Multi-purpose Co-operative Society for each community had been formed with 100% managerial subsidy and 100% subsidy for construction of godown-cum-shops. The aim behind the formation of such Society for each community was to supply of free ration. They could also sell their coconuts, forest products like resin and honey through the Co-operatives would guarantee that they would not be cheated by the outsiders. They could purchase the essential goods from here at reasonable prices. The co-operative is run by the Senior-Social Executive at Dugong Creek and Social workers at Strait Island.

Fishing

Fishing in sea is a means of the livelihood of the tribal of Andaman and Nicobar Islands. In the Fifth Five Year Plan, the Great Andamanese had been supplied with a fishing *dinghi* (boat), fishing net and other necessary materials. In the Sixth Five Year Plan an outlay of Rs. 0.25 lakh was provided for similar fishing materials to be given to the Onges. Rs. 0.35 lakh was provided for the maintenance of fishing *dinghi* and other fishing material for the Great Andamanese[27]. The Fisheries Department had posted a Fisheries Inspector with two fishermen at the Dugong Creek to teach the Onges modern methods of fishing. It had been proposed that during the Seventh Five Year Plan to provide essential fishing requirements to the Onges and the Great Andamanese for supply of essential fisheries requisities an outlay of Rs.1.25 lakh was sanctioned[28].

Domestication of Animals

Under the rehabilitation and welfare scheme, the Samiti had proposed to learn the Great Andamanese and the Onges about domestication of animals like cows for consuming milk and milk products. During the Sixth Five Year Plan, the Samiti had proposed to supply milch cows to them. The main target was to encourage the tribesmen to consume milk as food items. During the Seventh Five Year Plan period, an outlay of Rs. 0.878 lakh had been provided for maintenance of cattle unit of Great Andamanese. The stationing of cow unit consists of two cows for four Onges families. The cost was estimated of each cow to be Rs. 2000/- annually for per unit. The total outlay for this purpose was Rs.0.90 lakh[29].

Pork is the main food item for both the communities—the Great Andamanese and the Onges. But this resource became uncertain for them due to excessive poaching and hunting by the outsiders. So the administration had considered the measures of the domestication of pigs. For these purpose the administration was provided piggery units at Strait Island and Dugong Creek for the Great Andamanese and the Onges respectively. Though Rs. 0.75 lakh was the outlay for the supply of milch cows, fodder for cows and piggery units during the Sixth Five Year Plan period. To maintain the existing milch cows and piggery Rs. 0.257 lakh was the outlay for pay and allowances to Livelock attendents at Strait Island for the Sixth Five Year Plan[30]. It was also proposed to supply them goats, cows for domestication.

Vocational Training

Handicraft work is an important indigenous culture of the primitive tribes of India. The tribal people in the Andaman and Nicobar Islands are also very much engaged in carpentry and other home industry for their own needs. The craft materials for carpentry are provided from their own territory. Theyknow the art of making net, baskets, canoe, bows and arrows for their daily use. The Administration intends to encourage the natives in the practice of the indigenous craft culture and popularise it in the localities. The Samiti chalks out programmes to teach them the modern craft work in Industrial Workshop at Port Blair by supplying materials. Under the scheme it was proposed that every year, 5 adults would be selected for training with a monthly stipend of Rs. 100/-. In this way, within four years from 1981 to 1985, a total number of 20 adults would be trained about wood craft. For this purpose an outlay of Rs. 0.24 lakh was fixed. Moreover, Rs. 0.06 lakh was incurred for providing machinaries, tools and raw materials during the training period[31].

The Programme of training of cane crafts centre at Dugong Creek had been extended to the Seventh Five Year Plan with an outlay of Rs. 1.55 lakhs. It was proposed that a Black-Smith-cum-Carpentry centre would be opened at Dugong, Creek. Materials for running cane and crafts centre would be procured. For teach them about domestication of cows, during the same plan period, it was proposed to train 4 Onges at Dairy Firm at Port Blair for 3 months. A stipend of Rs. 150/- per month for 3 months would be provided. A total outlay of Rs. 0.14 lakh was fixed for this purpose[32]. For encouraging the womenfolk of their handicraft works, sweeing machine with craft teacher had been provided to the Great Andamanese and the Onges.

Education for Children

The education programmes among the small primitive communities like the Great Andamanese and the Onges is one of the important aspects of their development. Education is one of the vital measure for modernisation of new generation. Through modern education, the future generation will be benefitted for leading a modern life and culture. In between 1969 and 1976, before the existence of the Andaman Adim Janjati Vikas Samiti, an initiative was marked among the social workers of the localities for educating the children of the Great Andamanese and the Onges. Particularly, the social workers of "Sangh"had been trying to teach the children in the Hindi medium. Later Samiti was also proposed to post a teacher-cum-social worker and work out a scheme at Dugong Creek. During the Sixth Five Year Plan, an education centre-cum-Balwadies was proposed to set up one each at Strait Island, Dugong Creek and South Bay with an outlay of Rs. 0.354 lakh. It was proposed to import simple lessons of the Great Andamanese and the Onges in their respective habitats[33].

During the Seventh Five Year Plan, the educational schemes was extended further. The aims and objects were to educate the children through books and through vocational methods of teaching. A total outlay of Rs. 1.10 lakh and Rs.0.65 lakh was sanctioned for procurement and supply of educational materials, sport goods, furniture and other stores to the Balwadi centres and the community halls and providing snacks to the children of the Onges and the Great Andamanese respectively. Further, a scheme had been proposed for extending the facilities for education. A sum of Rs. 0.63 lakh was set up as the outlay for boarding and.lodging; of the three Great Andamanese children admitted to the Seva Niketan, at Port Blair. It was reported that an adult centre was also functioning at Dugong Creek where 20 adults attend the classes. It was run by local social worker[34].

Medical and General Health Centre

The general health condition of the two tribal communities was an important question before the government. Most of the adults were suffering from sexual diseases. After independence, the decline of population of both the ethnic groups—the Great Andamanese and the Onges had been continuing. Most of the adults of both sexes among the Great Andamanese were addicted to opium, tobacco and liquor. They were staying in Japanese bunkers in unhygienic conditions. For fighting against the health hazards of the tribals, the Indian Council of Medical Research deputed a team of medical experts in February, 1969[35] to study the cause of decline in the total population. Medical team found that the causes of the dwindling of population were high mortality and sterlity of women.

For improve the health hazard condition of the Great Andamanese and the Onges during the Sixth Five Year Plan, the Samiti considered it necessary to continue the services of a team of experienced and dedicated medical workers. A Medical Officer, Staff Nurse and a Ward Attendent-cum-Helper were posted with an outlay of Rs. 1.674 lakh for the five year of the plan period at Dugong Creek settlement[36]. During this period, some measures had also been taken through establishing a dispensary, a patients ward, with five bed. Maternity facilities had been made available. For the Great Andamanese, a well equipped dispensary with a compounder was set up. During the Seventh Five Year Plan period, a sum of Rs. 0.57 lakh was the outlay for the procurement of medicines and stores for the dispensary at the Strait Island. Also, an outlay of Rs.80 thousand was earmarked for the same purpose at Dugong Creek settlement for the Onges[37].

Infrastructure

Transport

To keep regular contact with the Onges of Dugong Creek, South Bay and the Great Andamanese of Strait Island, firm orders for purchase of a 78 feets long all-weather vessel was placed by the Samiti through administration on a Visakapattanam firm in 1976. The ship was constructed out of a grants of Rs. 20 lakh[38]. It was realised that the major handicap in implementing the welfare measures in the far off islands, where primitive groups are settled, is lack of communication facilities. It was proposed that the boat could be best used for the transporting the goods produced by the tribesmen like coconuts, resin and honey from settlements to the headquarters and for continuing the supply of rationed goods and construction materials from the headquarters to the settlements.

The total outlay of Rs. 14.644 lakh[39] was sanctioned for the payment of salaries of the vessel's staff and other servicing purposes during Six Plan and during Seventh Plan an outlay of Rs. 25.328 lakh was proposed for maintenance and other expenditure to run the Samiti's vessel "Melale" for meeting the requirements of primitive tribals[40]. Two small pucca jetties were constructed to facilitate the berthing of ferry vessels of the Marine Development and the Samiti's vessel, "M V Melale" at the Strait Island and at Dugong Creek.

Water facility

Under the welfare amenities programme, water facility was given the first and formost priority. Construction of pucca wells were chalked out between 1975 and 1976. During the Sixth Five Year Plan, under the water supply scheme, 3 pucca wells at different points were constructed to provide drinking water for the Great Andamanese. At the same time, 6 pucca wells at Dugong Creek and 2 pucca wells at South Bay Onge settlements were constructed for providing the same facilities to them. During Six Five Year Plan a sum of Rs. 0.525 lakh was sanctioned for construction of pucca wells.

Supply of Electricity

Under the modern amenities measures, the Samiti provided electric supply to the tribal colonies alongwith the staff quarters. Installation for electric supply provision for generator sets with distribution lines internal wiring service connection an outlay of Rs.4.410 lakh was incurred during Six Five Year Plan period[41]. For further maintenance of power supply of both the settlements, a sum of Rs. 30.5 lakh was sanction in the Seventh Plan periods[42]. But no power supply is provided to South Bay settlement.

Road and Footpath

During the Fifth Five Year Plan period construction and servicing of a half-mile metalled road and footpath with proper drainage facilities and street lights were proposed. The road would be linked from the seashore to the individual houses of both the settlements for the Great Andamanese and for the Onges. During Six Five Year Plan an outlay of Rs. 1.000 lakh was incurred for the road and footpath at the Onge settlements[43].

Radio and Television Media

The Radio and Television are the foremost essential media of communications for the community marching towards modernisation. During the Fifth Five Year Plan, the Administration of the Andaman and Nicobar Islands undertook a measure to set up one radio set at each of the settlements. Further,the Samiti linked them with one Direct Receiving Television Station for the Great Andamanese at Strait Island and for the Onges at Dugong Creek. It was proposed by the Samiti that, through the observation of current events on the Television screen, they can learn and also have entertainment through the audio-visual process in different languages.

During the Seventh Five Year Plan period a helipad was set up at Dugong Creek settlement. The aim behind its construction was mainly for fast and emergency medical relief for Onges. Dugong Creek settlement is situated at a distance of 46 km. away from the Hut Bay. Indeed, it is a long distance on foot or into the sea shore, also quite difficult to negotiate in the rainy season.

The Samiti started publication of brochures on primitive tribes and encouraged the participation of the Great Andamanese and the Onges in the Republic Day and the the Independence Day celebrations at New Delhi and at Port Blair. Traditionally since its existence, the Samiti, has proposed that tribesmen should be involved more and more with the outside world so that they have to, know-how about the means to modernisation. For these purpose, the Samiti started since the Seventh Five Year Plan period sending

2 youths each year from either the Onge,or the Great Andamanese alternatively to take part in the national celebrations. An outlay of Rs. 1.46 lakh was proposed during the Seventh Plan period[44].

Modern Economy and Employment Scheme

Cultivation was unknown to both the Great Andamanese and the Onges. Their primary occupations were hunting, fishing and collection. After contact with British rulers, the Great Andamanese changed their occupations system. Since independence, they have been gradually accustomed to monetary economy and wage-based occupations. After independence for few years, some Great Andamanese adults were employed as Buch Police by the Forest Department for vigilance in the border area of Jarawa territories. During the earlier seventies, the Onges were engaged in collection of coconuts, honey and resin from their settlements for sale to meet their necessities like food, clothes and tobacco. The Administration in many cases, has offered the Onges and the Great Andamanese, the status of casual workers. Some are employed as permanent workers in various departments under the Administration.

Administrative Management

The "Andaman Adim Janjati Vikas Samiti" is known as "Samiti" is an autonomous organisation fully financed by the Government of India. It has been functioning for all practical purposes as part and parcel of the Tribal Welfare Department of the Andaman Administration. It is found to systematise and co-ordinate the primitive tribal welfare programmes. The objects of the Government were to accelerate the extended welfare measures scientifically and methodically for these communities. Two types of officials are engaged in the management cadre. Some are connected with the Samiti, indirectly, who are involved in chalk out plans and programmes. Others are employed by the Samiti itself, who are professional and technical staff posted at the settlements and at headquarters. Usually, these managerial staff belong to various government organisations. All these made their joint efforts with the help of the Administration for the welfare work. Obviously, the Lieutenant Governor is the chairman of the "Samiti" as a Head of the Administration of the Union Territory. There are three administrative bodies are functioning. Those are Executive Council, Advisory Committee and General Body[45]. The Executive Council consists of the Lt. Governor, the Chief Secretary, as Chairman and Vice-Chairman and other members of the Council are the following:

Chairman, State Social Welfare Board, Principal (Chief) Conservator of Forest, the Finance Secretary, the Deputy Commissioner-curn-Development Secretary, the Judicial Secretary; the Deputy Commissioners of two districts, the Inspector-General of Police, the Director of Tribal Welfare; the Director of Medical and Health Service; Regional Officer, Anthropological Survey of India, Chief of Great Andamanese; Executive Secretary; Samiti and Assistant Commissioner (Tribal Welfare) of the Andaman and Nicobar Administration. The General Body of the Samiti comprises of all the heads of the departments and the senior officers of the Administration and the Anthropological Survey of India, Port Blair, Andaman.

The Advisory Committee consists of Lt. Governor as the Chairman and other officials are the Joint Secretary, Tribal Development, Government of India; Director General, Anthropological Survey of India; and Director of All India Institute of Medical Science. All the above administrators are the ex-officio members.

The permanent field staff of the Samiti's are Senior Social Executive, Social workers, Plantation-in-charges, boat Master, Engineer and other staff of the Samiti's vesselo. The casual workers are Mali, Ward attendents, massengers, Balwadi teacher, cattle attenders, helpers etc. Further, the Samiti has deputed few numbers of professional workers with special pay and allowances from other departments. For health care a doctor,compounder, Ward Boy, Midwife have been deputed. Police has been posted for vigilances and wireless operators with helpers for speedy communication. Engine drivers have been deputed for electric supply.

All welfare schemes and programmes generally originate at the level of the Executive Secretary. He is a non-field staff. All the managerial and administrative functions are headed by him. The non-field staff of the Samiti's are accountants, clerks, peon and jeep driver, who are posted at headquarters of the Samiti.

In the Sixth Five Year Plan, an outlay of Rs.4.454 lakh was sanctioned for payment of the field staff posted at the settlements. Moreover, an outlay of Rs. 2.281 lakh was incurred for maintain of the Samiti's office establishment at Port Blair for welfare of the tribesmen[46]. During the Seventh Five Year plan, a sum of Rs. 13.220 lakh was allotted for the field staff, who are posted at the tribal settlements and staff of the Samiti's head office at Port Blair[47].

Sector-wise Proposed Schemes and Outlay Shown in the Table of Plan Periods for the Great Andamanese and the Onges

Name of Scheme (Sector)	*Proposed outlay for 6th Plan 1980-85 (in lakh)*	*Proposed outlay for 7th Plan 1985-90 (in lakh)*	*Total proposed outlay during two Tribal sub-Plan (in lakh)*	*Remarks on the individual scheme*
1. Agriculture	3.00	4.375	7.375	Maintenance and improvement of cocoanut Plantation-cum-vegetables gardens at Onges and Great Andamanese settlements. Supply of agricultural implements and clearance of additional areas for raised plantations.
2. Bee-keeping	0.090	1.050	1.140	Proposed to supply 60 Nos. bee-colonies along with bee-hives to the Onges and the Great Andamanese.
3. Animal Husbandry	1.007	1.838	2.845	Supply of milk cow, and piggery units to the Great Andamanese and the Onge families of cattle Maintenance units.
4. Fisheries	0.60	1.250	1.850	Maintenance of fishing dinghies and cost of fishing gears for Onges and the Great Andamanese.
5. Poultry Farming	-	0.50	0.50	Supply of poultry units to each Onge and the Great Andamanese family.
6. Vocational	0.24	0.14	0.38	For improve craftmanship, proposed to impart training to adults

training				wood, cane and crafts and dairy development.
7. Establishment of small scale and cottage industries	0.60	1.55	2.15	It was proposed to establish a Blacksmithy-cum-carpentry and cane craft centres at Onges and Great Andamanese settlements.
8. Education	0.354	2.380	2.734	For better education, supply school furniture books, snacks and games articles for the tribal children.
9. Medical and Health Services	1.674	1.370	3.044	Procurement of medicines and stores for dispensaries and special treatment for the Great Andamanese and the Onges.
10. Food, nutrition clothes and gifts and cash allowances.	7.634	25.650	33.284	Supply of free rations and clothes and gifts to the Great Andamanese and the Onges, and Cash allowances to the unemployed Great Andamaneses.
11. Power Supply	4.410	3.050	7.460	Installation of Generator sets and distribution of lines internal wirings service connection for procurement of electric supply.
12. Infrastructure	14.644	25.328	39.972	Maintenance and other expenditure to run the vessel for transporting cargo and payment of the vessel's staff.
13. Establishment and maintenance of office and staff of the Samiti	6.375	13.196	19.931	For office establishment and payment of the staff of the Samiti at the settlements.
14. Providing Welfare amenities.	1.525	9.350	10.875	Improvement of water supply, road and footpath construction, raised model houses for Onges, maintenance rest houses and individual houses for both the tribal groups.

15. Miscellaneous	- 1.460	1.460	Publication of brochureson prinutive tribes and participation of Onges/Great Andamanese in Republic and Independence Day at New Delhi and Port Blair.
Total outlay (in Rs.)	42.153	92.487	229.000

REFERENCES

1. India, Constitution, *The Constitution of India,* Ministry of Law and Justice, New Delhi, (1973), pp. 6-123.
2. Verma, R.C., *Indian Tribes Through the Age,* Publication Division, Ministry of Information & Broadcasting, Government of India, New Delhi, (1990), p. 179.
3. Das, Nityananda, "The safeguards for tribes: past and present" in *Adivasi,* Tribal Research Bureau, Orissa, vol.8 (2), (1966), p.58.
4. Dhebar, U.N., *Scheduled Areas and Scheduled Tribes Commission Report, 1960-61,* Govt. of India, Ministry of Tribal Welfare, Delhi,(1961), pp. 155-450.
5. Whitakar, Romulus, "Endangered Andamans" in *Environmental Services Group World Wildlife Fund,* India and MAB, Deptt. of Environment, New Delhi, (1985), p. 6.
6. Andaman and Nicobar Administration, *Annual General Administrative Reports.* Port Blair, (1973), p.74.
7. Krishna R. Shyamji, "Survival of the Weakest, Symposium: Island Culture", on *Post Plenary Session International Congress of Anthropological and Ethnological Science,* Port Blair, (1978), p. 3.
8. Kochar, V.K., "The Great Andamanese today", in *Man in India,* v. 49(3), (1969), p. 248.
9. Chakraborty, D.K., *The Great Andamanese: A Study of Persistence of Culture in the Face of Biological Extinction, A Preliminary Report,* An.S.I., Port Blair, (1974), p. 1. (unpublished)
10. Sarkar, Dipak, Personal statement of D.K. Sarkar, *teacher, Education Department, Andaman* attached to P.S. Havelock 6. In 1967, he was incharge of welfare activities of the uprooted Onges. His statement was recorded by the researcher in an interview held on 12.3.1990 at Havelock.
11. Arya, Prem Chand and Greesh B. Mathur, "Tribal Development through Bharatiya Adimjati Sevak Sangh" in

Tribal Souvenir, p. 178. Here the researcher reffered "Bharatiya Adimjati Sevak Sangh" as the name of "Sangh" throughout his paper.

12. Sarkar, Dipak, *School teacher* attached to Primary School, Havelock:6, Andaman, ex-incharge of the Onges of Little Andaman in 1967.
13. Department of Social Welfare, *Report of the Study team on the Negrito Tribes of the Andaman*, Anthropological Survey of India, (here also referred as An.S.I. by the researcher) Govt. of India, Port Blair, 1969; p. 5 (unpublished).
14. Andaman Adim Janjati Vikas Samiti, *Retrieval From Precipice*, Port Blair, Here the researcher reffered "Andaman Adim Janjati Vikas Samiti" as the name of "Samiti" throughout his paper.
15. Andaman Adim Janjati Vikas Samiti, *Retrieval From Precipice*, Port Blair, 1977, pp. 44-47.
16. Verma, R.C., *Indain Tribals Through the Age*, Ministry of Information and Broadcasting, Government of India, New Delhi, (1990), pp. 174-177.
17. Das, Hare Hara and Rabindra Nath Rath, *The Land of the Coral Beds: Andaman and Nicobar Islands*, Behrampur, Orissa, (1988), pp. 102-103.
18. Vidyarthi, L.P., "Development plans of the tribes of Andaman and Nicobar Islands: An action oriented report," *Iournal of Social Research*, V. 19(2), (1976), pp. 78-79.
19. Krishnatry, S.M., "Report on the work done and achievements", in *Journal of Social Research*, vol. 19(2), (1976), p. 107.
20. Andaman and Nicobar Administration, *Tribal Sub-Plan for Sixth Five Year Plan, Port Blair*, (1980-85), pp. 60-61.
21. Andaman and Nicobar Administration, *Tribal Sub-Plan for Seventh Five Year Plan*, Port Blair, (1985-90), p. 77.
22. *Ibid.*, Tribal Sub-Plan for Sixth Five Year Plan and for Seventh Five Year Plan, p. 59 and p. 75 respectively.
23. Andaman and Nicobar Administration, *Tribal Sub-Plan for Six Five Year Plan*, Port Blair, (1980-85), p. 61.
24. *Ibid.*, *Tribal Sub-Plan for Seventh Five Year Plan*, (1988-90), pp. 75-76.
25. *Ibid.*, Tribal Sub-Plan for Seventh Five Year Plan, p. 76.
26. *Ibid.*, Tribal Sub-Plan for Sixth Five Year Plan and Seventh Five Year Plan, pp. 65 and 76 respectively.

27. *Ibid.*, Tribal Sub-Plan for Sixth Five Year Plan, pp. 59-61.
28. *Ibid.*, Tribal Sub-Plan for Seventh Five Year Plan, p. 67
29. *Ibid.*, Tribal Sub-Plan for Seventh Five Year Plan, p. 76.
30. *Ibid.*, Tribal Sub-Plan for Sixth Five Year Plan, p. 43.
31. *Ibid.*, Tribal Sub-Plan for Sixth Five Year Plan, p. 66.
32. *Ibid.*, Tribal Sub-Plan for Seventh Five Year Plan, pp. 76-78.
33. *Ibid.*, Tribal Sub-Plan for Sixth Five Year Plan, p. 45 and p. 59.
34. *Ibid.*, Tribal Sub-Plan for Seventh Five Year Plan, p. 78.
35. Department of Social Welfare, *Report of the Study team on the Nerito Tribes of the Andaman,* An.S.I, Port Blair, (1969), p. 5 (unpublished).
36. Andaman and Nicobar Administration, *Tribal Sub-Plan for Sixth Five Year Plan, Port Blair,* 1980-81, p. 35.
37. *Ibid.*, Tribal Sub-Plan for Seventh Five Year Plan, p. 61.
38. Andaman Adim Janjati Vikas Samiti, *Retrieval From Precipice,* Port Blair, (1977), p. 54.
39. *Ibid*, Tribal Sub-Plan for Seventh Five Year Plan, pp. 71 -77.
40. Andaman and Nicobar Administration, *Tribal Sub-Plan for the Sixth Five Year Plan,* Port Blair, 1980-85, p. 49.
41. *Ibid.*, Tribal Sub-Plan for Sixth Five Year Plan, p. 37.
42. *Ibid.*, Tribal Sub-Plan for Seventh Five Year Plan, p. 78.
43. *Ibid.*, Tribal Sub-Plan for Sixth Five Year Plan, p. 61.
44. *Ibid.*, Tribal Sub-Plan for Seventh Five Year Plan, p. 79.
45. Awardi, S.A., *Master Plan (1990-2020) for Welfare of Primitive Tribes,* Director of Tribal Welfare, Port Blair, (1989), pp. 24-25 (cyclostyled paper).
46. Andaman and Nicobar Administration, *Tribal Sub-Plan for Six Five Year Plan,* Port Blair, (1980-85), pp. 31-51.
47. *Ibid.*, Tribal Sub-Plan for Seventh Five Year Plan, pp. 72-73.

3

Nature and Extent of Benefits So Far Available

Agriculture and Horticulture

Both the Great Andamanese and the Onges were hunting and nomadic communities, did not know anything about agriculture and settled life. They lived a simple life. With the establishment of coconut and vegetable gardens in their respective settlements, the government has introduced a new economy for them with agriculture as a livelihood. The administration, through various plan periods have developed 95 acres of coconut plantation and 5 acres of vegetable and fruit gardens for the Onges. Similarly, for the Great Andamanese, 5 acres of coconut and 5 acres of fruit and vegetable gardens have been raised. The aim behind the development of horticulture was to make the tribal population an economically self-supporting community. It was expected that, they would utilize the coconuts, vegetables and fruits as items of their food as well as cash crops. Nuts were expected to sold to purchasers. Other requirements would be supplied to them through their Multi-purpose Cooperative Society. Coconut plantations were created for these communities with the idea that the coconuts would be consumed by them to compensate for the loss of fat intake in their diet. Now-a-days all the natural food resources in the area have become rare and their availability is uncertain due to the excessive poaching by the non-autochthons. Under such circumstances, the local tribe could manage to keep the supply of their essential food somewhat regular by consuming the coconuts, vegetables and fruits as substitutes. About 2500 coconut trees at Dugong Creek and at South Bay yield fruits out of a total of 4000 trees. Recently around 3000 coconuts were collected during a month after local consumption[1]. At Strait Island, all the 200 coconut trees yield around 500 coconuts per month[2].

During various Tribal Sub-plan periods, 10 acres of orchard-cum-kitchen garden has been proposed to be raised at Dugong Creek and the South Bay. But only 5 acres of orchard-cum-kitchen garden at Dugong Creek has been developed with vegetables, bananas, papayas and other edible fruits. On the other hand 5 Hectres of land allotted for developing the orchard-cum-vegetable garden at Strait Island have not yet been raised. The area was fenced with barbed wire around. This vast area is now lying unutilized.

Now the basic question is to what extent, the said communities are benefited and how far the schemes have been successful.

Table 1 has given in details about the individual willingness and benefits of the Great Andamanese and the Onges of the modern agriculture and horticulture schemes. At least 5 acres of plantation yield 500 coconuts for the Great Andamanese per month. Beside this plantation, they have to separate large areas of plantations at Interview Island and at English Island. These were developed by their progenitory[3]. For along time they are not getting any share of the nuts. Outsiders taken them away secretly or by force. Now the Government also sells them. So the Great Andamanese are not getting the money they are entitled to selling these coconuts. Now the plantation is under the authority of the Forest Department. So, due to lack of communication and less interest on the part of the Samiti, Great Andamanese are unable to collect the coconuts. They themselves have not been made interested in the wealth which should be shared by them.

Table 1

Name of the Tribe	*Name of the schemes*	*No. of persons inter-viewed*	*No. of respon-dents*	*N.A.**	*Provided schemes*		*Willingness to accept scheme*		*Use as food-stuffs*		*Getting financial benefits*	
					Yes	*No*	*Yes*	*No*	*Yes*	*No*	*Yes*	*No*
Great Andamanese	Coconut	15	15	-	15	-	15	-	-	15	4	11
	Vegetable/ Fruits	15	15	-	15	-	3	12	3	12	-	15
	Honey bee	15	15	-	-	15	-	-	-	-	-	-
Onges	Coconut	70	58	12	58	-	50	8	50	8	-	58
	Vegetable/ Fruits	70	60	10	60	-	-	60	-	60	-	60
	Honey bee	70	40	30	-	40	-	-	-	-	-	-

Source: Field Survey conducted by the researcher on the spot during 1988-1990.

*Here the researcher used the terms NO Answer, as N.A. in all the Tables througout the paper.

The Samiti has divided the trees at Strait Island unofficially and unequally among the Great Andamanese family. So, some families have shared only a few trees while some shared a good number to trees. Thus all the families are not equally benefitted as expected. Only a few trees yield fruits and even these fruits are shared by one or two families[4].

Out of 15 Great Andamanese respondents none of the individuals has prefered the coconut as food items. In reality, however, each of the Great Andamanese does not consume even one coconut a week. Only one family has developed a small areas of vegetable on personal initiative. 12 out of 15 are not interested in consuming and raising vegetables and fruits. Collection of coconut from the plantation takes place on individual as and when needed and the fruits are sold to outside market as in the Long Island, Havelock and Port Blair. The people prefer to sell the products to the staff of ferry boats of the Marine Department at cheap rate. There is every possibility of they are being cheated by the outside consumer. The office records of their Co-perative Society at Strait Island have shown that only on two occasions, they have sold their coconuts through the Co-operative Society to the Samiti at Port Blair[5]. Meanwhile, a large number of fruits and coconuts are being taken by the staff of the Samiti posted at the settlement without any money in return to the owners. The "Samiti" itself has not tried to prevent them from such activities. In short, it has failed to convince the tribals to sell the coconuts and fruits through the Co-operative Society at a fair price. If they sold through their own Co-operative Society, then they could also get benefits and profits from the Cooperative Society on the basis of a fair price.

From this, one could imagine the overall position of the benefits of the Great Andamanese in this particular scheme. They are not getting benefits from the administration as were expected under the welfare scheme. The plans for development of coconut, vegetable and fruit under the horticulture schemes have partially failed. The Samiti staff have never sought the opinion of the tribesmen on these schemes nor have they encouraged them to consume the products.

As far as the Onges are concerned, the plantation scheme has given them three types of benefits—first, they use the coconuts as a food items. Secondly, by selling them, they earn, and thirdly, they are getting money by working in the plantation as wage labourers. Perhaps the horticulture scheme has not benefited the Onges so much. This scheme simply employs them as daily wage labourers to clean the undergrowths of the coconut, orchard, and to collect the coconuts. Now 62% of the Onges at Dugong Creek are employed as daily wage labourers at the rate of Rs. 21/- per day for 10 days in a month. Table 1 shows that 50 out of 58 Onge respondents like coconut as food item. They also use its oil as a food item. But all 58 respondents out of 70 interviewed have narrated that now-a-days the income from selling of coconuts is nil. For last two years, the coconuts are not sold by the Co-operative Society due to lack of transport. At least 15,000 coconuts at Dugong Creek are kept in store. All the nuts get damaged due to lack of instant transport from the Onge settlements to the headquarters. The Samiti's own vessel, "M V Milale" has not been able to make more than one trip for transport. The nuts are sold to outside markets through the Samiti. The same condition exists at South Bay settlements where due to difficult over land communication, the coconuts are not brought from the settlement for sale at the proper time. Moreover, the Onge tribals have not been taught about horticulture or kitchen garden seriously. About likeness of vegetable, every Onge individual has offered negative answer to the question of consumption of vegetable and fruit as food. All 60 Onge respondents stated that they are not getting any benefits from the orchard-cum-vegetable garden. They are not interested in developing garden. This is because they are not encouraged by the authorities. Rather their enthusiasm in this regard is to get money from the wage labours. During all these years, the Samiti has not made any headway in introducing horticulture or agriculture among the Onges.

At Dugong Creek, a 50 acres new cocoanut plantation has been developed. But it is not being properly maintained by the Samiti. All the trees are at the fruit-bearing stage. But due to negligence of the Plantation-in-Charge, all trees have been covered by thick jungles. The remaining 25 acres are not also properly maintained. The coconut plantations at Dugong Creek is not cared for long time. They are not getting any coconuts from their 50 acres areas of coconut plantation properly. More or less most of the nuts are poached by the outsiders reported by the Onges of Dugong Creek. The Samiti has neither taken any initiative to refrain the outsiders from this plantation directly. This result is not upto the expectation, because they are not getting any benefits from the major portion of their plantation. Similarly, the income from selling of coconut is uncertain. Due to the negligence on the part of the Samiti they cannot sell their nuts properly and have not been taught about horticulture.

Under the horticulture scheme, the Samiti was supposed to introduce bee colonies for the Great Andamanese and the Onges. They are very fond of honey. It is an important and favourable item of food. But now they find it difficult to collect honey from their surroundings jungles. So, during the Sixth plan period there was a proposal to keep 60 bee-colonies along with bee-hives for them. It was also proposed to provide them with the technical knowhow by training them in the modern process of extraction of honey and with market facilities for sale of the surplus so as to supplement their income. But according to survey report, one 40 out of 70 Onges respondents and all 15 Great Andamanese respondents have denied any supply of honey bee for their settlements. That means, the Samiti has not implemented this welfare scheme either of the two communities. So, there is no question of benefits, success or failure of the project. The tribals are being deprived of their favourite food items and of the additional source of income. Apparently it is clear that the Great Andamanese and the Onge respondents reported that they are not interested to cultivate honey bee.

Domestication of Animals and Poultry farming

Under the rehabilitation and welfare measures, the local administration through (AAJVS) Samiti proposed to teach the Great Andamanese and the Onges about domestication of animals and poultry farming for their food purposes and financial benefits. They were provided with milch cows for

Table 2

Opinion Regarding Domestication of Animals and Poultry Farming

Name of the Tribe	*Name of the schemes*	*No. of persons inter-viewed*	*No. of respon-dents*	*N.A.*	*Provided schemes*		*Willingness to accept scheme*		*Use as food-stuffs*		*Getting financial benefits*	
					Yes	*No*	*Yes*	*No*	*Yes*	*No*	*Yes*	*No*
Great Andamanese	Milch cows	15	15	-	15	-	3	12	3	12	-	15
	White pigs	15	15	-	15	-	-	15	-	15	-	15
	Poultry	15	15	-	-	15	-	15	-	-	-	-
Onges	Milch cows	70	60	10	50	-	-	60	-	60	-	60
	White Pigs	70	50	20	50	-	-	50	-	50	-	50
	Poultry	70	60	10	-	60	-	60	-	60	-	60

Source: Field survey conducted by the researcher on the spot during 1988-1990.

this purposes. But both the communities have not any experience of domesticating any animal except dogs. The tribals become much fond of pork. But hunting the wild boar become difficult due to the indiscriminate hunting by the outsiders. As a substitute for wild boars, the Samiti supplied them white pigs at Dugong Creek and at Strait Island in 1982 with the objectives of restricting the traditional wild boar hunting of the Great Andamanese and the Onges. Milch cows was introduced for milk consumption.

All these schemes started under the supervision of the Samiti to certain extent. A lot of money and labour was spent for the implementation of the welfare measures during the various plan periods. The effective schemes had been reviewed from field survey by the present researcher. It has been found from Table 2 that all 60 out of 70 Onge respondents and 12 out of 15 Great Andamanese respondents do not like milk and so they are not inclined to domesticate the cow. Similarly about 50 Onge respondents expressed their displeasure about the consumption of white pork and the domestication of white pigs. Even the Great Andamanese dislike to domesticate any white pigs. The piggery programme, started with an improved variety of white pig was also a failure. All the pigs either died, or disappeared in the forest, as the Great Andamanese and the Onges never cared to domesticate them. They did not get poultry from the administration for farming. In the same manner, the scheme of goats, ducks, and cows have failed as the Great Andamanese and the Onges do not like the chicken nor are they willing to know how to take care of the birds. They did not get any financial benefits from these schemes. The Samiti has failed to convince them and try to encourage their interest on domestication of the animals. The Onges of South Bay did not get milch cow and piggery units for domestication. All the cows at Dugong Creek and at Strait Island are now roaming like wild animals. The Onges did not know milking and so they were not interested in consuming the milk at all. It is reported that the milk is consumed by the field functionaries posted there. Even during the Seventh Five Year Plan periods, the Samiti proposed to provide with training the Onges at Dairy Farm at Port Blair.

But the training scheme was not organised. The failure of the above schemes gives the impression that the welfare schemes of the Great Andamanese and the Onges were formulated according to the personal whim of one authority or the other with no knowledge of the tribal culture and tradition. Without the willingness and lack of proper guidance, welfare schemes failed to serve any real purpose.

Modern Fishing Facilities and its Usefulness

Both the communities—the Great Andamanese and the Onges are good fishermen. All their economic activities were concentrated on subsistence. By nature they are experts in fishing and hunting both the sea and in the creeks. The administration proposed to introduce modern fishing techniques for them. Simultaneously, the tribesmen have been encouraged to develop their traditional fishing culture by the Samiti supplying them with mechanised boats attached with big nylon nets, fishing hooks, ropes etc. It could be easy and speedy for them to get sea fishes with the help of mechanised boats they could go out into the deep sea and even their nearest Island for fishing. At its initial stage a Fisheries Inspector with two fishermen were posted at the Dugong Creek to teach Onges modern fishery method.

From the Table 3 it is found that no training for modern fishing technique has been provided for the Great Andamanese. Even they did not get fishing nets from the Samiti. So this particular welfare measures has been a total failure. All 55 Onge respondents do now know the use of mechanised boats and modern big nylon nets and gears. Only 2 out of 14 Great Andamanese respondents know little about the use of mechanised boats. They even dislike to go out for fishing by boat. The new generation of the Great Andamanese and the Onges are not interested in fishing. The old experienced persons are still practising fishing and hunt turtles and dugong by using their own canoes. The Samiti did not arrange any training to them about the use of mechanised boats and nets. So now the modern boats are lying useless. Neither the Onges nor the Great Andamanese are in a position to repair the boats and the use of the boats again. They do not know the technical difficulties regarding

Table 3
Willingness of the Individuals about Modern Fishing Methods

Name of the Tribe	*Name of the schemes*	*No of persons inter-viewed*	*No. of respon-dents*	*N.A.*	*Provided scheme Yes*	*No*	*Knowledge of usefulness Yes*	*No*	*Subsistence financial benefits Yes*	*No*
Great Andamanese	Mechanised Boats	15	14	1	14	-	2	12	-	14
	Fishing Equipments	15	14	1		14		-	-	-
Onges	Mechanised Boats	70	55	15	55	-	-	55	-	55
	Fishing Equipment	70	55	15	55	-	-	55	-	55

Source: Field survey conducted by the researcher on the spot during 1988-1990.

the boats. The Samiti itself has not yet arranged training for repairing the boats. So, regarding fishing culture and profession, both the communities have not secured any benefits. Naturally, the Great Andamanese and the Onges neither got financial nor got subsistence benefits from the modern fishing schemes.

Infrastructure

Transport communication is one of the urgent infrastructure for hastening constructive welfare measures for the Great Andamanese and the Onges. Practically, the Dugong Creek and the South Bay and Strait Island settlements are far away from the headquarters. The Dugong Creek and South Bay are 46 k.m. and 22 k.m. away from Hut Bay, the headquarters of Little Andaman respectively[6]. Both the Onge settlements are linked by land, but they are cut off by several creeks. On the other hand, the Strait Island, the Great Andamanese settlement, is an isolated island. It is situated of a distance of 57 km. North-east from Port Blair[7], the headquarters of the Union Territory. For sea communication, the administration has purchased a separate vessel for the purpose. It has proposed that all the forest products including coconuts, resin and honey should be carried from the settlements to the headquarters for sale by the vessel. Sometimes the materials which related to welfare programmes for the tribesmen should be transported from the headquarters to the settlements. For berthing the ferry boats and the cargo boat, two pucca jetties have been constructed at Dugong Creek and at Strait Island. But no sea route facilities have been arranged for the Onges at South Bay. However, most of the time, the vessels are being engaged for serving to Jarawas and the Sentinelese contact party for developing friendly relations with the Jarawas and Sentinelese gifting food articles.

Now all the rationed articles for Dugong Creek are carried either personally by the Onge themselves on road or by the sea. For such works, the Samiti has been using tractors for local transport and mechanised boats in the sea route. At South Bay, all the rationed articles and construction materials are transported by Inden tractors of other departments. Tractor brings their coconuts from the settlement allowing a high rate as transport charges. The main purpose are not served thereby. Due to lack of cargo vessels, all the collected coconuts at Dugong Creek get rotten. At Strait Island, goods are transported through ferry boats of the Marine Department. But such service is also uncertain at the rainy season or heavy monsoon due to rough weather. The construction works are not completed in due time because of short supply of materials and irregular transport services. Moreover tractors and vessels are not available all the year round because they are needed for repair and maintenance after a certain time. In this period, no service is available for the Onges and the Great Andarnanese.

One wireless centre has been opened for each settlement except at South Bay, for emergency and speedy communication between the settlements and headquarters. The wireless centres are controlled by the Andaman and Nicobar Police Department. So it is not used and controlled by the Samiti itself. Naturally the police outpost vigilance parties have been using the wireless system for their own purposes. Indeed, all the emergency calls relating to welfare purpose have also to be channelled by the social workers through the wireless system. A helipad has also been constructed at Dugong Creek for emergency service to deliver the required speedy relief. Journey by boat is also impossible during the rainy season. So, there should be air-service for meeting emergency calls. The helicopter service is not being used for such purpose, rather it serves visiting high officials.

Electric light and fan constitute another facilities provided by the welfare agency to the Onges and the Great Andamanese under the group of modern amenities. The power house works with diesel and supplies electricity to the residential areas of the Samiti's workers and the tribesmen colonies. No power supply has been provided to South Bay Settlement. The Supply of power is often disturbed by breakdown of the DG. sets or lack of diesel supply at Strait Island and at Dugong Creek[8]. The power houses are operated by the helpers. But they do not know the intricacies of its mechanism. Most of the time the operators go out from the settlements. Due to mishandling by the helpers, the power supply usually suffers from frequent break-downs. If the Generator is out of order, then it takes a lot of time for repairing. There are no repairing facilities and spare parts are also not available at the settlements. Operators have no much knowledge to repair the defects. Most of the time they depend on headquarters for changing any parts and repairing the Generator. The timing of electric supply covers a period of four hours from 6 p.m. Most of the Onges habitually take their dinner at sunset and go to the bed immediately thereafter. So the supply of electricity is not very useful to the tribesmen.

The Samiti has provided the tribals with some sort of facilities by opening a Direct Relay Station of television at Dugong Creek and at Strait Island. By these relay stations, the tribal population could see and listen to the programmes which are broadcast through the network programmes. They could enjoy the programmes of tribal dances and songs as well as the cultural programmes of other communities. They could thus be accustomed to broad base their culture. But unfortunately, the centres do not function regularly. No initiative is taken by the Samiti to stop this irregularity. Onges can not understand the language of the programmes. Further, they do not usually go out from their houses at night, and so they cannot enjoy the cultural programmes of the television at night in the community halls or centres. A few tribals individually posses radio sets and even tape-recorder sets. These have been either purchased by themselves or gifted to them by visitors. The Onges often listen to film songs without understanding the meaning of the songs. The Onges of the South Bay are deprived of these cultural amenities which their counterparts at Dugong Creek and the Great Andamanese of Strait Island enjoy.

Pure Drinking Water

Providing pure drinking water to the tribals is an important project at the islands. For these purpose, three pucca wells have been constructed at different points at the Strait Island. Six at Dugong Creek and 2 at South bay. Four wells at Dugong Creek and one well at South Bay are not in working conditions. The wells of both the Onge settlements always remains uncovered and the water gets polluted. The

Onges have not yet developed hygienic habits. Children often throw leaves, other dirty articles and even garbage into the wells. The Onges of both the settlements like to collect water from the natural stream in the jungle. They drink the dirty water without boiling or filtering it. The Samiti Staff neither take any initiative by spreading anti-bacterial medicines nor prevent them from polluting the water. They have never bothered to take much care of the wells and their water. Hence, supply of pure water is also a problem at the Strait Island. The Great Andamanese suffer more from anaemia, diarrhoea, dysentery and frequent worm infections probably due to the use of polluted water from the wells[9]. Even the supply of water is discontinued at the dry season. All the settlers face the crisis of inadequate supply of pure water from the wells.

Medical Aids

Medical facilities are the first and foremost measures, provided to the Great Andamanese and the Onges by the Administration. The urgent task of the authority was to prevent the tribals from fatal diseases, which caused high rate of mortality among them. The Great Andamanese were addicted to opium and tobacco. According to Dr. Verma[10] (1976) and Dr. Patnaik (1982)[11], most of the adult Great Andamanese and the Onges were suffering from rnalnurition and bronchial infection. They also suspected to be suffering from diseases like venereal and Tuberculosis, skin diseases, loss of fertility and syphillis.

For eliminating these harmful diseases, the administration prepared history sheet for every individual, specifying the diseases which he is suffering. One of the most serious health hazard is the addiction of the tribals to opium and intoxicating liquors. Both the settlements have been provided with medicine and physicians with well equipped instruments for first aid. A permanent doctor attends patients at Dugong Creek for a term of four months and a whole time compounder for Strait Island. Moreover a doctor from the nearest hospital at Long Island visits the settlement fortnightly. A special medical team with specialists from various institutions come frequently for the medical check-up of the

Table 4
Opinion on Acceptance of Modern Medicine and Healthcare

Name of the Tribe	*No. of persons inter-viewed*	*No. of respon-dents*	*N.A.*	*Likeness on modern medicine and treatment*		*Addiction on liquor/ intoxicants*		*Addiction*		*Place of availability of intoxicants/ liquor*	
				Yes	*No*	*Yes*	*No*	*Regular*	*Irreg-ular*	*Self made*	*Outside market*
Great Andamanese	15	15	-	15	-	13	2	10	3	5	8
Onges	70	60	10	5	55	30	30	20	10	-	30

Source: Field survey conducted by the researcher of the spot during 1988-1990.

aborigines. Steps have also been taken to prevent the smuggling of opium to the tribesmen. Those whose conditions were serious were sent to Madras and Calcutta as and when needed free of cost for treatment.

The authority has succeeded to eliminate many of the harmful diseases in the tribal population. The Administration has undertaken all possible measures to improve the deteriorating health condition of the aboriginals.

Health education is very much necessary in the tribal areas. A systematic programme with audio-visual equipments should be organised to spread the knowledge about unhyginic conditions and sanitory habits of the tribal people.

Table 4 shows that the Great Andamanese are very much believe on modern medicine and treatments. With the direct initiative by the administration most of the adult-males have been de-addicted so far as opium addiction among the Great Andamanese are concerned. But at present they are addicted to liquor in place of opium. Among the respondents interviewed by the researcher, 30 out of 60 Onge and 13 out of 15 Great Andamanese adults are addicted to liquor. The remaining adult population occasionally take liquor. It is surprising to note that among the Great Andamanese even female adults and children also take liquor. Many of them often visit Port Blair, and Havelock and consume liquor there. Some of them have learnt to brew the rice beer "the *handia*" from the other communities of the Islands like Ranchi, Telegus. They procure the patent herbal formula the "goli" from them and use the dole rice brew *handia* clandestinely. Even some of the staff of the Samiti itself are actively engaged in the supply of wine to the tribals. Sometimes supply them foreign liquor at high prices for exchange of coconuts or other sea-products like ambergris and medicated bird nets. The Onges generally consume country liquor from non-tribal villages at Little Andaman. The Samiti has failed to prevent such activities. However, it has arranged a supply of 250 grammes of tobacco leaves to every adult of both the tribesmen along with the rationed articles. Tobacco is also very harmful for health.

Patients suffering from tuberculosis and sexually

transmitted diseases are being attended to. But this programme is being followed with difficulty as the tribal people live in unhygienic condition, do not have knowledge of proper clothing and do not have clean, sanitary habits.

In case of the Onges settlement 55 out of 60 Onges respondents do not like to attend dispensary for treatment. They do not believe on the efficacy of alien medical treatment system. Rather they still take herbal medicines and are not hospital-minded. The dispensaries of both settlements are not well-equipped. Physicians sent there on deputation from the Health Department for four months. Consider their posting as a punishment. So, they never dedicate themselves to their work. Moreover, often the physician is a new recruit who just passed the MBBS examination without any orientation training about the people for whose medical care he is posted. Naturally as a new hand, he has no adequate knowledge about the complicated medical aids. Those physicians, who consider their posting as punishment, lack dedication. During their tenure, they take as much leaves as possible to avoid stay at settlements. There is no permanent physician at South Bay. A doctor from Hut Bay visits once in a week for the treatment of tribal patients. Emergency cases are referred to Port Blair hospitals. Language is a vital problem of both for the physicians and the patients. The Onges cannot express themselves as to with their problems are and the physician does not understand the ailment of the patient. After a physician gathers some experience and becomes able to understand individual cases, he is transferred by Health Department when his tenure is over. So, he could not take any initiative and measures properly. He cannot take any interest in their health problems as his tenure would be for a very short period.

The administrative efforts to improve the health and hygiene of the aborigines have yielded poor results and the tribesmen are not also happy. Till now they have not recieved any systematic health education. The millieu of the settlements are not clean. Often after cooking or eating, the tribesmen leave the utensils unwashed, dogs lick those utensils which are again used for the same purpose. The Onges eat together with dogs using the same plate. Many of them using the same clothes without washing for days together. The women usually wear petticoats which are not washed and remain dirty. The malefolk these days wear synthetic clothing, which are worn for days together without washing. So they sometimes suffer from fungal infection on the skin. Except a few, most of the tribesmen do not look healthy though they look cheerful.

To sum up, to the medical and health management for the two communities under reference has not been satisfactory. Unless these tribal people are educated about the modern medicines and develop faith on the "alien" treatment, the picture might not change. A few of them are getting modern medical benefits. Even, some doctors have been found successful at the dispensary under intensive care. Notably, the Great Andamanese are taking to modern medical aids. But until and unless they are refrained from excessive addiction to liquor and tobacco, no fruitful result can come out.

Multi-purpose Co-operative Society Ltd.

Multi-purpose Co-operative Societies are functioning— one at Dugong Creek for the Onges and the other at Strait Island for the Great Andamanese. All the adult, males and females, are active members of the Multi-purpose Co-operative Societies and have equal share in the respective society. The Societies were formed with the idea of collections cocoanuts, honey, resin and other forest products and sea products from the tribals and sold in the market. The profit is supposed to be kept as a fund for the welfare of them. Such process could remove exploitation by the middleman in the business transaction. The Co-operative Societies could get a fair selling price for the products. At the same time, free ration and other essential items like clothes would be supplied to the aboriginal people through these Co-operative Societies. However, the primitive tribesmen are only members and owners of the Co-operative Society, but it is run by a Social Worker who is the Treasurer-cum-Manager of the Society. All the records are maintained by him in the respective settlements.

The Multi-purpose Co-operative Society of the Great Andamanese does not also function properly. The people cannot collect forest products like resin or honey as these are not available in their place. So, there is no question of sale in respect of articles collected by them. The Co-operative Society, therefore, conducts activities like distribution of free ration to the tribesmen. The Individuals are now sell their little number of collected coconuts to the outsiders at an unfair price. The Co-operative Society is not also able to purchase their coconuts regularly. Only on two occasions, it purchased coconuts from the Great Andamanese. The office of the Social Worker has shown the following records about the transactions:- Coconuts were purchased from the Great Andamanese Multi-purpose Co-operative Society Ltd. Strait Island by the Executive Secretary, AAJVS, Port Blair on 15.5.88 and 12.9.88. The total number of coconuts sold through the Co-operative Society was 1700 at the total cost of Rs. 3400/-[12].

Now the Society is functioning as a loan-giving institution. From the Office of the Social Workers, Strait Island, the records have been collected. The Co-operative Society has supplied the essential commodities to the families of the Great Andamanese on Credit from 25.8.1987 to 24.5.1990. The cost of the goods was over Rs. 18,124[13].

Before the establishment of the Onge Multi-purpose Co-operative Society, the Onge sold cocoanuts and other forest products like honey, resin and various sea products to the Consumers Co-operative Stores at Hut Bay, Little Andaman. The Tahsilder, Little Andaman helped the Onges in the selling and purchasing processes. Exploitation of the Onges by middleman could thus be eliminated.

According to Pandit (1982), during 1973-74, the Consumer Cooperative Stores, at Hut Bay, Little Andaman purchased the following quantities of honey, resin and coconut from the Onges.

Table 5
Amount of Collection and its Values in the Year of 1973-74[14]

Item	*Year*	*Quantity/number*	*Value of sale proceeds in rupees*
Honey	1973	92 kg.	985.20
	1974	81.5 kg.	244.50
Resin	1973	3078 kg.	3847.50
	1974	6408 kg.	8010.63
Cocoanuts	1973	1642 kg.	985.20
	1974	3349 kg.	2009.40

From Table 5, it is found that initially, the Consumers Cooperative Store of Little Andaman's mission was highly successful. It increased the sources of income of the Onges. But unfortunately, it was not so successful in the later years. At present, the supply of forest produces and marine products has been virtually stopped due to lack of supervision and management of the Samiti. The Co-operative Society is not functioning according to expectation. Now the main function of the Co-operative Society is to supply the rationed articles and essential commodities to the Onges.

Recently, the "Samiti" has started a new project—offering payment to the tribesmen against their collection of coconut from the plantation. Payment was made only once since the system was started as reported by all Onge respondents. The coconuts cannot be sold by the Samiti through the Co-operative Society to the outside markets due to the inadequate transport system. So, the Co-operative Society could not keep the project steady and regular so far. The Onges are now suffering from frustration as the project could not be organised properly due to the mismanagement of transport and communication from settlements to the headquarters because the sale of cocoanut is also difficult. The Co-operative Society exists as an institution for the free supply of rationed goods to the Onges. Majority of the Onge respondents do not know what are the benefits they are getting from their Co-operative Society.

Dole System

Immediately after the settlement, of the tribesmen, it was the urgent task of the local authorities to ensure that the Great Andamanese and the Onges could get regular supply of food items and clothes. In their milieu, natural food items were not sufficient. The Administration planned to reduce their dependence on natural food due to scarcity of the food supply following difficulties in procurement. Since 1974, it has been providing the two ethnic groups with modern foodstuffs to get them habituated with them and make them adopt modern life-styles. Under the dole system, all the modern food articles like rice, and wheat, oil, soap, modern dress materials for men and women are being supplied.

The Onges often consume coconuts as food. But the Great Andamanese are not interested in consuming coconuts and vegetable as food. So they are very much dependent on the supply of dole. As the supply of dole items is insufficient it is reported by the 100% of the Great Andamanese before the researcher. So they are bound to take extra food items from their Co-operative Society on credit. Every family has taken a big amount of loan against goods from their own Co-operative Society.

The Onges are not suffering from food insufficiency, because they have adjusted to the insufficient food items by supplementing their food with consumption of coconuts. Both the ethnic groups are not getting any clothings from the authorities for a long time. They often purchase the dress materials on cash payment from the markets.

Shelter

Proper shelter is an important pre-condition of settlement. Under the rehabilitation schemefor the Onge settlers, 26 semi-pucca separate houses at Dugong Creek and 6 similar house at South Bay were constructed. The Onge houses are high-raised platform type buildings with wooden walls. All modern amenities like light, fan, cooking apparatus and mosquto-nets have been supplied to them. But for the Great Andamanese, 8 pucca houses with wooden walls have been provided. All the houses have two rooms each. For the Onge one room is totally open from three sides, used for cooking purposes. Both settlements have two big community halls for organising the festival and ritual ceremonies near the settlements. One rest house was also built at Hut Bay with one-room capacity for their two-way halt from Dugong Creek to South Bay and vice-versa. An Adibasera, a rest house is also made for the Great Andamanese by the Administration at Port Blair for halting purposes. Because while they come to Port Blair, they used to stay at the houses of their unscrupulous relatives. Here they could easily be exploited and addicted. So the administration has constructed one rest house for their temporary halting for avoiding such undesirable interactions.

House for Great Andamanese are very small and congested. All respondents complained that the house needed repair for living comfortably. Members of the big families are unable to adjust within this small space.

It is true that the Onges have been provided with all sorts of facilities for shelter. Shelter is, no doubt the primary amenity of the Onges. But South Bay is a very small settlement among the tribal settlements in the Andaman and Nicobar Islands, so they are very much neglected. The wooden houses provided to them are not to their satisfaction, as has been evident from the fact the most of the Onges do not like to stay there for the major part of the year. It has been observed that most of the Onges at Dugong Creek have constructed indigenous individual "Korale" type huts in front of their modern houses. Even bee-hive type communal huts are also under construction with individual initiative. The existing modern houses on raised platforms are very congested. These tribes, who have many members in their family, are unable to adjust themselves to live there. Some has combined sleeping room with a kitchen at the corner of the room. Naturally, at the cooking time, smoke is spread in the room as there is no system of ventilation in the room. The other room is not fit for cooking during the rainy season. The Onges still prefer to live in their traditional Korales which are more airy and cooler than the wooden houses. The Onges of South Bay are found living in nine Korales, adjacent to one another in an almost circular arrangement near the sea shore. They often abandon the settlement and move to a new settlement, constructed a few yards away near the sea shore. Among the respondent Onges, the present researcher finds that 40 out of 60 prefer to live at their indigenous huts made by themselves. Twenty Onges among the respondents preferred to live in the modern quarter-type houses though they feel uncomfortable. Houses are very small and become excessively hot. Besides, the houses are not repaired for a long time, which require repair as early as possible. The structural design of the community halls at Dugong Creek for Onges and at Strait Island for Great Andamanese is not similar to their bee-hive like communal huts. Perhaps it is the reason why the two tribals communities do not have any interest in performing their cultural programmes and social gathering. They seldom get together to perform dance, music and other socio-cultural functions. Now they perform all cultural functions at open air at the centre of the settlements. In fact, both the Great Andamanese and the Onges do not like to practice their age old traditional communal function. In this regards, the community halls have no utility rather than used as Balwadi Centres for teaching the minors.

Every settlement has been provided with pucca sanitary latrines, but none of them is ready for use. There is no system of water supply and the flushing system does not work. These latrines are in totally insanitary condition. The Onges are supplied with mosquito-nets but nobody uses it. They have a small rest house at Hut Bay, but it does not have the dormitory system where the halting tribals could sleep. The rest house which was constructed for the Great Andamanese at Port Blair is in a totally damaged condition as there has been no repair-work done. It is more or less abandoned. The tribesmen now halt either at the hospital when they come with a patient or like to stay with their old relatives in unhygienic conditions.

Education: Formal and Non-formal

Education is the most important question before the individual in civilised society. Without proper education, man cannot obtain the benefits of the modern thought and values. Education is the key catalyst to the development of human resources. For the Indian tribals, also education is the pivot on which their success depends. Education is very essential for the innocent tribesmen for attaining freedom from exploitation and poverty. Due to ignorance arising out of illiteracy, the tribes have not been able to take full advantage of new socio-economic benefits and march towards modernisation. The constitution of India has made specific provisions in Articles 15(4) and 46 for promoting education among the Scheduled Tribes. It empowers the State Governments to make special provisions for advancement of socially or educationally backward class of citizens of the Scheduled Caste or Scheduled Tribes[15]. Priority is also given for opening in the areas predominantly inhabited by Scheduled Castes and Scheduled Tribes, centres of non-formal education and adult education.

However, no clear-cut and well-thought-out programme seems to have been taken by any authority to educate the children of the Great Andamanese and the Onges. When the Great Andamanese came in the contact with the British authority, an attempt was taken by the ruler for educating the orphan children, with the establishment of the "Andaman Home[16]" in 1863. Homfray who was in-charge of the Andamanese Home, took much interest in the welfare of the Andamanese. He kept several Andamanese Children at the Home. He was the first in-charge of the Home who tried to teach the children. The Andamanese children were given instructions in the alphabets and in sums. Efforts were made to teach them English, but due to lack of proper official supervision many of the aboriginal boys living at the orphanage were not properly disciplined. Homfray's attempt to civilise a few very young Andamanese were found not successful[17].

Even after independence, the Government of India did not formulate to introduce any systematic education policy for the Great Andamanese and the Onge children. While they were living in and around the Port Blair, no child was in a school-going stage. According to Kochar (1969), only one child attended school, two other children were brought to school, but they were drop-outs. Some children of the

Burmese father also attended school for a short period; but the fathers were more interested in stipends and allowances rather than in the education of their children[18].

However, from the very beginning, with the settlement of the Great Andamanese and the Onges, the Andaman and Nicobar Administration undertaken initiative for educating the new generation. Through "Bharatiya Adim Jati Sevak Sangh", the Administration started to impart formal education to the children, in 1976, with the establishment of "Andaman Adim Janajati Vikas Samiti", the educational policies and programmes were extended further. For imparting modern education to the Onges and the Great Andamanese children the Samiti set up two separate Balwadi Centres for the two communities. To run the schools, a community hall was created at each settlement. During the various sub-plan periods provisions have been kept for all sorts of facilities like teachers, teaching materials, snacks supply, etc., for educating the tribal children.

But the main question is, whether the children of both the communities are really getting any benefits. To what extent has the welfare measure been a success? For over twenty years, the local administration and the Samiti have successively undertaken all sorts of positive steps to educate the children of the tribesmen of those two communities. According to the 1981 census, the literacy rate among the Scheduled Tribes was 16.35 percent against the general literacy of 36.23 per cent in India[19]. Whereas, the literacy rate (primary onwards) among the Scheduled Tribe in Andaman and Nicobar Island was 14.19 per cent for the Onges it was 1.03% and for the Great Andamanese it was 11.53% compared to their respective population[20].

Unfortunately, at present literacy rate among the Great Andamanese and the Onges has remained stagnant. In between 1981 and 1990, the progress of education among the two tribal communities is practically nil. At Dugong Creek, for a long time, the Balwadi centre has been closed due to the absence of teachers. At the South Bay Onge settlement, there is no school. At Great Andamanese settlement, the performance of the Balwadi Centre is poor. A lady belonging to the Great Andamanese community,

Table 6

Individual Opinion Regarding Present Education System

Name of the Tribe	*Name of the scheme*	*No. of persons inter-viewed*	*No. of respon-dents*	*N.A.*	*Provided schemes*		*School functioning scheme*		*Parents like modern education*		*Children like education*	
					Yes	*No*	*Yes*	*No*	*Yes*	*No*	*Yes*	*No*
Great Andamanese	Education for Children	15	15	-	15	-	15	-	15	-	5	10
	Education for Adults	15	15	-	-	15	-	15	-	15	-	-
Onges	Education for Children	70	50	20	50	-	-	50	10	40	10	40
	Education for Adults	70	58	12	-	58	0	58	-	58	-	-

Source: Data have been collected by the researched on the spot during 1988-90.

educated upto the 5th standard is teaching the children. She did not get any training and no knowledge of systematic teaching. She is formally in-charge of the School. It is her duty to record attendance and distribute snacks and other materials in among the children.

According to Table 6, at present children among the Great Andamanese are not going to school regularly. All 15 Great Andamanese respondents stated that though the school is functioning, it is not up to expectation. Both the teachers and guardians are not satisfied, because the children are not interested to go to school, due to lack of proper learning materials and snacks. Unscientific teaching methods disheartened and demoralised the children and parents. Both the teachers and the students are not frustrated. The teacher is facing a great problem in collecting the children to attend the school as most of them go out with their parents for collecting firewood and fishing.

The Onge children are not interested in attending and learning alphabets through the conventional type of teaching:- 'a' for apple, 'b' for ball etc. Formal education is altogether alien concept for the Onges and the Great Andamanese. Simply maintaining—school timing, regular attendance and discipline may not be effective. Special techniques relating to the communities should be carefully evolved. Success of basic education depends upon suitable trained teachers, the amount of interest taken by them and adequate provision for the necessary equipments for crafts teaching. The teaching of drawing and fine arts should be a part of the school curriculum. Tribal children should be given full opportunity to satisfy their creative urges through school activities involving education in visual arts. Agriculture hunting and dancing are essential parts of tribal life and the tribal children should be encouraged to display their talents for enriching their own tribal folk culture. Songs and dances are vital to tribal life and culture and the teaching of folk songs and folk lores, folk stories and myth and riddless should not be ignored. Tribal games and archery, as well as tribal music and dances that have special appeals to their own, should be organised as parts of the curriculum for tribal education.

The teacher in the tribal areas must have a thorough

knowledge of the respective tribal life and culture. He or she must speak the tribal languages. Language or medium of instruction is the great barrier of the Onge children. The medium of instruction is Hindi and English. So, the children can neither clearly understand language nor write the alphabets. Such type of education has no special relevance to Onge culture. Hence, though schooling for the Onges is being continued since 1976, there could be no "Literate" Onges boy or girl till now.

The second problem is that the Samiti never continuously provided the teacher and the appointed teachers have been paid a poor honorarium. Naturally, they did not like to continue their services. Most of the time the authorities have tried to appoint a homogeneous team of workers like social worker-cum-teachers. Thus a social worker is basically the in-charge of the settlement, naturally, he or she may not have time to teach the children or he or she may not have proper knowledge of systematic teaching. A retired teacher from Kinnour district of Himachal Pradesh was appointed by the Samiti on a monthly honorarium of Rs. 300/- only. He was found to be skilled and equipped with various techniques and teaching aids. He himself had evolved different teaching aids to suit the Onge Children. But unfortunately, he was neither helped nor encouraged by the Samiti and ultimately, he resigned and went back to his home. Also, the present Balwadi teacher at Strait Island does not like poor casual labour like payment. The teaching materials like books, charts, maps, sports articles are not provided by the authorities for a long time, so the children are not interested to come to school[21].

The teaching method is not connected with the tribal culture and tradition. Naturally, the children are not interested to learn. Whether teacher or social worker, whoever may be, does not have any special commitment for such works and sympathy for the pupils who are at the bottom of development, cannot introduce any radical change among the young learners effectively. At present among the total Onge children 66.67% are of the school going stage. Several times Mr. Tambolai[22], the spokesman of the community, who is also the member of Pradesh Council of the Andaman and Nicobar Islands, has been requesting the Samiti for appointing proper teachers and even he has put the matter before the

Lt. Governor of the Union Territory, on several occasions, but he could not succeed. No such facilities have been provided to South Bay children. At present, no school is running at Dugong Creek due to absence of teacher as said by 50 Onges.

During the Seventh Five Year Plan period some Great Andamanese children were brought to the Seva Nekatan "ashram" at Port Blair for their education. But they did not complete even their primary education.

Several reason have been responsible for the failure of educating the Onges and the Great Andamanese. So far there has not been any clear educational policy for the tribal students. In spite of the recommendation and suggestions made by various Committees and Commissions, no concrete policy for the tribals has evolved. However, it can easily be realised and concluded that to some extent the tribals referred to are benefitted through educational welfare scheme of the Government, but both the parties are responsible for the poor performance in respect of eradication of illiteracy from the Onges and the Great Andamanese. The factors towards this are: irregular posting of teachers, defective education policy, poor salaries to the teachers, lack of knowledge of teaching, inadequate supply of teaching materials and snacks. Lastly, both the parents and the children do not like to obtain education. Mr. D. Venkatesan (1988) has rightly listed the causes of failure of literacy programmes as follows: the allocated money which has been spent on the Onge education has not given proportional return as the administration expected. The main reason behind the very poor performance in Onge education is the introduction of cash economy. Plantation work is given more importance irrespective of age-groups than the schooling. Mothers rarely leave their children alone. Here, among the Onge, the cash economy and education do not seem to co-exist with each other. It may be agreed that the Onges are much motivated by the wage-based work in plantation than attending the school[23].

Education is invariably needed to adult tribesmen also. As long as they are not educated, injustice and exploitation of the innocent tribals would exist. Adult education is also a vital question before the tribal communities for understanding of the impact and benefits of the modernization. The Andaman and Nicobar Administration has laid down several welfare measures to educate the adult males and females of the Great Andamanese and the Onges. An adult centre has been proposed to be opened at Dugong Creek for making the tribals aware of their environment , health and sanitation, money transactions by identifying them with modern paper currency system and coinage. But the scheme has not yet been started by the Samiti. That is why there is no question of any further benefits acquiring from the welfare programmes. It is very strange that in spite of some modest schooling, the Onges have not yet learnt about counting money. According to a recent field survey 80% of the adult Onges can neither count nor identify the paper currency. Remaining adults can only count and identify the money on the basis of colour and size. But most of them are still unable to know the market price of the commodities. The unscrupulous merchants at time cheat the Onges by not returning the balance as the Onges themselves are ignorant of the face value of the paper currency and of counting and accounting. They have no knowledge of health and sanitation. The surroundings of the settlements are not clear, dirty utensils are left here and there. are having no concept of washing dresses and wear unclean dresses. Women often wear petticoats over the tassel.

So, it can be easily imagined to what extent the Onges are benefited by the adult education. All the adult Great Andamanese can count money but usually most of them do not know the prices of the commodities, which they purchase. The Samiti has failed to open any adult centre for both the tribal groups. It should have been the duties of the Social Worker and other staff of the Samithi to teach the Onges something about modern hygiene and life in general.

Vocational Training for Adult

Non-formal and vocational education centres are very successful in modern times and should be able to provide academic education as well as vocational training to help the tribal population of India financially. It provides knowledge which would not only be able to protect themselves from exploitation but would also be able to make them take full advantage of the various development programmes. Training in crafts not only helps them financially but also enriches their indigenous craft works. The primitive tribes like the Great Andamanese and the Onges are much experienced in handicrafts relating to cane, iron and wood.

To encourage their original primitive culture, the local Administration has undertaken several schemes. During the various plan periods, a detail provisions have been made to give training to the tribal youths in Cottage Industries at Port Blair in carpentry with adequate raw materials and financial helps.

After intensive field survey, it has been known that no tribal individual of the islands has been provided with any carpentry training in the Industrial training centres at Port Blair. No cane craft centres and black smithy-cum-carpentry centres have yet been opened by the Samiti in either of the settlements. One Black smithy centre is functioning at Dugong Creek and one at Strait Island on the ir personal initiative. Raw materials also are not supplied by the authorities free of cost. By their own efforts, the tribals of the areas are making iron digging sticks and harpoons for their personal use.

During the Seventh Plan Period, the Samiti was proposed to provide training to four Onges beneficiaries each year (who have been provided with milk cows) at the Dairy Firm at Port Blair to learn properly about the domestication of cows and utility of milk and milk products as food for three months. During the training periods each of the trainees would be provided stipends of Rs. 150/- p.m. But unfortunately, the training schemes have not been materialised. That means, the Samiti has not implemented many of the welfare schemes for either of the two communities. So, there is no question of benefits from the projects. All 60 out of 70 Onges and all 15 Great Andamanese are not willing to join such craft training camps. So, it is a fact that majority of the tribesmen are not yet interested to receive any training in dairy and carpentry.

Comments

For modernisation of the Great Andamanese and the Onges,

many welfare measures were proposed to be provided by the administration during various plan periods. There was no dearth of resources for the proposed schemes. All possible scientific and administrative measures were proposed to be undertaken for speedy and smooth development of these primitive tribesmen. After thorough analysis of all welfare projects, it has been observed that many proposed measures are not yet implemented. Some of those were implemented half-heartedly, and as a result either the scheme failed or stopped functioning immediately after its implementation. The non-implemented proposed schemes are culture of honey bee, poultry farming, vocational training in carpentry and black-smithy, establishing cane and bamboo craft centre at settlements and supply of raw materials for runing the centres, adult centres for adult persons imparting education about modern life and culture, health and sanitation, economy, dress, etc.

Rearing white pig for additional food and financial benefits were withdrawn due to lack of interest of the Great Andamanese and the Onges. They could not obtain benefits from rearing milch cows either as they do not like domestication of animals. Fruit and vegetable cultivation was also a failure as a means of food procurement and as an economic means of livelihood. Though coconut as a food was accepted by the Onges but not by the Great Andamanese. Due to lack of communication and absence of good market facilities, they could not sell the produce and get money from their coconut plantations. These people are not interested to adopt improved means of cultivation of coconut-cum-fruit orchards and vegetable gardens. They do not like to utilize modern fishing facilities. It is a discredit for the local authorities that it could not make the tribesmen either good agriculturists or horticulturists. Rather they were encouraged to become good wage labourers for their own plantations. Due to disfunctioning and negligence of the local authorities, relay of television programmes, power supply, transport communication are not serving them properly.

These people suffer from many diseases and need constant medical attention, but they show little interest to visit the qualified medical staff. Lack of formal education and of health consciousness might be the reasons behind their such attitude. They live in an unhygienic atmosphere having no idea of sanitation. Adults are addicted to intoxicating liquor, consume harmful tobacco, visit some places for entertainment, from where they are often transmitted with diseases. These tribesmen are yet to develop the habit of washing their garments regularly.

The future of their children is uncertain due to absence of proper education. Both parents and children loss their interest in formal education due to lack of teachers and teaching aids appropriate for the tribal children. Regular road and communication are yet to be established. Supply of pure drinking water and of foodstuffs as a dole are not sufficient to meet their requirements. Free clothes are not supplied. Modern shelters provided to them are uncomfortable due to small space and high temperature inside. The failure of the major developmental schemes give the impression that the welfare schemes for the tribesmen were formulated according to the personal whim of the local authorities with no knowledge of the tribal culture and tradition, which are hampering the tribesmen to march towards modernisation.

REFERENCES

1. This information have been gathered from the *Office of the Plantation-in-Charges* at Dugong Creek and at South Bay, Little Andaman, 1990.
2. This information have been gathered from the *Office of the Plantation-in-Charge-cum Social Worker* at Strait Island, Andaman, 1990.
3. Chakraborty, D.K., *Great Andamanese of Strait Island,* Port Blair, (1974), p.50 (unpublished).
4. Interview with *Mr. Habil Lakra, A Social Worker, Strait Island, 1990.*
5. This information has been gathered from the *Office of the Social worker-cum-plantation-in-charge, at Strait island,* 1990.
6. Basu, B.K., *The Onges,* Seagull Books, Calcutta, (199Q) pp. 14-17.
7. Chakraborty, D.K., *The Great Andamanese A study of Persistence of culture in the face of Biological Extinction—A preliminary Report,* An.S.I, Port Blair, (1974), p. l. (unpublished).
8. This information haste been gathered from *The Office of the power houses* at Strait Island and at Dugong Creek in 1990.

9. This information havebeen gathered from the *Offices of the Dispensaries at Strait Island* and at Dugong Creek in 1990.
10. Verma, Ishwar C., "Health problems of tribal communities in Andaman and Nicobar Islands," in *Journal of Social Research*, vol. 19(2), (1976), p. 16.
11. Patnaik, N., "Reading on Tribal Development administration" in Tribal Sub-Plan, New Delhi, (1982),p.258.
12. Data have been collected from the Office of the Social Worker, Strait Island, 1990.
13. *Ibid.*, 1990.
14. Pandit, T.N., "Economy of the Onges" in *Economy of the Tribes and their Transformation*, (ed.) by K.S. Singh, Concept Publications, New Delhi, (1982), p.191.
15. Verma, R.C., *Indian Tribes Through the Ages*, Publication Divisions, Ministry of Information and Broadcasting, Govt. of India, New Delhi, (1990), pp. 102-103.
16. Andaman Home, Mr.H. Corbyn, A Christian priest built huts, which to be known as "Andaman Home" on Ross Island in the year 1863 to civilize the Great Andamanese through English Education.
17. Mathur, L.P., *History of the Andaman and Nicobar islands*, Sterling Publishers, New Delhi, (1965), pp. 97-98.
18. Kochar, V.K., "The Great Andamanese Today", in *Man in India* vol. 49(3), (1969), p. 249.
19. Verma, R.C., *Indian Tribes Through the Ages*, Publication Divisions, Ministry of Information & Broadcasting, Government of India, New Delhi, (1990), p. 104.
20. Census of India 1981, *Andaman and Nicobar Islands*, Director of Census Operation, New Delhi, (1985), Sepcial Tables for Scheduled Tribes.
21. Interview with Mrs. Nau, Balwadi teacher, at Strait Island, 1990.
22. Mr. Tambolai, he is the spokesman and leader of the Onge community. He is designated as "Raja" by the Samiti itself. Now he is a member of the Pradesh Council, Andaman and Nicobar Islands. He is representing the whole primitive aborigines of the Andaman and Nicobar Islands in the Pradesh Council for the five years. He belongs to Onge Community.
23. Venkatesan, D., "Innovation and their impact on the Onge of Little Andaman" in *Man in India* Vol. 68(4) (1988) p. 421.

4

Modern Economic Scenario

Natural Resources

So far as the economic resources are concerned, the Andaman Group of Islands is remarkably enriched with natural resources. These Islands characterised by their extensive coral beds and hilly terrain covered by the tropical evergreen vegetation. Economically, it is attractive for its rich forest and marine resources. The vegetation of Little Andaman is very similar to that of the other islands of Andamans. The tropical Andaman forest, distinctly Indo-Chinese and Malayan in character[1], can be broadly divided into the littoral and non-littoral types of forests. The littoral coastal forest is characterised by an extensive growth of mangroves, pandanus, nipa-palm etc. which acts a shore protect and also has great economic value as source of firewood. The coconut and casuarina are the characteristic littoral flora of Little Andaman. The main part of the Andaman forest comprises of evergreen trees. In the forest, there are wild animals like wild boars, iquana, deer etc. whose flesh is taken as food along with edible vegetables, fruits, roots and honey. The important commercial forest resources consist of valuable timber like Padak, Koko, White Chuglam, Marblewood, Dhup (resin), Garjan and Lalchini (all are local forest official names), bamboo, cane, herbal plants etc. Similarly, all the coastal area is covered with sea resources like varieties of fishes, molluscs, crabs, turtles etc. In the surrounding maritime belt of Little Andaman, there are many varieties of fishes, turtles, crocodiles and Dugongs which constitute the important marine fauna.

The surrounding hilly and plain lands covered by thick forest and wide sea belt with open sea has been selected by the forest dwellers to live self-sufficiently. The tribals of these islands have traditionally been living on spontaneous natural food and supply. They follow primitive techniques of exploitation of natural resources. As a result, they have developed a close relationship with their surrounding forest, hills, sea etc. from which they get their day to day requirements. Of course, the amount of exploitation of natural resources in these islands is not the same due to various factors. As a result, they sometime face crisis situations in maintaining their economic balance.

Economy of the Great Andamanese and the Onges is considered to be a subsistence economy due to lack of diversification in production, and not adopting modern food producing techniques. All these natural resources, truly, may not have marketable value from modern market point of view, but obviously, these have economic as well as survival value.

The structure of the tribal economy is generally based on forest and sea. The tribals use simple technology in exploiting the nature. So far as the traditional economy is concerned, the tribal community acts like a cooperative unit. The distribution is generally based on gift and ceremonial exchange without any concept of profit. Due to spontaneous supply of natural food resources, the tribals never felt any scarcity of food. They need no food stores for future consumption. The family is often unitary in its economic process so that the whole job from extraction of natural resources to procurement of the consumable good is done by the family members. In the tribal family, there is an organised division of labour according to sex and age.

The methods of exploitation of these resources can broadly be divided into three categories—hunting, collecting and fishing. Here all members of the family join a common type of work. The Great Andamanese and the Onges have been exploiting sea and forest products in various ways under the category of hunting. For hunting purposes, they use self-made instruments like bows and arrows. They also take the help of dogs for hunting pigs and deer which were imported by the British rulers. They also use harpoons, canoe, rope etc. for hunting.

In collecting food, they collects edible fruits, roots, honey etc. from the forest and molluse, crabs from the sea-shore. Generally they use the instruments of digging like iron stick, hook, adze etc.

In fishing, they use iron hook, small self-made nets for fishing. Beside consumption, they exploit the natural resources for their livelihood. They have built their traditional bee-hive-shaped communal huts and lean-type individual huts with timber, bamboo and reeds that they collect from the forest. They also practise cottage crafts to some extent exploiting the local raw materials which they procure from the forest and from the sea. They also obtain herbs and medicinal plants which have therapeutic value to them both the curative and preventive points of view.

Past Economic Condition

The economic system of the Great Andamanese and the Onges was based on hunting, fruit gathering and fishing. These economic activities were divided into two types—primary and secondary. Tribal people of both sexes were involved in primary and secondary activities. So far as primary occupation is concerned, there was no class distinction or hereditary position in their, economy. More or less every male was engaged in primary occupation. In primary economic activities, involvement of the male was found throughout the seasons. They were involved in hunting, fruit.gathering and fishing. Men preferred to do any work in group. They hunted pig, deer and dugong: collected honey, turtles egg, resin, and fish in the forest and in the deep sea as well as in offshore with the help of harpoons, bows and arrows. In the rainy season, most of the males remain pre-occupied with pig and deer hunting in in case of Great Andamanese and only pig hunting in case of Onges. During dry season, they collected honey, turtle eggs and hunted dugong, turtle etc.

The secondary economic activities of the tribals consisted of making bows and arrows. A sharp iron piece is also set at the end of a long stick and another head is connected by a long rope for hunting by throwing the harpoons to the game. Digging sticks are made by iron bar by rubbing continuously for sharping the one end point of the iron stick. Adze is also made by a piece of iron.

The tribals made different types of containers out of wood and bamboo for storing water and honey. All their economic activities depended on seasons and were related to primary and secondary activities. At leisure time, the tribals were usually involved in making out-rigger canoes, for long sea journey.

Similarly, women of the both the Great Andamanese and the Onges also took part in their economic activities. They assigned light and less risky works in comparison to males. Like other tribal women, women of the Great Andamanese and the Onges kept themselves engaged in collecting roots, fruits and firewood. The Onges young and grown-up males were involved in hunting, fishing, honey collection etc. As primary occupation, women were involved in collection of edible fruits, roots, from the forest and catching fish, crabs, molluse etc. with the help of their self-made small nets near off-shore and island creeks. In these activities the grown-up children also helped their mothers. As secondary activities, women rear children and boil food. Moreover, in their leisure periods, women often engaged themselves in the making of small nets, buckets, sea-shell ornaments, bark made armlets, hand-belts and other decorating ornaments. They shave the hair of the heads of the husband and children, paint their bodies with white clay and red ochre done very carefully. Women were prohibited to take bows and arrows and harpoons on any occasion.

Present Economy of the Great Andamanese and the Onges

Tribals in India are also passing through a phase of economic change with the rest of the country. Similarly, the Great Andamanese and the Onges are slowly changing their economic pattern and occupation. While they still follow a great deal of traditional activities which have been described above, they are gradually adopting modern technological concepts for their economy. The overall economy and occupational pattern of both sexes somehow have been changed. New techniques and skills have been imported. So far as male occupation is concerned, in place of the traditional primary occupation like hunting, fruit gathering and collection, white collar jobs and skillful official and non-official works have been introduced. The Great Andamanese and the Onges males primarily perform the works in their own plantations for cleaning the undergrowth of the cocoanut plants and kitchen gardens. Some of them are involved in official works in hospitals, dispensaries, offices of the Samiti and other departments. Some are posted for outdoor jobs in their own islands while some work at their own settlements. However, all these works are mainly done by the adult males. Here the minor and disabled males do not perform any work. They rather help others in their household jobs. So far as present economy of the other ethnic groups is concerned, the Nicobarese economy is mainly based on coconut and betel nut plantations. Pig-herding is also a part of their economic activities from which they earn.

Under secondary occupations, the adult males of both the ethnic groups have changed their working performance. Some of them engage themselves in repairing their personal canoes and helping their wives in household works. The males often take part in works like collection of firewood from jungles, rearing of children, fishing by hooks etc. Moreover, the Onge adult males on rare occasion make bows and arrows, harpoons, knives digging sticks. Occasionally, they go for hunting wild boars, fishing turtle, small fishes, crabs, turtle eggs and collecting honey. Additionally, the males help the administrative authority by importing rationed articles from Little Andaman, the headquarters to their own settlements. They often unload the foodstuffs from the ferry boats. Great Andamanese occasionally go for selling the coconuts and fruits which they collect, taking them outside the island.

Females of both the ethnic groups have also changed their traditional primary occupations. Like their male counterparts, they often perform jobs in plantation for collection of coconuts, cleaning the undergrowth in their own plantations. Some of them perform official jobs like males. As the secondary occupations, the females of both tribal groups perform household works. Women help their husbands for making of sleeping cots, indigenous individual huts by the side of their settlements.

Role of the Administration and the Cooperative Societies in the Changing the Occupational Behaviour of the Two Tribal Communities

Since independence, the local administration of Andaman and Nicobar Islands have been trying to introduce striking changes in the tribal and non-tribal economy of the two groups of Islands. Steps have been taken for this purpose by introducing modern projects for welfare and for economic betterments. The Great Andamanese and the Onges are pre-occupied in agriculture and horticulture. In this connection, the local administration raised a 25 acre of coconts plantations at Dugong Creek for the Onges in the early sixties. For intensive care, the administration has handed-over the welfare department under the charge of an autonomous agency. For betterment of the uprooted tribals and modernising their utterly primitive economy, the "Bharatiya Adimjati Sevak Sangh" took charge of these tribesmen in 1970.

Simultaneously, to discharge their backward primitive occupations and enrich their economy, several new economic projects have been started. On priority basis, at first the authorities have raised an area of total 95 acre of cocoanuts and an area of 5 acre of kitchen gardens for the Onges at Dugong Creek and at South Bay. In a similar way, for the Great Andamanese an area of total 5 acre for cocoanut and 5 acre for fruits and kitchen garden has been started at Strait Island. In this regard, the Ministry of Rehabilitation, with the help of the Agriculture Department improved these plantations. The administration has also planned to make these tribesmen economically self-sufficient. So it has tried to reduce their dependence on natural food supply and change their non-productive economy into a productive, profit-oriented economy.

Under the various plan period, the authorities have taken several new occupational strategies to modernise this tribal economy. Since 1976, a new Tribal Sub-Plan project has been started specially for the tribals of Andaman and Nicobar Islands like the Tribal Sub-Plan of the rest of Indian Tribals. The local administration also set up an autonomous body called "Andaman Adim Janajati Vikas Samiti" in 1976 for the intensive care and speedy development of the primitive tribes of Andaman and Nicobar Islands. Immediately after the establishment of the (AAJVS) "Samiti", the "Bharatiya Adimjati Sevak Sangh" handed over all its tribal welfare charges to the Samiti. The Samiti has undertaken many new economic projects. Under the Tribal Sub-Plan, the Samiti attempted to improve the fishing activities of the Great Andamanese and the Onges. The authorities have planned to provide the tribals with new mechanised boats, nylon nets and other modernised fishing equipments. Moreover, two fishing technicians have been appointed to teach the tribal people new fishing methods and commercialise their fishing profession. For modernising the occupation of domesticating the animals, the administration has played an active role by providing the tribals with milch cows, goats, white pigs and poultry birds. The tribesmen are very fond of honey, but supply of wild honey is inadequate so the Samiti has planned to compensate for their honey supply by providing them with modern bee colony schemes. To commercialise the bee-colony and also has planned to provide the tribals with new technical knowhow. They are experts in the indigenous arts and crafts. To encourage the craftmanship on a priority basis, the Samiti has planned to provide the adult males at Port Blair with modern carpentry-cum-black smithy training. The Samiti has tried to develop the occupational pattern of the tribesmen. It has taken a plan to provide the tribals with modern poultry and dairy development training. Moreover, to develop their carpentry, cane and bamboo works, it has planned to supply the tribal people with required raw materials.

Further, the Samiti has taken over the duties to sell all the tribal products and surplus goods through the tribal's own Cooperative Society to the outside markets. To stop they are being misled by unscrupulous non-tribals like middlemen and outside merchants, it has arranged for collecting the goods from the tribesmen and sell them at reasonable prices to the outsiders. On the other hand, the Samiti has arranged for the supply of essential goods to the tribals through the Cooperative Society at reasonable rates on cash.

Modern Occupational Pattern Schemes

Under the modern occupation pattern schemes the administration has provided opportunity to involve adult males and females of the Great Andamanese and the Onge males into two categories of work. They are offered training in skilled occupations of a permanent nature. In this category one Great Andamanese and three Onge males are involved per unit. No female of either of the tribal group has come under this category of work for training. In the second category of occupation, both the males and females of the Great Andamanese and the Onges are engaged as unskilled casual workers. Among the Great Andamanese, 3 males and 1 female are now involved in this process. However, among the Onges 4 males and 1 female are engaged as casual workers. Under the Samiti's job scheme for the Onges, 32 males and 30 females have engaged themselves as daily wage labourers for ten days in a month. Besides, the basic occupations of the tribal groups like rearing plantations, orchards and vegetable gardens have been improved.

According to the industrial classification made under the 1961 Census a worker is defined as a person engaged in some economic activity. A non-worker, on the other hand, is not engaged in any such productive economic activity.

Table 1 refers the sex-wise occupational positions of the two ethnic groups the Great Andamanese and the Onges. The Table refers, among the Great Andamanese, 4 out of 9 workable males are engaged in "other services" and out of 7 workable females, 1 is engaged in other services. Under "Other Services", the males and females are engaged in skilled and unskilled manual work. Here among the Great Andamanese out of total 16 males and 14 females, 9 males and 7 females are considered workable persons. But here only 4 males and 6 females are considered to be non-workers. Non-workers means, those who have no specific works in which they are engaged for most of the year. We find 1 male among the Great Andamanese workers is engaged in the traditional hunting, fishing and plantation works.

Table 1

Sex-wise Occupational chart of the two Ethnic Groups—the Great Andamanese and the Onges

Name of the Tribe	*Sex*	*No. of population*	*No. of workable population*	*No. of workers involved in various works*	*Other service categories*			*Engaged in plantation, hunting & fishing like traditional*
					Permanent	*Casual*	*Daily wage labourers*	
Great Andamanese	M	16	9	5	1	3	-	1
	F	14	7	1	-	1	-	-
Onges	M	56	40	39	3	4	32	-
	F	44	34	31	-	1	30	-

Source: Field Survey conducted by the researcher on the spot during 1988-90.

It is found that among the Onges, none of the Onge male or female is engaged in his or her traditional occupation. More or less, the maximum males and females are involved in "Other Services". Here even males and females above 60 are also engaged in various economic activities. So the present researcher hold that they cannot be categorised as "invalid" or as "non workers". It is remarkable in the Onge economic history that the maximum number of Onge females are involved in "Other services". Out of total 56 males and 44 females in the Onge society, 40 males and 34 females are considered workable persons. While out of total 40 workable males 39 are involved in various economic activities. Similarly out of total 34 workable females, 31 are involved in various categories of economic activities. But none of them is engaged in traditional occupation like hunting, fishing etc.

Table 2

Sex-wise Occupational Chart of the Two Ethnic Groups in 1981 Census

Name of the Tribes	*Census of 1981*			
	Great Andamanese		*Onges*	
Sex	*M*	*F*	*M*	*F*
Total Population	21	21	51	46
Workable persons	12	5	43	28
Non-workers	7	12	8	18
Seeking for works	1	5	-	-
Other services	2	1	2	-
Traditional activities	9	3	41	28
Cultivation	1	-	-	-
Marginal Workers	2	4	-	-

Source: Census of India 1981, Andaman and Nicobar Islands, Directorate of Census Operation, New Delhi, (1985).

Data of the Table 2 indicate the occupational and functional patterns of the Great Andamanese and the Onges in the census of 1981. Here out of total 42 Great Andamanese and 97 Onges, 17 Great Andamanese and 71 Onges were considered workable persons. Among these 17 Great Andamanese workable persons 12 were engaged in their traditional hunting, fishing activities and 69 Onges were engaged in the same age-old traditional activities. Only 3 Great Andamanese and 2 Onges were engaged in Other services. Six Great Andamanese individuals were waiting for job. While only 2 Onges were seeking for job, six Great Andamanese were also considered as marginal workers. No marginal workers were found in the Census of 198l among the Onges. Similarly, no individual was engaged in cultivation among the Onges, while 1 Great Andamanese was considered himself as a cultivator. The above data indicated that a notable change has taken place in their occupation in between 1981 and 1990.

Nature of Work Under Various Categories of Occupations

The working composition of the Great Andamanese has been changed after India became independent. At present, we find only a few number of males and females being involved in "Other Services". The remaining males and females do not have any specific work apart from household works. Apparently, the working condition and the composition of workers in the Onges are fairly high. Here almost all adult males and females above 18 are engaged in various types of skilled and unskilled works. Non-tribals are mainly engaged in agriculture and horticulture activities. Under agriculture, they cultivate paddy, vegetables and orchard gardens like banana, coconuts, betel nuts, fruits etc. Educated individuals are engaged in white collar jobs both under skilled and unskilled categories of works. Non-tribals are mainly agriculturist.

However, those who are designated as "permanent workers", work in various offices as skilled workers at settlements as well as outside the settlements. Some of them work as assistants of the other workers in the Marine Department and the Medical Department. Some of them also work as Constables in the Andaman and Nicobar Police Department posted at Dugong Creek for vigilance purposes. Their duties are to keep watch on the intruders and stop poaching and hunting of animals in the forests, stealing forest goods.

Those who are designated as "casual workers" are may be categorised as "unskilled workers". Under this second category of casual work, both the sexes are involved as "unskilled workers". Their duties are to assist the staff of the Samiti in their official and non-official works at the settlements. Some of them work as teachers in the Balwadi centre for teaching the children and some act as Malis (gardeners), cleaning the settlement areas and maintaining kitchen gardens within the office boundaries. Cattle Attenders keep watch on cattle at the settlements. Ward Attenders help in the work of the Pharmacies and dispensaries. Switch Board Attenders often help machine operators at power houses at the settlements. Messengers perform correspondence works. Cash payments and other facilities are granted on a casual basis fixed by the Samiti as per Government Casual Mazdoor Payment rules. As per rule, nobody can claim himself or herself as "Permanent workers" in future. The Samiti has discretionary power to replace any casual worker by another one at any time on the ground of indiscipline or misbehaviour.

Under the "daily wage" category of occupation, a good number of Onge males and females are involved as daily wage labourers. It is their basic duty to clean the undergrowth of the coconut and kitchen gardens and often collecting coconuts from the plantation for sale. Even children below 18 years can work as half-wage labourer. However, none of the boys or girls are engaged in such work within the age group of 14-18 years. It is notable that the Great Andamanese are not given any scope to absorb themselves in this category of work by the Samiti.

Besides these compulsory works, the males often perform household work like making sleeping cots, drawing water, collecting firewood and fishing. The females take part in cooking, washing clothes, rearing children along with other housekeeping works.

Working Position

Under the influence of modern welfare measures adopted by the Government, both the ethnic groups, the Great Andamanese and the Onges are changing their occupational pattern recently by absorbing themselves in various skilled and unskilled works. But their working performance, is not satisfactory. The permanent and casual staff often do not work as per schedule. The non-tribal staff of the Samiti often engage the permanent and casual tribal workers for their personal works like collection of firewood, drawing water, maintaining personal gardens, collection of honey, resin, sea-shell, crabs and fishes from forest and sea as the case may be.

Among the Onge males and females, out of total population of 100, (62%) 62 are daily wage workers. Usually, it is their duty to clean undergrowths around the plantations and collect coconuts. Women have been found better workers than their male counterparts. Daily working hours is 8, but the male and female daily wage workers hardly work for 4 hours on an average in a day. Moreover, they work for a total of 10 days in a month. It has been has observed that without guidance or order of the leader (Raja), the individuals do not work properly. If they had worked properly for 8 hours in a day, then half of the individuals could have done the same amount of works. Apparently, it can be said that the same amount of work can be finished within 5 days by the same workers in a month if they worked for 8 hours in a day.That means, every individual is now wasting 50% of his/her manpower by doing half of his/her scheduled works. Naturally, 62 individuals do the works which could be done by 31 individuals. Therefore, this additional 31 (or 50%) of the daily wage labourers are considered to be "marginal labourers".

Further, all the 62 daily wage workers can generate 1860 man-days in a month, if they worked for 30 days in a month. But now 62 workers generate only 620 man-days within 10 days. It must be remembered that they generate 620 manpowers working for only 4 hours in place of 8 hours every day. That means actually now they generate only 310 man-days as half-day workers. So it can be said that now they lose almost 1550 man-days (or 84%) of their total 1860, man-days in a month. However, the authorities pay an amount of Rs. 12820 in a month as wages for these labourers against their total work of 310 man-days instead of 620 man-days. This 310 man-days can be produced by 10 (approx) individuals in a month. Therefore out of total 62 daily wage workers 52 individuals are to be considered as unemployed.

The following Table shows the real working composition of the Great Andamanese and the Onges. In"the overall Indian context, the employment position of the tribal society is very poor and is considered to be an acute problem. The employment situation of the Great Andamanese and the Onges is not so good.

The Table 3 indicates that out of total 16 workable population of the Great Andamanese only 6(37%) are reported to be employed taking into consideration of the various categories of occupations. The remaining 10(63%) of the population capable of working are unemployed. Similarly, out of total 74 workable population of the Onges 18(24%) of the individuals are reported to be employed, which is 13% less than that of the Great Andamanese. The remaining 56

(76%) are considered as unemployed. Among the Great Andamanese, out of 16 individuals capable of working, only 6 are reported to be employed and out of total 74 such Onge individuals, only 18 are employed. Data regarding employment position of the Great Andamanese and the Onges are given in Table 3.

Table 3
Employment Position of the Great Andamanese and the Onges

Name of the Tribes	*No. of workable population*	*Permanent workers*	*Casual workers*	*Daily Wage labou-*	*Plantation workers*	*Total Employed*	*Unemployee*
Great Andamanese	16	1	4	-	1	6	10
%	(100)	(6)	(25)	-	(6)	(37)	(63)
Onges	74	3	5	10	-	18	56
%	(100)	(4)	(7)	(13)	-	(24)	(76)

*Field Survey Conducted by the researcher on the spot during 1988-90.

Sources of Income

The present economy of the Great Andamanese and the Onges is based on plantation and other occupations. The people depend upon them for their livelihood. As cash crops, the Samiti has developed a number of good coconut gardens and orchards for the both tribal groups. Since 1974, the local authorities have been supplying foodstuffs to them free of cost. Further, a good number of milch cows were provided for supply of milk products for enabling them to earn money. The sale of fishes after consumption is another source of earning for the tribesmen. Besides, those adults Great Andamanese who are unemployed, are being provided with "Pocket Money" in cash per month by the authorities to enable them to meet their additional expenses apart from their purchase of foodstuffs.

A permanent worker of the Great Andamanese community gets an amount of Rs. 1250/- per month, while of the Onge workers get an amount of Rs. 1500/- per month on an average. The casual staff of both the tribal ethnic groups get an amount of Rs. 475/- per month. However, those are daily wage labourers among the Onges get Rs. 210/- per month for 10 days work in a month. That means per day, every worker gets Rs. 21/-. On the other hand, the unemployed Great Andamanese get Rs.75/- per month and their leader (Raja) gets an extra-amount of Rs. 200/- per month as honorarium or pocket money from the authorities. Among the Great Andamanese, 60% of the families get an amount of Rs. 100/- per month on an average by selling their coconuts and fruits on a casual basis. The researcher has found that among the Onge families none has got a single paise from their coconuts for the last two years due to non-selling of the nuts to the markets. While analysing the source of income of the Nicobare tribes of Chowra Island in Nicobar group of Islands, it has been found that their income is determined by the plantation and selling of canoes and pots. This income is the primary source of their income while fishing and forestry constitutes their secondary source of income[2]. The non-tribal's income is determined by the agriculture and horticulture i.e. selling of paddy, vegetables, coconuts, betel nuts, fruits, etc.

The histogram 1 and 2 indicate the per annum income position of the Great Andamanese and the Onge families. The horizontal lines of both the charts indicate the number of families and this is shown in percentage. In case of Great Andamanese family, one family means 12% (approx.) out of total percentage. One Onge family means 2.60% (approx.) out of total percentage. The vertical lines indicate the annual income of the every family in rupee. Income of the individuals vary according to their personal occupation and sources of income.

It is found from the Histogram 1 that among the total 8 Great Andamanese families interviewed, on an average every family earns an amount of Rs.5700 per annum. Out of total 8 families, 1 family earns an amount of Rs. 15000 per annum, 4 families earn on an average of Rs.5700 and 1 family earns its 3600 and remaining 2 families earn on an average of Rs.2100 per annum. Out of total 8 families interviewed, 7 families earn on an average an amount of Rs.4371/-(approx).

Histogram 1
Histogram of Annual Income of the Great Adamanese Family

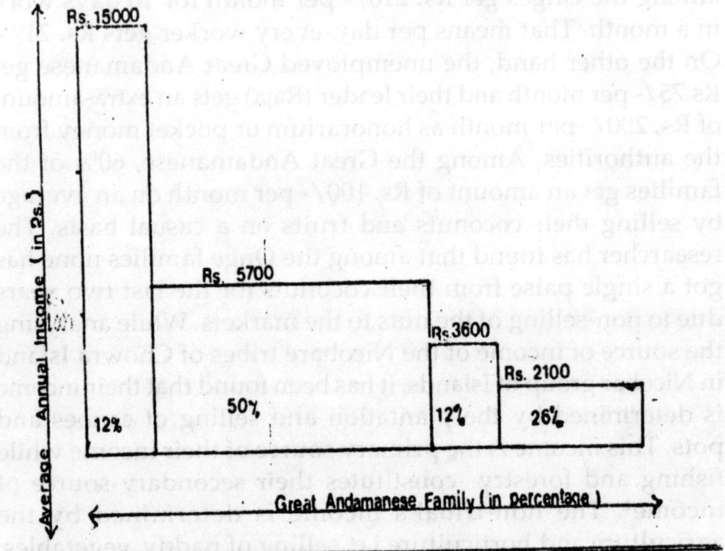

per annum, while rest one family earns Rs. 15000 per annum. A great income gap is noticed between lower income family and higher income families. Here out of total 100% of the families 88% of the families earn little amounts of money. Details about the annual income of the Great Andamanese families are given in Histogram 1.

Histogram 2 of the Onges shows the annual income of the Onges in details. Among the Onge families, the researcher has taken 38 families for assessing their annual family income position and thc incomc level. Among the Onge families, on an average, every family earns an amount of Rs.5753 per annum, which is more than the income earned by an average Great Andainanese family. It is found that out of total 38 families interviewed, only 3 families earn on an average an amount of Rs.21000 per annum, 5 families earn on an average an amount of Rs.5700 annually and the remaining 30 families earn a meagre amount of Rs.4238 per annum on an average. It must be remembered that only few families earn a heavy

Histogram 2
Histogram of Annual Income and of the Onges Family

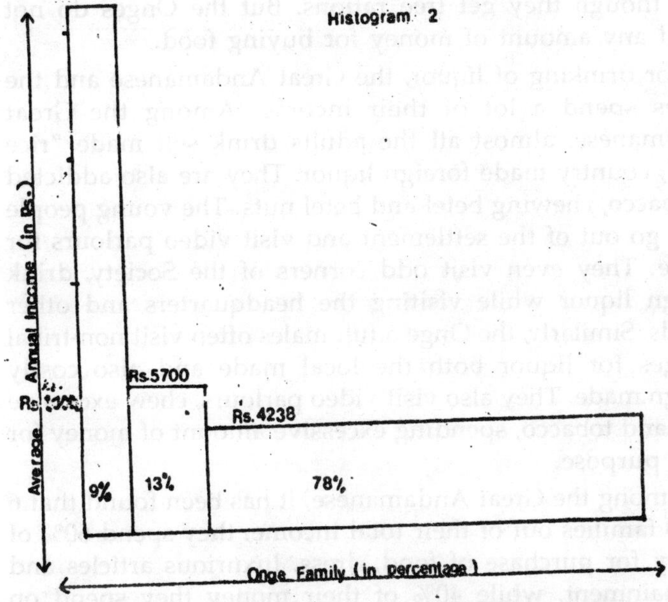

amount of money, while other families earn quite a poor amount. Only 3 families out of total 38 families earn fairly high amount than the rest of the 35 families. It has been found only 3 families on an average earn Rs.21000 annually, while 35 families get Rs.4446 per annum on an average. Thus there is a wide gap between higher income and lower income families. The per capita annual income of the Great Antlamanese is Rs.1520/- and in case of Onge, the per capita annual income is Rs.2186/- which is more than the per capita annual income of the Great Andamanese.

Nature of expenditure

Like the Nicobarese, the Great Andainanese and the Onges believe in the maxim "eat, drink and be happy". By nature they have no idea of saving. Naturally, they spend their income like extravagants. The main items of their expenditure are drinks and dress including luxurious items. They do not spend money for food, because all the necessary rationed articles are being supplied by the Samiti free of cost under the "dole system". The Great Anclarnanese spend some amount of their income for purchase of foodstuffs alone even though they get free rations. But the Onges do not spend any amount of money for buying food.

For drinking of liquor, the Great Andamanese and the Onges spend a lot of their income. Among the Great Andamanese, almost all the adults drink self made "rice beer", country made foreign liquor. They are also addicted to tobacco, chewing betel and betel nuts. The young people often go out of the settlement and visit video parlours for movie. They even visit odd corners of the Society, drink foreign liquor while visiting the headquarters and other islands. Similarly, the Onge adult males often visit non-tribal villages for liquor both the local made and also costly foreign.made. They also visit video parlours, chew excessive betel and tobacco, spending excessive amount of money for these purpose.

Among the Great Andamanese, it has been found that 6 (75%) families out of their total income, they spend 60% of money for purchase of food, dress, luxurious articles and entertainment, while 40% of their money they spend on liquor and other forms of addiction. Moreover, it is found that 2 (25%) of the families spend 80% of their income for purchase of liquor on an average. It is reported that the Great Andamanese families prefer to barter with outsiders their products like coconuts and fruits in exchange of tobacco, liquor and dress. Most of the elders, however, reported that they do not know the market value of their commodities which they sell to buy goods in exchange. Naturally, the non-tribal unscrupulous traders and customers often cheat them by not paying the exact or fair price at the current market-rate of the goods and traders often charge excessive price of the commodities they sell to the tribals.

Similarly, the innocent Onges are often exploited by the unscrupulous merchants at the time of business transactions. They spend a lot on local drinks and even on foreign alcohol. Adult males often visit non-tribal villages for drinking "rice beer", at high costs. It is reported that some of them procure drinks from the staff of the Samiti at a high price. It has been found that at present at least 80% of income they spend out of their total income on liquor, tobacco, pan (betel-leaf), video shows and the remaining 20% of money on purchasing dress and luxury articles. But every family does not spend the same amount of money for particular purposes.

It is the policy of the Samiti to supply two sets of cloths for every adult male and female every year, including the children. But Samiti has failed to supply cloths for the last four years to the Great Andamanese and the Onges. Naturally, both the communities have to purchase clothes from outside markets on cash. The males use shirt, half-pants and some shirt-like upper garments, while the Great Andamanese females wear the Burmese type of bright coloured dresses, including sari used for going outside the settlements. But the Onge females wear the Burmese type lungis and blouses as lower and upper garments respectively. Children usually use panties while some still remain naked.

Indebtedness

Indebtedness is caused by an imbalance between income and minimum requirements as well as lack of resources for carrying on gainful economic activities and unemployment. Indebtedness is an immediate major problem of the innocent tribesmen in India. This is also true for the Andaman tribals particularly, the Great Andamanese. The causes for their indebtedness are:- low income and high expenditure, lack of knowledge of economic transaction in the case of tribesmen cheated by unscrupulous outside traders, short supply of ration articles, excessive income and expenditure of the Great Andamanese family for consumption of liquor and use of luxury goods. So far as India is concerned, 85% of the tribesmen suffer from indebtedness[3], while 100% of the Great Andamanese families suffer from chronic indebtedness.

The family expenditure of the Great Andamanese and the Onges have been found to be increasing in such a way that most of the Great Andamanese families have failed to balance their lower family income against higher family expenditure. Their sources of income are inadequate to meet their family requirements. On the other hand, the number of members in the families are increasing fast in comparison to their family income.

Histogram 3 showing.the Income and Expenditure graphs indicates that every Great Andamanese family earns on an average an amount of Rs. 5700 per annum, while on an average every family spends Rs. 6472 annually. That means every family spends an excess amount of Rs. 772 per year.

Table 4 shows the indebtedness position of the Great Andamanese families in details. From personal interviews and office records of the Samiti, the researcher has found that every Great Andamanese family has taken some amounts of commodities on credit from their own Multipurpose Co-operative Society. Due to shortage of their food requirements, every family is bound to buy such extra-foodstuffs on credit. During the two years of the survey-period, all the 8 families have found to have borrowed an amount of Rs.18124 worth

Histogram 3
Histogram of Average Annual Income and Expenditure of the Great Adamanese Family

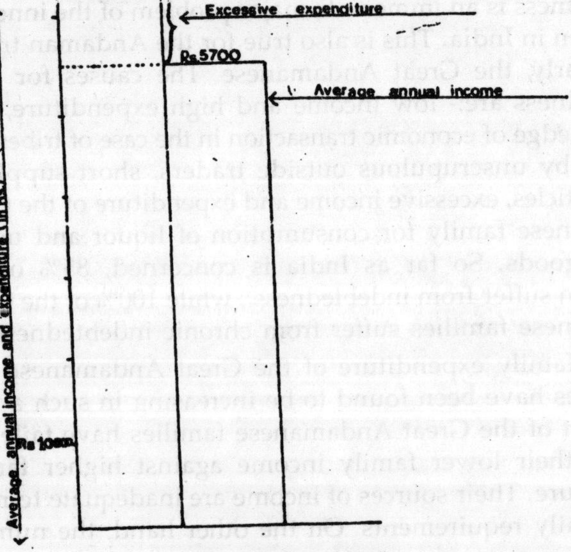

of commodities approximately and simultaneously these Great Andamanese families have been refunded an amount of Rs.5768 (approx.) upto June 1990. That means on an average every family owes Rs.772/- per annum to the Co-operative Society. It is found from the Table 4 that the average loan repaying position of the tribals is not upto expectation. On an average, a family has borrowed Rs.1132 per annum, while it has repaid only R.s.360/- per annum. Therefore, every family has incurred debt to the tune of Rs.772 to their Cooperative Society. That means every family has spent an excessive amount of Rs. 772 per annum beyond their annual income. If such flow of credit and refund system continues, then none of the family can clear up the dues in the near future.

Table 4

Indebtedness of the Great Andamanese families during 1987-88 to 89-90*

Name of the Tribe	*No. of families taken loan*	*Total amount of loan taken from 1987-88 to 89-90(Rs.)*	*Average loan taken per family*	*Total refunded (Rs.)*	*Average refunded per family*	*Indebtedness position on an average (Rs.)*
Great Andamanese.	8	18124	2265	5768	720	1544
Great Andamanese's yearly indebt	8	9062	1138	2884	360	772

*Data of the Table havebeen collected' by the researcher on the spot during 1988-90.

At present, the Onges do not face any debt problem. They have also the problem of shortage of foodstuffs. But they manage the crisis by taking natural food as much as possible.

The amount thus spent varies from family to family. Most of the tribes are suffering from indebtedness. Only a few permanent staff of both ethnic groups allow the deduction of a fixed amount of money from their payment at the time of pay disbursement as per government employees compulsory deduction rules. The amount thus deducted is deposited in their G.P.F. or other funds. Remaining head of the members of the families of the both ethnic groups have opened bank accounts in their nearest Public Banks. But the tribesmen in general have no concept of savings and saving benefits and so they take less interest to save money.

Further, the poor income of the tribals often discourages them to save. After spending for the family, they have no extra-money left over to save. Eighty percent of the families have deposited only Rs. 150/- to Rs.400/- at the time of opening their Bank accounts.

Modern economic activities, however, are changing the traditional tribal economy and this is also noted in the case of the two tribal groups referred to. The following modernising forces need to mention in the context of the changing economy of the tribes :- education, newly established link of tribal market with the big markets outside, the cooperative, labour unions, the concept of saving itself, a shift in the consumption pattern from need-based to impersonally need-based emergence of a type of commercial aptitude among the tribals, shift in the crop pattern from cereals to cash crops and open sale of minor forest produce as a means of cash economy[4].

Every economic system has some merits and demerits. Both in case of the Great Andamanese and the Onges, the economy is now under a process of transition. So, the main problem of these tribal groups is the lack of factors in the process of modernisation of the economy is absence of factors like education, inadequate markets, inactive Cooperative Society. Poor income prevents them from saving money. They cannot develop any sense of commercial aptitude in their economic activities. There is no organised method for collection of forest and sea products or produce as a means of enabling them to build up a cash economy. Even after a period of 20 years of uninterupted endeavour of the authorities, the spread of education among the tribals is not satisfactory. As regards their adopting new occupations and economy the chances are almost negligible. They do not like to commercialise their plantation and agriculture. Naturally, the tribesmen are neither ready to make themselves fullfledged agriculturist nor good labourers. The 'Dole System' which is available to them makes them idle, more suspectible to stick to go-old habits. Due to absence of transport and proper sales market, the Onges have not been able to sell their coconuts with reasonable margins of profits. The Great Andamanese sell their goods to the outsiders at so cheap rates that they are almost cheated. The Co-operative Society could not make any arrangement of marketing the products for them with fair profits. They did not get any facilities to absorb themselves in any meaningful jobs. Naturally, it is found that most of the Great Andamanese spend their time without any work. Even the Onge daily wage labourers remain unemployed for 20 days in a month. They have no scope to utilize their man-powers.

The new "spoon feeding" policies have not been able to create any confidence among the tribesmen and their self-survival attitude have almost been lost. Many of them do not like to continue their traditional occupations and remain under the traditional economy. Still the Onge oldmen practice hunting and fishing. The youths do not want to stick to such occupation, but they are helpless. The dole system has made them crippled both physically and mentally. If food does not reach their doors, they feel distressed.

The Co-operative movement have failed to be successful to pursue its role so far as the two tribal groups under reference are concerned. The Societies of both settlements cannot maintain regularly supply of free rations to the tribals and sell the rations to the Great Andamanese on credit. It has failed to pursue the tribesmen to sell their products through the Societies at reasonable prices. Only on two occasions the Co-operative Society purchased some coconuts from the Great Andamanese. At present, the Great Andamanese Co-operative Society does not buy any products from the people. Therefore, the tribals are bound to sell their coconuts and fruits to the outsiders at shockingly cheap rates and are often exploited by the outside buyers. Similarly, the Onge Cooperative Society has also not been able to purchase the coconuts and fruits from the tribesmen due to problem relating to transport, storage and export. For over two years, the tribesmen did not earn a single paise from their coconut plantations.

However, the Co-operative Societies have recently floated a scheme to supply all household articles to the tribesmen at cheap rates and stop exploitation of the tribesmen by supplying goods to their door on cash. Most of the time the Onge Co-operative Society does not offer them any payment on cash, but gives them commodities in return of the money value of things bartered. Unfortunately, the Society has been found to have given them such commodities which either they do not want or do not use. Naturally they take such goods home and keep them unused or throw them into the jungle.

The new economy neither encourages the tribal groups to produce nor enables them to buy these from the markets. The tribals have been removed from their traditional modes of subsistence without being replaced by any new type of food-producing economy. The present occupational structure has changed them into manual labourers, nothing else. The collection of coconuts has created a new sense of competition in them. This has developed a sort of environs or malicious attitude among the innocent Great Andamanese and the Onges. In case of Onge society the able-bodied persons collect more than that what the disabled and oldmen do and thereby they get more money. Those permanent workers are used to lead a better, somewhat more modern economic life than the unemployed and those with a lower income. It has created a class of distinction, a sort of inequality on economic basis. The present system and the mode of employment are highly objectionable. Most of the fit tribals are unemployed, though they get door to door supply of foodstuffs without rendering any contributory labour. They do not get any earning facilities. No endeavour has been made to utilize this unused man-power for development purpose. Such "spoon feeding" policies could not help them survive unless they are encouraged to eke out a living for themselves. The Samiti has failed to successfully develop animal husbandry and posiculture to improve the economic of the two tribal groups a lot. No honey bee-colony has been set up.

Table 5

Willingness of the Individuals Regarding Self-Employment Scheme*

Name of the Tribe	*No. of persons interviewed*	*No. of respondents*	*N.A.*	*Do you like to self-employment scheme?*	
				Yes	*No*
Great Andamanese	12	12	-	2	10
Onges	60	50	10	3	47

* Field Survey conducted by the researcher on the spot during 1988-90.

From the results of the interview recorded in Table 5, it is seen that 10 tribals among 12 interviewed Great Andamanese and 47 out of 50 Onge respondents do not like to start any self-employment project to solve the unemployment problems. Those Onges who gave affarmative answers, majority of them are not ready to open any self-employment projects themselves. Willing individuals of both ethnic groups desire light work projects such as opening pan shops or stationery shops. They do not agree to open carpentry-cum-blacksmithy or bamboo and cane workshops. They want to open their shops at the headquarters. They are personally interested to get jobs in office as unskilled workers. Majority of the Onge individuals have no idea about self-employment scheme and profit and loss. They want that systems like supply of free dole should continue which could help them to survive easily.

Comments

With the introduction of modern agriculture and horticulture, an effort has been made to change the traditional subsistance economy of the Great Andamanese and the Onges. Moreover, all modern welfare measures have been provided to improve their primitive economy during various plan periods. They have of course changed their primitive hunting-gathering occupation structure into a modern cash crops and wage-based economy. Under the new economic system, few tribal individuals are involved in white collar jobs and few are involved in wage-labourers. It is seen that majority of the able individuals of both sexes among these tribal communities are still unemployed having before them no scope to utilize their labour power. So it could not be ascertained whether the present generation could have adjusted themselves with the alien occupations and economy. They do not like to improve their plantations and vegetable gardens to produce more food grains, domestication of animals and use modern fishing techniques that could help them to become financially sound. Though they have been provided with all cash crops earning facilities, but, no income is ensured from their horticulture and agriculture due to lack of market and transport facilities. They have developed no sense of money matters and saving habits. Majority of the families are living under poor conditions. The Great Andamanese are suffering under the trap of indebtedness. The causes of their extravagance are—excessive wastage of money on liquor, tobacco, video shows, luxurious goods etc. Due to lack of knowledge about the modern currency and price index, the innocent tribesmen are often cheated by the unscrupulous non-tribal merchantmen during their business transactions. The new modern economy made their unified classless society into class-divided society on the basis of privilege, income and powers.

REFERENCES

1. Basu, B.K., *The Onge,* Seagull Books, Calcutta, (1990), p.6.
2. Chanda, Sudhendu, Economic Structure of a Nicobarese Villages: In "Chowra Island" in *Indian Journal of Social Work,* (1971), 32(1),25-33.
3. Verma, R.C., *Indian Tribes Through The Age,* Publication Divisions, Ministry of Information and Broadcasting, Government of India, New Delhi, (1990), p. 117.
4. Vidyarthi, L.P. and B.K. Rai, *The Triabal Culture of India,* Concept Publishing Company, Delhi, (1977), pp. 140-141.

5

Present Social Scenario

Man is a social animal. He does not and cannot live alone. Social life may be called the essence of human life. Man forms the family to fulfil his biological as well as social needs. The family is the primary unit of the human society. It is an essential part of the social organisation of man. The nature of social organisation varies from tribe to tribe and from place to place.

According to Vidyarathi (1977), the following five factors form the matrix of social life. *(1)* the natural environment, *(2)* population, *(3)* the human being, *(4)* material technology and, *(5)* social environment[1]. Change of any of the above factors affects the whole social life and organisation of man simultaneously. Under such circumstances, a crisis may arise in the social life of man, a disorderly situation may prevail over the social system as such.

The tribals of the Andaman and Nicobar groups of Islands are primitive. Particularly, the tribals of the Andaman Group of Islands are considered with the Negrito racial affiliation. The social organisation of this tribe is to be considered as paleolithic or belonging to the Stone Age. The five natural factors which have already been stated, help the tribesmen to continue to lead a primitive social life for centuries. The nature of isolation, limited population, poor technical knowledge, have helped them to form a special type of social organisation. The tropical climate, the evergreen forests as well as the sea around condition, the weather of this area have created a unique ecology in their material and social life. The deep forests and scattered islands bound them to live in groups. Apparently, the Andaman tribals are hunter-fruit gatherer communities. To follow these activities, to procure food they have been forced to form bands. The internal structure of the band is simple. Often a tribe will comprise several bands held together as a result of living together through the band of kinship[2].

Past Social History

The retrospective social history of the Great Andamanese and the Onges of the Andaman Islands, however, gives us a different experience. The Great Andamanese were the most populous ethnic group having ten different sub-tribes with separate names and territories for each group or sub-tribe. Their areas of movement were found in and around the Great Andaman Islands which is extended from South Andaman to North Andaman. The southern group of islands were occupied by tribes like Aka-ked, Aka-Kol, Aka-Juwai, Aka-Pucikwar (Bojigyab), Aka-Bea and Aka-Bale (Balawa). The northern group of islands were occupied by the rest of the four sub-tribes like Aka-Cari, Aka-Bo, Aka-Jero and Aka-Kora[3]. The Onges had several bands spread over the whole Little Andaman Island till the early fifties. Every group had a separate name and had a demarcated territory within the island. In 1888, Portman found six different sects or sub-groups among the Onge community[4]. Later, on the basis of the number of communal huts and small subsistence groups, Cipriani (in 1953), Nigam (in 1962) and Badal Basu (in 1987), record in their respective reports 29, 31 and 24 different groups or bands among the Onge tribal respectively[5].

But Dr. Mann has classified the Onges into four different groups with their separate names and definite areas of their movement,. He has reported that the people of Chholung group moved from Dugong Creek to Hut Bay. People of Maaye group lived in Western Coastal area of Little Andaman, mainly from West Bay to Sandy Point. People of Amiya group moved from Jackson Creek to Dugong Creek. The interior forests of the island were the exclusive areas of movement of the people belonging to the Aami group[6].

The spoken language of the ten different tribes of the Great Andamanese was closely related to one another. They had, however, same grammatical structure. But the Onge spoke the language and had the grammatical structure common to all different local groups. Social life of each band or group was concentrated on the communial hut or huts. The communal hut was their symbol of group unity, if not social unity. Members of each band or group which comprised a few families shared a bee-hive shaped communal hut called "beyra". The Onges identified themselves with the name of their communal huts, while the Great Andamanese identified themselves with the name of their territory where they lived. People of every group had several temporary huts for subsistence purposes along with their common and permanent huts. For subsistence purposes and on seasonal needs, the individual family often took shelter at a temporary hut, which was erected for a particular season only with individual efforts. However, the communal hut was made by the common efforts for common living. This permanent beehive shaped communal hut was the integral part of their social and cultural life of the people of all groups. During the monsoon when it rains heavily and as the venue of all important events and rituals associated with the life cycle and the social gathering the communal hut was the symbol of unity. At least 30-50 members belonging to 6-7 families took shelter sharing common meals at the communal hut for a particular period of time.

The Great Andamanese and the Onges maintained a different type of family which is uncommon in the definition of the family according to the social sciences. According to their nature of living, Radcliffe-Brown (in 1922) and Dr. Mann divided the Great Andamanese and the Onge families into three types. The first type of family was composed of husband, wife and their minor children below 6 years. The second type of family consisted of all unmarried males above 6 years along with widowers and the third type of family was constituted by all unmarried females above 6 years and the widows. The last two types of families lived in dormitories separately, according to their sex. Children above 6 of both sexes were to be guided by adult males and widows at their respective dormitories[7]. Similarly, the Nicobarese tribes of the Nicobar group of Islands also maintained lineage based joint family life comprised in a main hut or "pati" (Tuhet) a circular habitat[8]. The last two types of families of the Great Andamanese and the Onges are considered as two big families, which were constituted irrespective of family and blood relations. No separate family identity was available among the Great Andamanese and the Onges. As a matter of fact, there was a relationship of interdependence among the members of these three type of families formed by sharing meals and games. All unmarried adult males often took responsibilities of all minors, females and old individuals of the group. They taught the children about hunting, fishing and collecting foodstuffs from the forests and the sea. Apart from these groups, the bachelors and adult married males often extended their helping hands towards the old and the minors, providing them with food, shelter and protection irrespective of family or blood relations.

There was an organised division of labour according to sex and age in the tribal group referred to. The youths performed hard and risky works like hunting and fishing. Adult females did domestic and light work. All the children above 6 were treated as members of the community. No class distinction was found in the Great Andamanese and the Onge societies. Everybody was treated equally and respectfully without any discrimination of sex, age and family background. The greater the age, the greater was the respect. Parents-in-law were treated as though they were the actual parents. Men were, however, treated differently from women. Of course, the older people were more respected than the younger. But no family was in a higher position or more powerful than others socially or economically. There was no government, all decisions were taken by the whole community. Here obviously, the older males and females had more influence in the society than the younger males and females. There was no office of authority, no chief[9]. The position and status of the women were highly preserved by certain social norms and rules. The females above 6 lived at dormitories under the strict guidance of the widows. No male was allowed entry into the female dormitory without prior permission of the widows. Torture on the women was unknown. Marriage was totally prohibited between the widows of the younger brother and the elder brother of the deceased person. Communication between them was made through third parties. All matters relating to affairs of women were to be dealt with by the women themselves. The wife of the group leader often got power to hold discussion on such affairs. Women were, however, free to attend any meeting without any social obligations.

The concept of authority of senior over junior persons was unknown to the Great Andamanese and the Onges. It was strange for the tribesmen to think that one of them could pass orders to others. The subordination of Juniors was more a matter of obedience and respect for the senior than a principle of authority or order. Children of either society did not expect that somebody even their father, mother, elder brothers, should order them to do certain things and stop them from doing certain other things. Children could only take suggestions and advice. Likewise, an elderly tribesman also expected that he would not have to bear with disrespect in the form of his suggestions, advice or request being dishonoured. The advices given was mainly limited to the family. Every elder tribesmen got equal respect from the younger individuals, whatever might be their relations.

Individual life was marked by different socio-cultural functions. From birth to death, several ritual ceremonies were observed to demarcate the various stages of their social life. Women of the Great Andamanese and the Onges gave birth to their children at temporary delivery huts, exclusively made for such purpose beside their permanent hut. In between pre-natal and post-natal periods, the expected mother followed several norms along with food restrictions. Among the Onge, the pregnant lady was ritually offered some food items like pork, turtle's meat by an elder of either sex. The person who offered the food entered into a kind of ceremonial relationship with the child to be born and the parents of the unborn baby. In the Great Andamanese society, the elder of either sex chose a name of the child to be born after his or her name or to perpetuate his or her name by naming a future child of the tribe after him or her. And a new relationship was established between the person who chose the name of the unborn baby along with its parents. Among the Great Andamanese, same name could be chosen for either sex. The elder Onge could adopt as many children as he or she liked. Both the cases, the adopted children and the actual children of both societies were treated as original children by these elders. The husbands and wives of these families were treated as foster-parents by these children. Equally, these children also bore all responsibilities of their foster-parents in their old age.

Transition from adolescence to adulthood period was the next stage of the children. During this period, he or she followed certain food restrictions. After certain periods of time, several food-eating ceremonies like eating pork, turtle, dugong and honey were celebrated by offering these "forbidden" food to them. In case of maiden, immediately after the first sign of her menses, she was separated from the rest of the individuals of the society. At the end of her first menstruation period, she was purified following a secret bath in the sea, and a ritual was observed by giving a new name to her after a flower of the season. She was painted with white clay on her whole body and offered boar blood and meat, which was followed by a cultural function in her honour for the whole night. The boy also observed certain food restrictions during his first sign of adulthood. Like maiden, he was purified by a sea bath and painted the whole body with white clay. Later, he was offered boar-meat which was followed by a traditional group dance and song ceremony for the whole night.

The third stage of the individual life of the tribals was celebrated through marriage performance. Both males and females of either society were free to choose their life partners. Marriage between close relatives was strictly prohibited. Even marriage between children of the foster-parents and adopted children were not permitted. Among the Great Andamanese, marriage was never permitted between same name bearable individuals. No marriage was practised forcefully. For marriage, the parents of the bridegroom never approached the parents of the bride directly. Usually, a third person offered a marriage proposal to the parents of the bride on behalf of the parents of the bridegroom. In the early Onge society, widow re-marriage was prohibited. Later this band has been removed. Nobody was permitted to marry again before the death of his or her life-partner. In case the wife was unfertile, then only the husband was allowed to marry another woman with the full consent of his first wife. Monogamy was the only form of marriage. Divorce was usually rare. In case of any illicit relationship between either of the married couples is found, then only the individual could have separation. No illegal sex relationship was tolerated in the society. Different types of punishment were sanctioned by the elders of the society against culprit according to the nature of the fault. The tribal elders tried to perpetuate their social norms and traditions very carefully. No written rules and regulations existed in the society. Every law was adopted by the elders in a social gathering. Nobody was above the law. Everybody was bound to obey and respect the social systems and norms.

Marriage with other tribe or sub-group was strictly prohibited. According to Mann, marriage between Chhalung and Aami groups was not practised. Similarly, marriage was not permitted between Maaya and Amiya groups due to their having close relations[10]. Likewise, in the Great Andamanese society, no marriage took place among ten different recognised tribes. They often performed their marriages within their own tribe having so many local groups. For example, the people of Aka-Jero often had their marriage relations within the Aka-Jero tribe. Child marriage was banned in their societies, though in the Onge society, the betrothal system existed. No marriage was practised before the initiation or ritual performance of the boys and girls respectively. The marriage ceremony was always performed at the communal hut, in the presence of all relatives of both the wedding parties. Usually, the wedding couple was introduced by an elder of the group at a social ceremony which was attended by all relatives and people of both local groups. The bridegroom often held the hand of his partner and made her sit on his thighs. The two embraced each other for a few moments and later the marriage was ceremoniously celebrated with grand feasts with a colourful group dance and song.

The funeral ceremony was marked as the last celebration of an individual's life. Death was mourned by the relatives of the deceased person along with the people of the whole local group by stopping all their entertainment for a certain period of time. The dead body was often buried under the bed of the deceased person by his or her relatives and they abandoned the settlement temporarily. After the mourning period was over, they came back to the camp to live there.

Present Social Conditions

The recent developmental activities have greatly affected the social organisation of the Great Andamanese and the Onges among the Andaman tribals. The on-going developmental activities, sudden exposure of the outsiders, behavioural change of the individuals among the tribals, import of allien technology in their primitive economy and de-population along with disordered socio-environment conditions are considered to be the factors that influenced the general features of the social organisation of the Great Andamanese and the Onges.

In accordance with the modern programmes, the two tribal ethnic groups referred to, were settled in different corners of the two Islands. The Great Andamanese were settled with an exclusive authority over an isolated island with an area of 3.11 sq. km. instead of the whole Great Andaman Islands. The Onges were settled down in two small isolated remote corners of the Little Andaman, within a restricted area instead of the whole island. Both the ethnic groups were settled in these places irrespective of local group or tribal affiliation. At present, among the Great Andamanese six, out of the ten tribes almost disappeared. Now the Aka-Jero, the Aka-Kora, the Aka-Bo and the Aka-Cari tribes number 30. Within such a small population, neither the territorial affiliation nor the separateness of the tribes or local groups could be retained. Similarly, the Onges have a population of 100 living in two settlements without any clan-like local group affiliation.

Demographic Situation

Under the present social set-up, the two communities have separate living accommodations, every individual family being given a wooden house. All the communal huts have vanished and the tribals have to live in closed types of settlement. They have been settled in a limited place permanently stopping their nomadic social life irrespective of bands, clan-like affiliations. The present demographic situation of these tribals is shown in Table 1. The total number of population, their sex ratio, production situation are shown in details in this Table 1. The Table hat been produced with the help of the data collected by the researcher during his field survey in 1988-90.

Through field survey and direct questionnaire, the researcher has found in 1990 from the Table 1 that the Great Andamanese are 30 and the Onges are 100 in number. Out of the 30, only 6 males and 4 females of the Great Andamanese have been found under the reproductive age group of 15-49. The Onges have a total number of 29 males and 23 females in the same age group. The sex ratio of the Great Andamanese is 667 and the Onges is 793 females per 1000 males. From the Table 1 it is found that only 14 Great Andamanese and 30 numbers in the Onge society are within the age-group of 0-14. The remaining individuals are found belonging to the age-group of above 49 in both societies.

Table 2 shows that the population profile of the Great Andamanese and the Onges in 1975 and 1970 was total 23 and 121 respectively. During the period, the Great Andamanese numbered 7 and the Onges 76 in the reproductive age group of 15-49 and the sex-ratio was 1333 females and 948 females per 1000 males respectively in the same age group. This sex ratio is more than the present (1990) sex-ratio of both the ethnic groups. At present, on an average, the sex-ratio of the Great Andamanese has been increased from 642 in 1975 to 875 in (1990). While on an average, the sex-ratio of the Onges has been decreased from 952 (1970) to 785(1990) females per 1000 males.

These two Tables which recording the demographic position of the Great Andamanese and the Onges indicate an acute de-population problem in these two societies. The present population situation indicates that the re-productive persons of these two ethnic groups are few in number in comparison with their respective total population. Nonetheless, the continuous dwindling of population which is hampering the tribesmen to maintain their family, their basic social institution, their marriage-relations, population growth, status of the females etc. and to sustain their social customs and traditions.

Table 3

Nature of the Composition of the Families of the Great Andamanese and the Onges societies in 1990[12]

Different types of families	*Great Andamanese*		*Onges*	
	Total no. of families	*Total no. of members*	*Total no. of families*	*Total no. of members*
1. Family composed of husbands and wives and their unmarried children.	3	20	13	51
2. Family composed of husbands and wives.	1	2	21	42
3. Family composed of other than husbands and wives.	2	6	-	-
4. Family composed of bachelor/widow/widower without blood relations.	2	2	4	7
Total	8	30	38	100

The family is the basic social group and its forms and functions in different communities are of various types. Murdock (1949) states that the family is a social group characterised by common residence, economic cooperation and reproduction. It includes adults of both sexes, at least

Table 1

Age and Sex structure of the Great Andamanese and the Onges in 1990*

	The Great Andamanese				*The Onges*			
Age Group	*M*	*F*	*T*	*Remarks in 1990*	*M*	*F*	*T*	*Remarks in 1990*
0 - 4	2	2	4	M-7,F-7,T=14	8	4	12	M-17,F-13,T=30
				Total (0-14)=14				Total(0-14)=30
5 - 9	0	5	5	Percentage =46.67	4	5	9	Percentage=30
10 - 14	5	0	5	Sex Ratio=1000	5	4	9	Sex Ratio=764
15 - 19	1	1	2	M-6.F-4, T=10	1	1	2	M-29,F-23,T=52
20 - 24	-	-	-		3	3	6	Total(15-49)=52
25 - 29	2	2	4	Total (15-49)= 10	4	3	7	Percentage = 52
30 - 34	2	-	2	Percentage = 33.33	1	3	4	Sex Ratio = 793
35 - 39	1	1	2	Sex Ratio = 667	7	2	9	
40 - 44	-	-	-		9	6	15	
45 - 49	-	-	-		4	5	9	
50 - 54	-	1	1	M-3,F-3,T=6	6	1	7	M-10,F-8,T=18
				Total (50-above)=6	1	4	5	Total(50-above)=18
55 - 59	1	2	3	Percentage = 20				Percentage =18
60 - above	2	-	2	Sex Ratio = 1000	3	3	6	Sex Ratio = 800
Total	16	14	30	Sex Ratio = 875	56	44	100	Sex Ratio- 785

*The table has been produced with the help of the data collected by the researcher during the field survey in 1988-90.

Table 2: Age and Sex Structure of the Great Andamanese and the Onges in 1975 and in 1970 Respectively

	*The Great Andamanese in 1975**				*The Onges in 1970***			
Age Group	*M*	*F*	*T*	*Remarks*	*M*	*F*	*T*	*Remarks*
0 - 4	1	1	2	M-4,F-3,T=7	5	4	9	M-18,F-16,T=34
				Total (0-14)=7				Total(0-14)=34
5 - 9	-	-	-	Percentage =30.50	8	4	12	Percentage=28.1
10 - 14	3	2	5	Sex Ratio=750	5	8	13	Sex Ratio=888
15 - 19	-	-	-	M-3.F-4, T=7	5	6	11	M-39,F-37,T=76
19 - 24	2	1	3	Total (15-49)= 7	5	3	8	Total(15-49)=76
25 - 29	1	-	1	Percentage = 30.50	9	5	14	Percentage = 62.8
30 - 34	-	-	-		8	8	16	
35 - 39	-	2	2	Sex Ratio = 1333	4	5	9	Sex Ratio = 948
40 - 44	-	-	-		4	6	10	
45 - 49	-	1	-		4	4	8	
50 - 54	3	1	4	M-7,F-2,T=9	3	3	6	M-5,F-6,T=11
55 - 59	1	1	2	Total (50-above)=9	-	3	3	Total(50-above)=11
60 - above	3	-	3	Percentage = 39.00	2	-	2	Percentage =9.1
				Sex Ratio = 285	3	3	6	Sex Ratio = 1200
Total	14	8	23	Sex Ratio = 642	62	59	121	Sex Ratio= 952

**Chakraborty, D.K., *Great Andamanese of Strait Island*, An.S.I., Port Blair, (1975); p. 2 (unpublished).

*De, D.C., "A demographic study of the Onges of Little Andaman", in *Bulletin of Department of Anthropology*, vol. 19(2), (1970); p. 118.

two of whom maintain a socially approved sexual relationship, and one or more children, own or adopted, of the sexually cohabiting adults. At present, the Great Andamanese and the Onges have changed their joint family structure which was so far based on local group affiliation or bands.

From the Table 3 it is found that now-a-days both the ethnic groups are maintaining four types of families. Here the first type of family consists of husbands, wives and their unmarried children. Under this type of simple family, the Great Andamanese have a total number of 3 families, while the Onges have a total number of 13 families. The unmarried children of both sexes have no separate dormitories. Now the children do not like to live alone. The Great Andamanese have 7 children within the age group of 6 to 24 and the Onges have 12 children within the age-range of 7 to 19 living with their parents.

The second type of family consists of only husband and wives. Some families have children but after their marriage, they have separated from their parents and maintain separate families. The researcher has found that one female in the Great Andamanese society and 8 females in the Onge society are barren. Under the second type of family, the Great Andamanese have one family and the Onges have 21 families.

The third type of family consists of members other than husbands and wives. Sometimes, the family is bound by blood relations. Here, the Great Andamanese have 2 families, where widows and their children have formed family. But no such type of family is found in the Onge society.

The last and the fourth type of family is composed of a single member or more than one members. Few cases have been found, where a single bachelor or a widow or a widower forms the family unit. Two families are found, where single bachelors have formed a family each in the Great Andamanese society and four such families exist in the Onge society. In short, the family structure of both tribal ethnic groups has been found to be changing and the change is due to break-up of the big family into small families. At present, the Great Andamanese have a total number of 8 and the Onges have a total number of 38 families.

From the Table 4 it can be seen that in 1975, the total number of the Great Andamanese families were 9. Out of 9 families, 3 were found to consist of husbands, wives and their one child, 2 families of husbands and wives and the remaining 4 families of a single widow or father, son and relatives, which is composed of one or more than three members.

Table 4

The Structure and Size of the Families of the Great Andamanese and the Onges

	Year of survey	*No. of members per family*										*No. of family*	*No. of persons*	*Av. size of the family*
		1	*2*	*3*	*4*	*5*	*6*	*7*	*8*	*9*	*10*			
No. of families of the Great Andamanese	1990[13]	2	2	-	2	-	1	-	-		1	8	30	3.75
	1975[14]	2	2	3	1	1	-	-	-	-	-	9	23	2.55
No. of families of the Onges	1990[13]	2	22	6	5	2	1	-	-	-	-	38	100	2.63
	1988[15]	-	15	8	2	2	1	-	-	-	-	28	96	2.90

From the same Table 4 it can be found that in 1988, that means just two years back from 1990, the Onges had a total number of 28 families. Out of these 28 families, 15 were comprised of husbands and wives, 8 families were comprised of 3 members. The rest of the families were comprised of more than three members, average size of the family of the Great Andamanese was 2.55 and the Onges 2.90 in 1975 and 1988 respectively. The total number of families in the Onge society has been increased from 28 in 1988 to 38 in 1990. But the total number of the families of the Great Andamanese has been decreased from 9 in 1975 to 8 in 1990. Now the average size of the family of the Great Andamanese is 3.75 and the Onge is 2.63. The causes of the increase of the Onge families is the increase of child marriage. Moreover, the researcher has considered bachelors and widows as comprising a single family due to their separate household existence.

Table 5

Likeness to live at Communal huts under joint family and like to leave their children to live at bachelor dormitories of the Great Andamanese and the Onges in 1990*

Name of the tribe	*No. of inter-viewed*	*No. of respon-dents*	*NA*	*Those who like to live at communal huts under the joint family system*		*Those who like to leave their children at dormi-tory for living separately*	
				Yes	*No*	*Yes*	*No*
Great Andamanese	15	15	-	4	11	4	11
Onges	70	60	10	28	32	26	34

* The data collected by the researcher during his field works in 1988-1990.

It is found from the Table 5 that out of 15 Great Andamanese 4 are olds, who like to live under the joint family system, while all 11 young respondents have indicated that they do not like to live under the joint family system. On the same question, out of 60 Onge respondents, 28 majority of them are olds said that they like to go back to their traditional communal lives. While other 32 Onges, most of them are young respondents do not like to live jointly under the common shelter. These unwilling individuals of both ethnic groups prefer to maintain simple type of family system. They do not like to bear the burden of the whole members of the community on their shoulders as before.

The second direct question which the researcher asked to tribals was whether people of the present generation like to leave their children at separate dormitories for living. He found that the majority of the old individuals of the both

Table 6

Marital Status of the Great Andamanese and the Onges

Name of the Tribe	*Year*	*No. of population*	*Unmarried*						*Married*						*Widow/ widower*		*Divorce separation*	
			Age (0-14) child		*Age (14-ab) adult*		*Total*		*Age (0-14) child*		*Age (14-1b) adult*		*Total*					
			M	*F*	*M*	*F*	*M*	*F*	*M*	*F*	*M*	*F*	*M*	*F*	*M*	*F*	*M*	*F*
Great	1990[16]	30	7	7	3	1	10	8	-	-	4	4	4	4	1	2	1	-
Andamanese	1975[17]	23	4	3	2	-	6	3	-	-	4	4	4	4	4	-	-	2
Onges	1990[16]	100	16	8	5	-	21	8	1	5	33	29	34	34	1	2	-	-
	1970[18]	121	18	16	8	5	26	21	-	-	35	35	35	35	-	2	1	1

ethnic groups agreed to re-start their past traditional accommodation system, while all 11 young individuals in the Great Andamanese society and 34 Onges, majority of them are young do not accept the proposal to keep their unmarried children away for living at a dormitory under the guidance of the widows or widowers. Young respondents of both societies want to keep their children under their own custody for their own care. But 4 Great Andamanese and 26 Onge respondents, majority of them are old, wants to keep their children at dormitories for maintaining their traditional and social customs and norms.

Table 7
Increasing Rates of Child Marriages and Unmarried Individuals*

Name of the tribe	*No. of persons inter-viewed*	*No. of respo-ndents*	*NA*	*Causes of child marriage: Like child marriage*	*Social system and norms*	*Scarcity of marri-ageable males/ females*	*Due to non-avail-ability of marriage-able mates unmarried case is increasing: Yes*	*No*
Great Andama-nese	15	15	-	-	-	15	15	-
Onges	70	56	14	-	-	56	56	-

* Field Survey conducted by the researcher on Great Andamanese and the Onges during 1988-1990.

Due to de-population problems, the people of the Great Andamanese and the Onges have failed to perpetuate their traditional marital status. From Table 6 it is found that among the Onges, child marriages still take place. Here one male, and 5 female children are married below the age of 14 years. Except one female, the rest of them are below 10. Such types of child marriage are not found in the reports of 1975 and 1970 among the Great Andamanese and the Onges respectively. Although, it has been found that the former society does not practise child marriage. Not a single case of Polygamy has been found anywhere. Enquired about the causes of the gradual increase of child marriage in the Onge society, most of the respondents replied that due to non-availability of marriageable girls, the Onge youths often bound to marry any girl or female irrespective of age, band, etc.

The data shown in Table 7 indicate that all 15 Great Andamanese respondents think that scarcity of marriageable mates causes the increase in the number of child marriages or unmarried individuals in both males and females. It was found that out of 70, 56 respondents among the Onges also felt the same. Individuals of both ethnic groups do not like to accept the child marriages and unmatched marriages. 4 Onge girls below 10 were found married to men between the age group of 12 to 40. Due to non-availability of marriageable mates in this tribal group, 5 youths were found to remain unmarried. In the Great Andamanese tribal group, 3 youths and one maiden above 18 were found to be unmarried. No such marriage problems were recorded in the census report of 1970 and 1975 on these two ethnic groups. In those reports, no child marriage case was recorded. Most of the respondents remarked that they did not like or prefer such child marriages, but that they had no alternative to marry minor girls or remain unmarried. They remarked that marriages should be performed after the attainment of puberty. All the surviving members of the Great Andamanese were relatives to each other or had blood relations. Therefore, it was not possible for them to have marital relations within the community. Unless, they made marriage relations with outside the ethnic group, their future generation would be extinct.

Table 8
List of unmatched married couples in the Great Andamanese and the Onge societies in 1990*

Sl. No.	*Name of the Husband & Age*	*Name of the Wife & Age*	*Husband's remarks*	*Wife's remarks*
		The Great Andamanese		
1.	Nao(Sr) 75	Bowa 55	Married for the third time has no issue	Married for the third time has no issue, barren
2.	Jirake 58	Surmai 33	Married for second time has children of his first wife	Married for the first time has one girl
		The Onges		
1.	Tambolai 40	Tolata-bege 60	Married for the second time	Married for the second time
2.	Balls 39	Malai 50	Married for the first time	Married for the second time, barren
3.	Koira 40	Togagigi 49	Married for the first time	Married for the second time, barren
4.	Nebekutti 52	Demburai 62	Married for the second time, no children now	Married for the second time, she has children of her first husband
5.	Chogegi 27	Botalai 37	Married for the first time, one child	Married for the second time, she has children of her first husband
6.	Kekele 47	Kamegi 58	Married for the first time	Married for the second time,barren
7.	Totauegai 42	Chobai 44	Married for the first time	Married for the second time has child
8.	Bellai 37	Nambero-legie 42	Married for the first time	Married for the second time has child
9.	Tanagiri 42	Nambemboi 58	Married for the first time	Married for the second time has child
10.	Notijirale 45	Malambabi 55	Married for the first time	Married for the second time, barren
11.	Otalatai 64	Tankitai 29	Married for the	Married for the

			second time has child of his first wife.	first time has children
12.	Langati 40	Kapita 9	Married for the first, time	Married forcefully
13.	Chotaokalai 54	Tinai 24	Married for the second time has children of his first wife.	Married for the first time has child
14.	Kanju 54	Sheela 28	Married for the second time has children of his first wife	Married for the first time has children,
15.	Botalai 30	Daldakumari 8	Married for the first time	Married forcefully

* Field Survey conducted by the researcher on the Spot during 1988-1990.

From Table 8 it is found that among the Great Andamanese, two cases were found where husbands were 25 and 30 years older than their respective wives. Among the Onge families, out of 34 married couples, 10 were reported to be incompatible as the wives were older than their respective husbands. Similarly, 5 cases were found, where husbands were too aged that is, more than 32, 31, 22 years older than their respective wives. From the same Table it was found that due to the de-population problem, both ethnic groups have lost their traditional marital status and customary rules. Now no body could bother to maintain any social or customary norms. For these reasons, such dissimilar married couples could be found. The aged males and females could easily be married to young boys or girls who married for the first time. Even the widows or widowers or barren females could easily be married to young partners.

All the young unmarried and married males and females reported before the researcher that they do not like to marry aged or widows or widowers, and that they do not have any alternative to live with widows or widowers or aged males or females as husband and wife. After the death of either of the couple, the man or woman wants to live with any partner irrespective of age or kinship relations. Due to scarcity of marriageable girls, boys have to choose any female irrespective of the fact as to whether she is barren or above the age of child bearing capacity. Nonetheless, the widows or barren women get married at the earliest sometime with a young man who is marrying her for the first time and vice versa.

Among the Great Andamanese, some marital relationships have now been made, which broke the social norms and the past social traditions. One case was noticed where the name of the wife of an individual was the same name of his mother, which was not sanctioned by the customary marital norms existing in their ethnic group. Mr. J. (aged 58) and Mrs. S (aged 34) were uncle and niece respectively. But they got married. Mrs. N (aged 28) married her mother's brother's son Mr. P (aged 40). Mr. N (aged 78) married three times. He marrying for the second time, married the wife of his younger brother. Few cases were found, where the tribals married half-bred and non-tribals. Mr. J(aged 58) at first married a half-bred girl, whose mother was a Great Andamanese but whose father was a Burmese, second time he married a women of 36, named Mrs. S (36). Mr. L (age 32) married a non-tribal popular lady. But she could not adjust herself with the tribal society and later she obtained divorce and took custody of her one year girl. Another tribal youth was waiting for the permission from the Samiti (AAJVS) to marry a non-tribal girl with whom he had a love affair[19].

Some unprecedented social norms and rules have been prevailing over the Onge societies in their disordered social system. All their traditional social rules and regulations regarding, marriage, family life and social life have broken down. It is found in the Onge society that Mr. T (40), Raja and his step-father Mr. K (58) were married again after the death of their wives respectively. Mr. T(40) married a widow Mrs. T (60) had one son, aged 27 by her first husband. But the old widower, Mr. K (58), married a much younger woman, Mrs. S (28) instead of marrying an old lady. Mr. N (52), former Raja of the Onges, married Mrs.D (60), a widow, who has one son and two daughters by her first husband. Mr.O (64), a widower, married Mrs. T (29). He has two daughters by his first wife[20].

Table 9
Choice of the Mate[21]

Name of the Tribes	*No. of person interviewed*	*No. of respondents*	*N.A.*	*Selected by the bridegroom/bride*		*Selected by the parents of the bridegroom/bride*		*Selected by other than parents of bride or bridegroom*	
				Yes	*No*	*Yes*	*No*	*Yes*	*No*
Great Andamanese	15	15		-	-	3	-	12	-
Onges	70	60	10	10	-	50	-	-	-

So far as marriage proposal is concerned, the Table 9 indicates that out of total 15 Great Andamanese respondents 12 reported that instead of parents or brides or bridegrooms, now the Samiti (AAJVS) often arranges all marriage matters. The Samiti itself chooses the partners, fixed up marriage-date and also performs the marriage ceremonies. It was reported that since the past few years, in place of parents of the bridegroom and the bride, the Samiti has been selecting the marital partners. Therefore, the parents of the bridegroom or bride have no freedom to choose their daughters-in-law or sons-in-law. No marriage can now be performed with any outsiders without prior permission of the Samiti. But no such obligation was found, as evident from reports of the 60 Onge respondents. Now instead of the bridegroom and the bride, the parents still decide the marriages according to their own choice. However, a few respondents also replied that they had some voice in selecting their marital partners. Marriage within the community is being disliked by some individuals. Sometime force would be applied in the matter of marriage. Mrs. L (28), an adopted daughter of Late Mr. K (ex-Raja) of the Great Andamanese society did not like to marry Mr. G (30) and Mrs. S (34) to Mr. J (55). But after a long negotiation by the Samiti and the elder of the society the women agreed to marry these mates.

Table 10
Choice of Marital Partners by Young Males and Females of the Great Andamanese and the Onges*

Name of the tribe	*No. of person inter-viewed*		*No. of respon-dents*		*N.A.*		*No of respondents like to marry*				*Causes behind marry-ing non-tribals/ outsiders*			
							Within commu-nities		*Outsiders*		*Like them*		*Non-avai-lability of marriage-able mates*	
Sex	*M*	*F*	*M*	*F*	*M*	*F*	*M*	*F*	*M*	*F*	*M*	*F*	*M*	*F*
Great Andam-anese	7	4	7	4	-	-	3	4	4	2	4	2	4	2
Onges	20	15	15	10	5	5	10	10	5	-	5	-	5	-

*Field Sruvey conducted by the researcher on Great Andamanese and Onge Youths on the spot during 1988-90.

From Table 10 it is found that out of the total 11 young males and females of the Great Andamanese, 4 males and 2 females preferred to marry outsiders. Out of the total of 35 young Onge male and female respondents, only 5 young males expressed their choice to marry outsiders, because they like the non-tribal girls as marital mates. Another cause is that they have no suitable marriageable mates within their own community. But rest respondents of the Great Andamanese and the Onges agreed to choose their mates from their respective societies provided they could have marriageable mates among them. One case was noted in the Great Andamanese society, where a maiden of 19, denied to marry a boy of her own society. She wants to marry an outsider. An Onge boy also refused to marry a widow of his own society, as he developed intimacy with a Nicobarese girl whom he wanted to marry, while the father of the girl did not agree to the proposal.

In their social system, the Great Andamanese and the Onges often follow the patriarchal system. The father is the main guardian of the family. After marriage, the bride does not lose her fathers local group recognition. But the children are identified with their father's local group or tribal affiliation. Due to the stoppage of their nomadic social habits, the newly married couple cannot change their living place and join either of the local groups as they like.

Table 11

Response of the Present Young Generation of the Great Andamanese and the Onges Regarding their Local Group or Tribal Identity*

Name of the tribe	*No. of person interviewed*	*No. of respondents*	*N.A.*	*Knowing the name of their own local group or tribe or clan-like local group*		*Knowing the name of the place where their forefathers resided*	
				Yes	*No*	*Yes*	*No*
Great Andamanese	11	11	-	-	11	-	11
Onges	35	30	5	10	20	10	20

*Field Survey conducted by the researcher on Great Andamanese and the Onge Youths on the spot during 1988-1990.

Table 11 refers, at present, a total of 11 young Great Andamanese males and females, who are unable to recall the names of their respective tribe and the place, where their forefathers lived. Similarly, 20 out of a total of 30 Onge young males and females respondents do not know what was their original territory and the name of their respective clan-like local groups. All the young people of both tribal societies known themselves as Great Andamanese and the Onges.

Status of Women

Women of India are often neglected by the male-dominated societies. Social prejudice and injustice have created many problems for the women-folk. Even now they suffer from many evils like child marriage and illiteracy. They are mostly ill-treated by the males in every sphere of social life. But women of the tribal societies of India hold a remarkable position in the society as they participate equally in the social activities with the male-folk. Sachchidananda (1978), reveals that the status of the women in tribal society is not a function of her economic role but determined by the principle of the social structure on which a particular society is based[22]. This is true in respect of the Great Andamanese and the Onges. The position and status of these tribal women have been changed to some extent in comparison to their past social life. In these two societies, the position of a woman as a daughter is fairly satisfactory. She is equally welcomed like a boy. She lives with her parents till she is married. The parents of the girls now get their daughters married with male partners who are 30 to 32 years senior to these respective girl-brides. Girls have no freedom to choose their life partners. They have been forced to get married with aged males or with widowers. Due to non-availability of female partners in the Onge society, the teenage girls are bound to marry any male within their society. It was reported by all the Great Andamanese that the young females, both married and unmarried, feel unsafe outside their society. For their innocence and helplessness, the unscrupulous males outside often tried to exploit them or lead them to the wrong way. That is why the maidens are forced to stop their education and come back home to save themselves from such dangers.

Women now perform the same activities as the men do. In the Onge society, all the adult women take part in jobs like weeding under-growths from their own plantations, working in the hospital as an assistant, collecting coconuts from their gardens as casual and daily wage labourers. One Great Andamanese female was even found engaged in teaching the children at Balwadi centre. Women often help their husbands in the outside works along with collecting firewood for cooking, rearing children, cooking, food for families and washing clothes etc.

The status and position of the women of the Andaman and Nicobar tribal societies have been interacting after contact with the outsiders. Women have been living under a helpless condition since the British rule. During British rule, they were sexually exploited by the Muslim convicts as well as British navalmen. According to Majumder (1975) a more serious grievance was the misconduct of the Naval

Brigademen and the convicts who were associated with Andamanese, as Portman mildly puts it, which evidently includes misconduct with women inmates of the "Andaman Home"[23]. Which later, was proved definitely as will be mentioned in connection with the infection of syphilies[24]. Later, the Burmese and other Indians, also illegally used these helpless women sexually and the women bore their children. Women were forced to live with these unscrupulous people without formal marriages. Kochar (1969) reveals, "The addiction to opium, wine and tobacco has often led the Andamanese to odd corners and subject to pressures of various sorts...... parents of young girls are thus forced to give their daughters to Burmese in marriage or concubinage. The Jero Women, it is said, used to "marry" Burmese more frequently. Kota's father was a Burmese. Konmu, now married to a Burmese, was the daughter of Burmese father. Loka...... his present wife was previously attached to a Moslem convict"[25].

Due to the bad socio-economic conditions of the Great Andamanese the women were often forced by their husbands to have illegal sexual relations with unscrupulous people. Women have been still suffering and are exploited by the non-tribals. As a result, most of the present children are of mixed blood. The mother may be an Andamanese but the father might be a Burmese or an Indian Tamil or Malayalee. It was observed that most of the Great Andamanese Women also developed illegal sexual relations with non tribals for earning money for family. They often want to take financial and other advantages from the non-tribal individuals concerned. Unlike the Great Andamanese, the socio-economic conditions of Onge women is not so bad. They have no scope to be exploited by the non-tribals. But it is found that they have been forced by the authorities to perform dance with their semi-nude traditional dress before the visitors.

Old women of these two societies are still under bad conditions even when they are free from all social prejudice. They have no restriction on dress, food and participation in social functions. But it was found that the widows and old ladies are surviving by their own initiative or by the kind help of the Samiti. No younger or other individuals of the society is ready to help the old women and old widows by taking care of them during their helpless conditions. No literate female is found in the Onge society. In the Great Andamanese society, a few married and urimarried females were found to be literate, who obtained education upto the primary and middle levels. The Onge women are yet very safe from any kind of exploitation from outsiders. However, the time may not be far when they reach a stage where the Great Andamanese are today.

Table 12

Literacy and Educational Standards of the Great Andamanese and the Onges in 1990*

Name of the tribe	*No. of population*		*Illiterate*		*Can read and write without educational standards*		*Primary standard*		*Middle standard*	
Sex	*M*	*F*	*M*	*F*	*M*	*F*	*M*	*F*	*M*	*F*
Great Andamanese	16	14	11	11	3	1	1	1	1	1
%	(100)	(100)	(69)	(79)	(19)	(7)	(6)	(7)	(6)	(7)
Onges	56	44	51	44	5	-	-	-	-	-
%	(100)	(100)	(91)	(100)	(9)	-	-	-	-	-

* Field survey conducted by the research on the spot during 1988-90.

The literacy Table 12 indicates, that the literacy rate of the Great Andamanese and the Onges is usually underestimated. Education is a vital part in the socio-cultural life of an individual. Several initiatives have been taken by the authorities for upliftment of the Great Andamanese and the Onge Communities for modernisation through education. Out of a total of 30 people of the Great Andamanese, 11 males and 11 females could be considered as illiterate. Out of a total of 100 Onge people, 51 males and 44 females could also be considered as illiterate. Among the Great Andamanese, only 3 males and one female were found to be literate without, however, any systematic educational standards. They could only sign their names and count money. One male and one female obtained primary education and one male and one female were obtaining middle standard education. While in the Onge society, out of 100 members, only 5 males could be considered literate without any systematic standard. Except the few persons, none of the male or female could count money or sign their names. Even these people do not know the face value of the money. Due to irregular posting of teachers and lack of interest of the tribesmen, education could not be spread among them. Most of them do not know the market price of the consumer goods. Due to their illiteracy and ignorance of face value of the currency, they are often cheated by the unscrupulous non-tribal merchants.

Human life is mostly regulated by social system and environment. Due to change of circumstances, like the change in social structure and system, the individuals also change their traditional social life, customs, rites and rituals. Among the Great Andamanese, three cases were found out of 5, where mothers did not follow any food restrictions during their pre-natal or post-natal periods. 50% of the Children were not given any proper names before their birth. Out of 7 youths, 4 and out of 4 females, 3 did not follow any initiation, ritual and puberty ceremonies or food restrictions. No secret bath was performed for these 3 females during their first menstruation periods. No new name was given to them after their first menstruation ritual. These younger individuals reported that they do not like to perform or observe food restrictions and other taboos during their transition from adolescence to adulthood. Similarly, it was found that 5 males and 4 females among the Onges did not follow rituals and initiation ceremonies, while they had already passed their adolescence periods. The females had already married without observing the puberty ceremony strictly and formally. It was found that five females married before reaching the adolescence periods. It was reported that at least 7 mothers gave birth to 14 children, though these mothers did not follow any customary food restrictions during their conceive periods. At present, child birth does not take place at separate self-made delivery houses. Now-a-days, except in the case of one delivery, all deliveries take place either at the individual huts or in the jungle. Food intake for a pregnant woman is, however, restricted but such restrictions have been somewhat relaxed. No traditional relationship is. supposed to be developed between the tribal individual offering food and the baby of the mother who takes the food. There has been no case for adoption of a child by a tribal individual. Scarcity of children in the society prevents parents from handing over their own children to others for adoption. One betrothal case was found in the Onge society.

Due to absence of separate houses for unmarried girls, no ritual ceremony is now being practised immediately after the first menstruation of the maiden. Similarly, due to scarcity of natural food at proper times in the Great Andamanese society, no food-offering ceremony is followed by young boys and girls.

Among the Great Andamanese, there were 2 cases out of a total of 14, where the children were named after the suggestion of the elders. 4 out of 6 parents do not like to put traditional tribal names for their children. Only one case of adoption of a child was reported. The parents of the present society prefer to put non-tribal modern names after their children such as Pinki, Babu, Baby etc. in place of their traditional names like Mao, Bowa, Jeraka, Biya etc. Every traditional name carries certain socio-cultural and environmental significance. For example, 'Mao' means 'stone', 'Bowa' means 'land', 'jeraka' means 'enemy', etc. The tribals could understand the meaning and significance of every such individual name. Similarly, in the Onge society, every Onge child has been given a non-tribal name, such Champa, Ramesh, Dalda Kumari, Pankaj, Ramu etc. instead of their traditional names like Tambolai, Otalatai, Betabegi, Chaibai, Bairaggegi and Danka-Lanka. These traditional names carry special meanings in the traditional Onge language and related to their socio-cultural and environmental backgrounds. The name Chaibai, for example means 'rate', Bairagegi means 'Oar', Danka-Lanka means 'helicopter'. When the parents of these children were asked about the meanings of the new modern names of their children, none could explain the meaning of the modern names of their children. They reported that all the names were given by the staff of the Samiti (AAJVS) and it asked the parents of such children to call them by these names.

Emergence of New Classes

At present the social status of a family in the Great Andamanese and the Onge societies is decided on the basis of the economic status of the male leader of the family. Better economic condition of the family may add to their social status in the society. Birth is to be considered as providing an accidental social status. The Great Andamanese and the Onges societies were classless in the sense that no hierarchial position in the society existed. They had no concept of private property and no idea of saving. From the interview, the researcher knew that the Great Andamanese families get individual ownership of their surrounding movable immovable property recently. They have been given the private ownership of the houses they dwell in. The standing cocoanut and fruit trees are distributed among all the families. The distribution has been made by the Samiti (AAJVS) itself. Children of the Great Andamanese have now acquired the right to inherit their parents' property. Moreover, those who are involved in various categories of work are receiving money for individual family maintenance and for personal expenses. But no private ownership has been given to the Onges over their plantations and orchards. Nonetheless, every Onge family has equal rights over the existing cocoanuts and fruit frees in and around their respective settlements. But income from personal collection of cocoanuts and personal employment under different categories of work is to be considered as private property. This personal property must be transferred to their successors. Out of 8 families in the Great Andamanese society, one is earning a considerable amount of money from his respective employment, while the income of the rest of the 7 families is low and they live under conditions of poverty. Similarly, in the Onge society, out the total 38 families surveyed, 3 are living under good conditions due to their higher incomes. But the other 35 families are very poor due to their lower incomes. Most of them are unable to provide dress and necessary articles to the members of their families. However, the families of the higher income group often try to establish themselves as a moneyed class by adopting proper modern dress, using modern articles and taking modern food. More or less, the maximum number of Great Andamanese families are under heavy burdens of indebtedness mainly due to their low incomes. The present occupational structure gives scope to the tribals to secure various types of occupations and earn incomes. The white collar employees get a higher remuneration in comparison to manual labour or those who are unemployed. The present younger group often try to mark themselves out as a new class by adopting alien cultures and their incomes are higher. It is observed that the economically well established families often consider themselves as superior Classes. Comparatively, the old individuals and economically poor families try to recognise themselves as separate and inferior classes before the society by displaying their shabby dress and sticking to old habits and tastes.

The leaders of both the communities, along with the permanent and casual workers, do not get involved in any manual work but they get more money and extra facilities. Subsequently, majority of the individuals among the Onges perform manual work like loading cocoanuts from their respective settlements to cargo boats and carry and unload foodstuffs from their cargo boats to the settlements, weeding grass and cleaning the jungles from their plantations and settlements. Due to the inertness and language problems, the majority of the Onges do not get proper scope and often try to keep themselves aloof from their advanced fellow-folks. Anthropologist Majumder narrates an example—Slavery in various forms persisted in the tribal society decades ago. Though slavery is a thing of the past in most parts of the world, the dominant-dominated relations still form a part of the tribal psyche. However, a new elite is emerging in every Indian tribe. They consist of politicians and businessmen.[26]

The head of the Great Andamanese and the Onge families earns for his own family. Now the old men and women and disabled persons are surviving through their own initiatives and by the aid of the local administration. The researcher observed that not a single younger individual is ready to help the olders. The Samiti supplies them with foofstuffs as dole. Individual life is regulated by the individuals themselves. There is no existence of any "Elder Council" and nobody is ready to accept any guidance of the elders whether they are parents or other individuals. In the Great Andamanese and the Onge societies, the traditional leadership system does not exist.

Though the Onges have now a traditional leader along with their elected modern leader, both are called "Raja". The elders of the society have no authority to select the modern leader of their community. No professional leader is in either of the societies. Now the modern leaders have recognised themselves as men of higher status and intelligence. They have been provided with all extra-facilities like honorariums and transport facilities, high respects etc. for maintenance of their higher status and dignity. The whole society is now being regulated by the leader of the society along with the help and guidance of the Samiti. Socio-cultural matters like, marriage, divorce, family disputes, illicit sexual relations are settled by the leader of the community and the Samiti. All developmental activities are now undertaken with the guidance and joint supervision of the leader and the Samiti. The leader of the Great Andamanese is nominated by the Samiti from the senior most members. Though the leader of the Onges is now elected by the people of the Onges, leader does not involve himself in manual work, but guides the manual workers for proper works. The leaders of both societies have grown with a sense of superiority which is prevailing in their activities. Once they had not sense of privilege and non-privilege. Nobody could imagine that one could subsist on other's labour or he gets extra-facilities whether he is a leader or is an elder of the society. Moreover, under the new socio-political background, a group factionalism has been developed among different, local groups or tribes in connection with the choice of leadership of the society. An individual is chosen by the Samiti, the Samiti being considered as a leader of the society, the people of other tribes or groups may not like to accept him as their leader. Nonetheless, the leader often fails to work properly, because the people in the opposition often vehemently oppose the proposal without understanding its reality. Under such a critical social juxtaposition, the old men and women feel themselves helpless. No young male or female able-bodied individual is ready to render his or her help to the old individuals by providing them with financial help nor does he or she respect the old individuals. The situation can be revealed in few words that under such circumstances, the two ethnic groups, the Great Andamanese and the Onges could neither give up their previous social system nor could sustain or welcome the modern social system and attitude. Now they are surviving within the framework of an uncertain and illicit social and family life.

Comments

Both the Great Andamanese and the Onges led a paleolithic social life. But the on-going developmental activities, sudden exposure to the outsiders, behavioural change of the individuals among the tribals, import of alien technology in their primitive economy and de-population along with disordered socio-environment conditions are considered to be the factors that influenced the general features of the social organisation of the Great Andamanese and the Onges.

In accordance with the modern settlement programmes, the two tribal ethnic groups referred to, were placed into different corners of the two islands. Their place of settlements are remarkably isolated and conjusted and so even now the tribesmen are restricted to their nomadic character and tradition-band or grouplike social organisation. Their number of population has been dwindling sharply since mid of the last century. Continuous depopulation has thus been affected the size, structure and marital status of the respective tribal family. The present family system has further weakened their social and community feelings. Nobody bothers about maintaining any social or customary laws in their life cycle. Child marriage,dissimilar marriage, marriage with outsiders are increasing. Aged widows or barren females have to be married to young boys, who marry for the first time and vice versa. As a result, the individual life is disturbing by increasing divorce and illicit relations. The local administration often interferes with the social affairs of the Great Andamanese and the Onges in matters like marriage, divorce and marriage with outsiders. The new economic system has been divided their society into haves and have-nots on the basis of income and other sociopolitical facilities.

So far as the present social situation is concerned, the elders have mostly lost their age-old social status and powers. Women and old people are feeling themselves somewhat helpless. Women are often exploited physically and mentally by the unscrupulous outsiders on their socio-economic weak points. Youths are not ready to render help to the old by providing them with food and protections. Once socially coherent and unified tribal people are now suffering from distrust and disintegration in their family as well as in their society. The new hierarchial system in the society exists on an evolving economic and socio-political infrastructure.

REFERENCES

1. Vidyarathi, L.P. and B.K. Rai, *Tribal Culture of India,* Concept Publishing Company, Delhi, (1977), p. 145.
2. Winick, Charles, *Dictionary of Anthropology,* Littlefield Adams and Co., Totawa, New Jersey, (1970), p.59.
3. Basu, Badal K., *The Onges,* Seagull Books, Calcutta, (1990), pp. 39-51.
4. Radcliffe-Brown, A.R., *The Andaman Islanders,* Illinois: Free Pree, Glencoe, (1922), pp. 11-12.
5. Mann, R.S., *Bay Islanders,* Institute of Social Research and Applied Anthropology, Simla, pp. 77-79.
6. *Ibid.,* pp. 80-82.
7. Radcliffe-Brown, A.R., *The Andaman Islanders,* Illionis: Free Frees, Glencoe, (1922), p. 35.
8. Chanda, Sudhendu, "The Socio-economic and political structure of Car-Nicobar", in *Khadigramodyog,* Vol. 16(9), (1970), p. 626.
9. Service, Elman R., "The Andaman islanders", in *Island Culture of India,* (ed.) G. Prakash Reddy and V. Sudarsan, (1989), pp. 34-37.
10. Mann, R.S., *Bay Islanders,* Institute of Social Research and Applied Anthropology, Simla, (n.d), p. 77.
11. Murdock, George Peter, *Social Structure,* The Macmillan Company, New York, (1949); p. l.
12. The data collected by the researcher during his field survey in between 1988 and 1990.
13. The Table has been produced with the help of the data collected by the researcher during his field survey in 1988-1990.
14. Chakraborty, D.K. (1975), *The Great Andamanese,* Seagull Books, Calcutta, (1990), p. 21.

15. Danda, Depali, G. and Sumit Mukherjee (1988), "A study on Onge population", in *Journal of Indian Anthropological Society,* vol. 24(l), (1989), p. 58.
16. Researcher collected the data of the table from the field survey during 1988-1990.
17. Chakraborty, D.K. (1975), *The Great Andamanese,* Seagull Books, Calcutta, (1990), p. 17.
18. De, D.C. (1969), "A demographic study of the Onges of Little Andaman," in *Bulletin of Department of Anthropology,* 19(2), (1970) pp. 111-126.
19. Mr. J (58) = Mr. Jerake, Mrs. S (34) = Mrs. Surmai, Mrs. N(28) = Nau, Mr. P(40) = Mr. Pucher, Mr. N (Sr)(78) = Mr. Nao (Sr), Mrs. B (60)= Mrs. Bowa, Mr. L (32) = Mr. Look, Mrs. L(28) = Mrs. Lachu, Mr. G(30) = Mr. Gulate, Mr. K(Late) = Mr. Kota.
20. Mr. R (38) = Mr. Ramesh, Mr. T (40) = Mr. Tambolai, Mr. K (58) = Mr. Kanju, Mrs. S (28) = Mrs. Sheela, Mr. N (52) = Mr. Nabekutti, Mrs. D (60) = Mrs. Damburai, Mr. O (64) = Mr. Otalitai, Mrs. T (29) = Mrs. Toukitai, Mrs. T (60) = Mrs. Totatabege.
21. Field survey conducted by the researcher on the spot during 1988-90.
22. Sachchidananda, "Social Structure, Status and Mobility patterns The case of Tribal women", in *Man in India,* vol.58(l), (1978), p. 11.
23. Andaman Home, The Rev. H. Corbyn, a Christian Priest built huts. Which came to be known as the "Andaman Home" on Ross Island in the year 1863 to civilize the Great Andamanese through education in English.
24. Majumder, R.C., *Panel Settlement in the Andaman,* Ministry of Education and Social Welfare, New Delhi, (1975), p. 87.
25. Kochar, V.K., "The Great Andamanese Today" in *Man in India,* Vol. 49(3) (1969), p. 249.
26. Majumder, Diptosh, "Arunachal worried over disharmony among tribals", in *The Statesman,* Calcutta, March 20, (1991), p. 2.

6

Political Scenario

Man cannot live without politics. The political instinct said Aristotle is ingrained in man. Politics and society go together. Formally and non formally, a triditional political system evolves in every society. Among the tribal communities, the political organisation is not so complicated as it is in the advanced societies. It has no separate identity but it is mixed up with the social and cultural life of the community. Like their simple social and cultural life, the political life of the tribal people is also very simple. It is quite surprising that they follow a more democratic way of life than most others in India. Even though they have no constitution, Nehru once remarked, they are able to function democratic and carry out the decisions made by elders or representatives[1]. This phenomenon exists all over the tribal world. The social norms and traditions are the main sources of their rules and laws. Social behaviour is the ultimate sources of their laws. They respect and try to preserve their social dignity through their peculiar political system. Every tribal individual respects his status-quo and tries to maintain the norms and hereditary positions in his society. The Andaman Islanders are not any exception. As they are highly respectful for their tribal culture and traditions. Till recently, they could preserve their traditional democratic political norms. In the words of Man, "Their domestic polity may be described as a communism...."[2]

Past Political system

Among the Great Andamanese and the Onges political structure, the existence of the leader was very informal. The people of a band or group usually recognised a man to sort out their differences with mutual obligation. The position of such leaders were neither hereditary nor acquired through formal election. Even age was not considered a vital factor for leadership or headmanship. Traditionally, the right handman would occupy the head's post after the death of the existence head. Disputes, regarding selection of the successor of the present leader would be decided by the wishes of the majority. There was no autocratic method in case of the selection of tribal leaders. No individual would try to occupy the post of the leader against people's decision. Ultimately views of the majority were given highest respect and priority in the decision making process. Every band members gave respect and recognisation to the head, his views also respected. The leader was not vested with authority and authoritative powers. It was his duties to guide and uphold democratic norms, not to exercise authoritative powers by order. Here, individuals had great freedom of thought and acts. The headman or leader himself did not by and large think of passing any special order of any individual of the society. After consulted with other people, he usually gave his consent or advice. He never be entertained unnecessary interference of his men or used his dictatorial powers on the people of his community.

There were so many leaders existed on different occupations among the Great Andamanese and the Onge societies. The professional leaders emerged on the basis of occupational expert. Their roles and functions were limited to that particular profession too. Among the Great Andamanese the hunting and fighting groups were led by a leader known as "erjum", while the group or band was led by a leader called *"ackachapan"*[3]. Among the Onges, hut making, canoe making, iron implementation making leaders were called "Okalai", "Kelorai", 'Kanjuf' respectively. While 'Kuvera' was address to a religious headman[4]. The tribals of Nicobar group of Islands had their own traditional leader called "ma-panam"[5].

The Great Andamanese and the Onges had no statutory or permanent "Elder Council". When needed the leader or head joined by a few other elderly persons to decide about socio-political and cultural matters of the society. Such men were no particular ones, those available at the moment were included. This informal existence of Elder Council was very powerful. Original authoritative powers were vested in the hands of the "Elder Council" of the band or group. Here the headman or leader of the group kept his leadership upto assemble the elders and propose the agenda before the council members. All socio-religious and political affairs were dealt by the elder council with democratic manners. Approach to elder council was opened to all irrespective of age and sex. Most of their verdicts were unbiased and free of prejudices. The leaders along with elders often settled matters related to the regulation of marriage, divorce, widow re-marriage, family disputes, penalty for illicit relations etc. Organise of fighting against any intrusion under the leadership of an individual was decided by the elder council. All religious and social rituals and taboos were regulated by the council to save the community from evil spirit and for solidarity of the society. The council very strictly prohibited all bad activities like cohabitation in the communal huts. Nobody was allowed sing or dance for about certain days after a death. Additionally, it was the duties of the council to fix a date for celebrating the initiation or puberty and rename ceremonies of the boys and girls. It is said that if any individual would try to violate such socio-cultural and religious rules was produced before the elders council for his or her expiation or atonement.

The political institution of the Great Andamanese and the Onges was fully based on their socio-cultural milieu. So, the change of their socio-cultural environs has changed their political system sharply. While they have been uprooted from their territories by outsiders, the dwindling of their population has set in simultaneously. This has affected their political status quo. Which was running for centuries.

Indian Independence and New Politics in the Islands

Immediately after independence, the Government of India has been concerted moves toward development and welfare of the backward communities in the Andaman and Nicobar Islands. To save the poor, neglected, isolated and backward tribals of the Islands, several rules and programmes have been started for the upliftment of these communities along with other backward communities in India. In the Island's political system, a new route was opened by introducing the provision of nominated persons in representative tribal bodies. Under the Representation of the People Act 1951, the Islands were allotted one seat in the Lok Sabha, to be filled by a person nominated by the President[6]. Sir Richardson was nominated for the first time as a Member of Parliament in 1952 for representing the Union Territorv in General and Nicobarese tribal in particular. Since then a radical change took place in the Nicobarese political system. For the first time, leader from this community is represented at the national and local administrative levels. Simultaneously, for the better popular administration and smooth development of the area, two Advisory Committees were set up namely, the Home Minister's Advisory Committee and the Chief Commissioner's Advisory Committee. In advisory capacity, they play important roles in regard to the administration and developmental activities of the islands. To represent the Nicobar Islands, the Chief Headman Mr. Fred of Car-Nicobar and Rani Chauge of West Bay Katchal were made members of the Home Minister's Advisory Committee. These two persons, along with Rani Laxmi of Nancawrie were also members of the Chief Commissioners Advisory Committee[7].

A new direct election system has been introduced under the Union Territories Direct Election to the House of People Act, 1965. For the first time, in the General Elections of 1967, One Member of Parliament was elected for the territory. At that time both the Great Andamanese and the Onges did not come forward to the administration with their representation. For the refugee re-settlement, the Administration and the local leaders started negotiation with the traditional leaders of the Great Andamanese and the Onges. In this connection, the administration was trying to persuade the leaders of the tribals to leave the occupied areas and islands for the settlement of the outsiders. For successful to missions, the administration selected an individual from among the Great Andamanese as a leader. After a prolonged negotiation, the administration was successful to make negotiations with the Onge leaders to reopen the Little Andaman island for refugee settlement along with adequate plans for tribal development.

Modern Political Set Up

The Administration for Islands benefits in general and tribal welfare in particular interfered the internal political system of the tribesmen of tribal groups. Particularly, in these regards, those tribesmen who were friendly came into contact with the local Administration. Among the Great Andamanese, Late Mr. Loka was the first leader who was selected by the local Administration. He was the first leader of this tribe, under the emerging political system. For the re-settlement of the uprooted Great Andamanese, the urgent task of the Administration was to choose an efficient and skilled person who could organise the community. Yet it was the first time in the Great Andamanese traditional political history that the 'democratic' norms was broken by the Administration by selecting an individual as a leader on its own choose. The Government of India, along with the local administration realised that unless the leader of the tribesmen representing his community in the administration agreed and convinced his brethern speedy and smooth rehabilitation and developments could not be possible.

With a view of giving more representative to the tribals of the Andaman and Nicobar Islands, on the Chief Commissioner's Advisory Committee and the Home Ministry, the Government of India decided in October, 1975 that one member shall be nominated each year by the Ministry of Home Affairs from amongst the three tribes, namely, the Great Andamanese, the Onges and the Shompens to the Chief Commissioner's Advisory Committee and Home Ministry. With the same ideas, the Samiti's General Body Committee also decided at a meeting on August 8, 1976 to include one Onge individual on the Sub-Committee to be constituted their welfare in the Little Andaman. The same Onge leader was also nominated to the General Body of the Samiti. The above decisions opened a new chapter in the traditional political history of these communities. Since then two individuals have been included in the national and local administrations. The Administration has created a new type of leader in place of the traditional leaders of the tribesmen. Nomination is made on the basis of its own choice. Moreover, such political system has created a vacuum in between the leaders and the elders of the society. The leader is being given some importance by the administration resulting in the traditional "Elder Council" become neglected. We know that no nomination system existed in the political system of the Andaman tribes. Even the post of the leader was not hereditary. So, it was the first time that the authority had broken the status-quo regarding the selection of the leaders from the tribesmen. The Administration, on its own consideration, select one person as leader from the Great Andamanese and from the Onge communities.

A new chapter was added to the political system of the tribesmen with the establishment of a Pradesh Council in this Union Territory. The inauguration of the Andaman and Nicobar Pradesh Council is a very significant milestone in the history of the Island's quest for development and self-identification. Since June, 1981, the Pradesh Council, Consisting of 29 members has been constituted. Among these 29 members some are directly nominated by the Head of the Administration (the Lt. Governor). Under this new popular administration, provision has been made for nominating one member from the primitive tribals by the Head of the Territory. Mr. Tambolai belonging to the Onge community was nominated as a Member of the Pradesh Council in 1981. Some members are also represented from Nicobar district. The Chairman of Municipal Board is also an ex-officio member of the Pradesh Council. The remaining members represent the Andaman district through indirect election. Every four year the Members of the Pradesh Council are indirectly elected by the Gram Panchayats in the Andaman district. The Gram Panchayat is formed on the basis of direct adult franchise of the local people under the Panchayati Raj system of India. Afer election the Panchayat members further elect their Panchayat Pradhan and form the Gram Panchayat for local Administration. Under this form of local self-Government system, adequate representation facilities are also given to women as per the Andaman and Nicobar Islands Gram Panchayat Regulation 1958[8]. As per the Pradesh Council rules, the Members of the Pradesh Council is elected by the Gram Pradhans. Some seats are reserved for women here also.

The Panchayati Raj system is not yet in force in the Nicobar district however. Nontheless, the Nicobarese have their own Tribal Council. They have a traditional village tribal panchayat system. There are three captains in every village and an Elder Council looks after the socio-political matters of the village tribesmen. The second and third captains look after the village affairs in the absence of the first captain. Moreover, for controlling the island administration one 'Island Council' is set up for the Island. All the village captains are the members of the 'Island Council' of the particular island. The Council elect the Chief Captain and the Vice-Chief captain from among them for the 'Island Council'. But under the new Pradesh Council system, the Nicobarese are also sending their representatives from the Island Council to Pradesh Council as members of the Pradesh Council. The Nicobari tribal political system was further modified by added election system of the village captains. In 1978 for the first time the Nicobarese village captains were elected by the people of above age of 15 years of the village[9].

Among this 29 members, five councillors are appointed by the Head of the Union Territory. These members are not elected on the basis of any party colour. But it is equally true that indirectly every council member wins by a particular party support. Naturally, the party which gets the majority,usually forms the council and appoints five councillor from among the members. All the important departments are divided among these five councillors to look after departments like health, forest, transport, revenue, education, Labour Welfare, Tribal Welfare etc. A new provision has been made that one councillor must be chosen from the tribal representatives. Therefore, a councillor from the Nicobarese community now represents the tribal groups of the territory. He takes the charge of the tribal welfare department usually. This system is democratic.

Like the leader of the Great Andamanese, the member of the pradesh Council from the Onge community is called the 'Raja' The term 'Raja' is not found in the Onge and the Great Andamanese nomenclature. Though the term was introduced by the administration for the convenience of communication, Rajas have been working on the basis of nomination. But in 1985, the Tribal Welfare authorities have introduced election system in place of the nomination of Raja by the administration from amongst the Onges. Since 1985 the Raja of the Onge community has been elected by the adult individuals of the Onges.

India has successfully established a real democracy from the village level to the national level through periodical elections. In the Indian political system, the tribals have also been given rights and privilege to bring them closer to the mainstream of national political process. In the democratic system, exercise of the voting rights is the main method which makes the people politically and socially conscious and get themselves educated about local as well as national politics and administration. Universal adult suffrage irrespective of religion, sex, caste, creed and language is the basic of the success of Indian democracy. People's awareness and willingness, their determination to utilise the benefits of universal adult suffrage become the primary instrument of political modernisation.

Like other tribals, in India, the tribals of Andaman and Nicobar Islands: the Nicobarese, Shompen, the Onges and the Great Andamanese have gradually become acquainted with the modern democratic political system of India seeking to perpetuate a new set of community leadership and functions. The main question is to what extent have these tribal groups accepted this new set up. Political consciousness of the Great Andamanese and the Onges should be analysed for determination of their response to the present political set up in India.

Table 1
Opinion Survey on Acceptance of Modern Political System and Leadership*

Name of the Tribe	*No. of persons interviewed*	*No. of respondents*	*N.A.*	*Favouring acceptance of present political system and leadership.*	
				Yes	*No*
Great Andamanese.	15	12	3	4	8
Onges	70	60	10	24	36

* Field Survey conducted by the reserarcher during 1988-90.

Table 1 shows that majority of the Great Andamanese and the Onge respondents do not favour acceptance of the modern political system and leadership. The data indicate that 8 out of 12 Great Andamanese and 36 out of 60 Onge respondents, are against the new political system. It is found by the researcher that the old Onge respondents claim that their traditional political system and its leadership were better, because they felt a sense of belongingness so far as their elder council and leadership were concerned and because their traditional leaders were their own folks, having a common tribal heritage. So they had a better understanding with their traditions, customs and manners than the present young leaders.

Table 2
By Whom and How the Leader of the Community is Chosen*

Name of the Tribe	*No. of person interviewed*	*No. of respondents*	*N. A.*	*Leader is nominated*	*Leader is elected*	*Leader is chosen by Adult Franchise*	*Elder Council*	*local authority*
Great Andamanese	15	13	2	13	-	-	-	13
Onges	70	60	10	-	60	60	-	-

*Field Survey conducted by the researcher on the spot in betw een 1988 and, 1990.

Table 3

Tenure of Office of the Present Community Leader*

Name of the tribe	*No. of person interviewed*	*No. of respondents*	*N.A.*	*Elected for five year*	*Elected for life*	*Nominated for five year*	*Nominated for life*	*Depends on leader himself*	*Depends on government/ samiti*
Great Andamanese	15	14	1	-	-	-	-	-	14
Onges	70	56	14	56	-	-	-	-	-

*Field survey conducted by the researcher on the Great Andamanese and the Onges in between 1988 and 1990.

They think that their old organisation never did injustice, while with the present system, they feel that there is always a risk of injustice. The old organisation was created by their forefathers and was handed over from generation to generation. In their traditional political system, the elders and 'Elder Council' had equal power on socio-political affairs as the leader or Chief of the Society. Now all their powers have been concentrated only in the hands of the present leaders.

It is found that few young Great Andamanese respondents seemed to be disinterested whether the system is traditional or modern. The young individuals among the Great Andamanese respondents have expressed their discontentment on the present political system and its leadership, because as the young respondents said, under the present system they have no authority to select their leader by election as their own choice.

On the same clue, the researcher extended the question and asked the individuals of both the ethnic groups, by whom and how their community leader was chosen. 13 out of 15 Great Andamanese respondents said that the leader of their community is nominated by the Samiti itself from amongst the oldest persons. But 60 out of 70 Onges expressed that their leaders are elected by the adult Onges. Details are given in Table 2.

Table 4

Name of the tribe	*No. of person*	*No. of respon-*	*N.A.*	*Want election by Adult franchisee*	*Elders*	*Want nomination by Local authority*	*Elders*
Great Andam-anese	15	12	3	8	-	4	-
Onges	70	56	14	32	24	-	-

* Field survey conducted by the researcher on the spot during 1988-1990.

Moreover, majority of the Great Andamanese said that it was the reserved right of the Samiti and the sitting leader of the community to decide jointly, who would be the next leader of the community.

The respondents were asked to spell out some qualities which they would prefer in the case of selection of leaders. Data on this account has been recorded in Table 5. Out of 15 Great Andamanese, all 14 respondents said that age would be the basic quality for a person for his selection as leader. Forty two Onges out of 62 respondents, however, informed that they were bound to cast their votes for a candidate, who was referred to them by the Samiti on the basis of his good leadership qualities. But a few of them thought that none of the above mentioned qualities are necessary for selection of the leader as even a new candidate is given a chance.

Table 5 : Opinion Survey Qualities of the Leaders*

Name of the tribe	*No. of person inter-viewed*	*No. of respon-dents*	*N.A.*	*Qualities of the leader for election* Age	*Leadership capacity*	*Physical ability*	*None of the above*
Great Anda-manese	15	14	1	14	-	-	-
Onges	70	62	8	42	-	20	-

*Field survey conducted by the researcher on the spot in between 1988 and 1990.

Table 6

Interest in Election Results*

Name of the tribe	*No. of person inter-viewed*	*No. of respon-dents*	*N.A.*	*Interest in election results of*			*Not interest in any election results*
				Commu-nity	*Pradesh Council*	*Parli-ament*	
Great Anda-manese	15	14	1	12	2	-	10
Onges	70	64	6	8	2	-	54

*Data of the table collected by the researcher on the spot in between 1988 and 1990.

Interest in the announcement of election results indicates one's involvement in the democratic process. Interest in knowing the election results, therefore reveals a person's consciousness on political system and administration. Data collection on this awareness as recorded in Table 6 shows that 10 Great Andamanese out of 14 respondents and 54 out of 64 Onge respondents did not express any interest to know election results or selection results either of their community leader or in the case of Pradesh Council or Parliament. Only 4 Great Andamanese and 10 Onges indicated their little interest to know election or selection results.

Table 7

Participation in Elections

Name of the tribe	*No. of person inter-viewed*	*No. of respon-dents*	*N.A.*	*Participation in election campaign or slogan-shouting*	*Not partici-pation in election activities*	*Like to be engaged in election activities*	
						Yes	*No*
Great Andam-anese	15	15	-	-	15	3	12
Onges	70	58	12	2	56	2	56

* Data of the table collected by the researcher on the spot during 1988-90.

Elections are the basis of the process of political participation. They give chance to the people concerned for attending meetings and coming to contact with various propaganda materials. Elections also bring the tribal voters face to face with non-tribal government officials and leaders of the political parties and their ideas and programmes. Table 7 shows that among the Great Andamanese, all 15 reported their non-participation in any political meeting and campaigning. They also indicated that they had no interest in election campaigning and slogan-shouting. Similarly, except 2 Onge, other 56 respondents reported their non-participation in any election activities.

Table 8
Political Awareness*

Name of the tribe	*No. of inter-viewed*	*No. of respo-ndents*	*N.A.*	*Knowing the name of the local M.P. and his supported party*	*Name of at least two poli-tical parties at the national level*	*Can recog-nise the symbol of one party*	*Know how many times the respo-ndent voted for Lok Sabha Election*
Great Andam-anese	15	15	7	3	5	5	5
Onges	70	60	10	10	8	8	12

* Field survey conducted by the researcher on the spot in between 1988 and 1990.

Though the Great Andamanese and the Onges cast their votes for Lok Sabha Elections they reported that no candidates of any political party come to their places before the elections for campaigning. Nor did their community leaders teach them about the significance of the elections and approach them to cast their votes in favour of a particular candidate Detail are recorded in Table 7.

People of both the ethnic groups have a poor consciousness or awareness on modern politics and the political system of India. It is indeed, a great set back for a popular democracy that the majority of the local tribesmen exercise their adult franchise without realising or knowing the significance and importance of the voting rights. It is found from the data in Table 8, that only 5 out of 15 Great Andamanese and 12 out of 70 Onge respondents knew how many times they had exercised their voting rights for Lok Sabha elections. Except a few young Great Angamanese and Onges along with the leaders of the both communities, no individual knew the name of his/her seating Member of Parliament and the name of the political party he belonged to. Few of them could speak about the symbol of one or two political parties at the national level. Most of them knew the existence of one political party in India that is, the Congress (I). They have no idea that India is a multi-party system. Details are given in Table 8.

Present Position of Leadership and Functions of the Modern Leaders

Under the present political system it seem to be necessary to evalute the importance and role of the leader or "Raja" of the Great Andamanese and the Onges. The leader is the only representative of the tribal society, who communicates between the society and the administration. To what extent the leader can influence or dominate over the society as well as on the local administration depends upon the personal potentiality, intelligence and ability of the leader.

Under the present political set up, the roles and functions of the leaders have not only been modernised but also diversified within as well as outside the society. The first and foremost functions of the leaders are to project the community problems before the local authorities and draw the attention of the authorities for increasing the welfare of the society concerned. The Onge leader is also a member of the Pradesh Council who represents, all the primitive tribes of the Andaman and Nicobar Islands. Moreover, leaders of the both ethnic groups are members of the General Body of the Andaman Adim Janjati Vikas Samiti (AAJVS) committee. The normal functions of the leaders are to be considered as follows:

The necessary advice is given by the leaders to the local administration and the Pradesh Council on the welfare measures with the provision that every new issue would be discussed and decided with the full consent and willingness of the leaders. They attend the annual review meeting of the Samiti, where the authorities find out the causes of success and failure of the policies relating to the welfare of the tribals. Before implementation of any new plan or programme, the consent of the leaders is thought to be necessary. The Onge "Raja" as a member of the Pradesh Council, attends every session of the council as well as every emergency meeting of the council. No session of the Council is summoned without prior intimation to him. The Head of the Administration of the Union Territory calls on the leaders of the two communities for discussing the matters relating to their welfare. The staff of the Samiti and other departments who are posted at settlements, are always confined to their local duties. They also maintain regular contact with the leader of the respective community. It is the primary duty of the leaders to keep watch on the individual performance of the staff regarding their duties. If necessary, complaints should be placed before the higher authorities against the field staff of the settlements. Delegates and visitors from outside are at first introduced with the leaders by the Samiti. The leader plays a role of the middleman, while any expert team or committee visits the settlement for official purposes relating to their welfare measures. All problems are to be highlighted by the leader to these delegates. It is the day to day duty of the leaders to collect the individual grievances of the people and the same are placed before the person in charge of the Samiti. Later, discussion at the table of the Pradesh Council on these problems takes place.

Moreover, it is the main functions of the leaders to look after the matters like health, sanitation, education, food supply, means of communications and housing facilities. The leaders guide the people in their works in the plantations. They settle all family disputes, arrange community festivals, marriages etc. Leaders decide as to who would be provided with what types of jobs or amenities.

Table 9

Opinion Survey on the Identity of the Dominant Authority in Socio-Political Fields*

Name of the Tribe	*No. of inter-viewed*	*No. of respo-ndents.*	*N.A.*	*Dominant authority on socio-political field*		
				Community lead r	*Elder of the community*	*Government official*
Great Andamanese	15	14	1	-	-	14
Onges	70	60	10	-	-	60

* Field Survey conducted by the researcher on the spot in between 1988 and 1990.

It is found from the data in Table 9 that the position and functions of the present leaders of the tribal communities have developed to some extent of modernity, though 15 Great Andamanese and 70 Onge respondents have expressed different views.

The responses have been codified in Table 9 regarding identification of the dominant authority in the present politics of the community. The hypothesis of the researcher was that the present community affairs run by the leader of the community with community consent. But the data indicate that the present socio-political scene in the two tribal communities is dominated by the staff of the Samiti. This was indicated by all 14 Great Andamanese and 60 Onge respondents. The leader has diversified his activities, though he is unable to perform all his duties independently. In most of the cases, the Samiti takes all decisions alone, without consulting the leader or the people. The Great Andamanese respondents said that the leader has no specific duties, because the Samiti interferes with all socio-political and religious matters of the community. The Onge respondents said that they do not like interference of the samiti in these matters. They prefer to solve their family disputes, marriage matters etc. themselves along with the leader.

Inconsistencies in the Present Political System: The Politics of Groupism

With the introduction of modern political system, there was a return to the traditional Onge chief as the member of Pradesh Council. However, subsequently another Onge was brought as the representative of the tribe, in place of the traditional leader. This resulted in groupism among the once extremely coherent community of the Onges. Moreover, all the tribesmen have settled in a single place or in two places irrespective of their local group affiliation. But a local group attitude is now continuing in their behaviours in connection with the selection of their leaders. That is why, while a leader is elected or nominated from one group, the tribesmen of the anti-group do not like to allow the exercise of powers by the new leaders as their common leader. This was disclosed by 5 Great Andamanese respondents like Late Mr. Loka who, as a Raja, was very successful in his lifetime. But most of the surviving persons at that time were not satisfied with his leadership, because he was from the local "Puchikwar" tribe, while the rest were from other local tribal groups. Even they expressed this discontentment on the selection of the new place of their settlement.

Table 10

Opinion Survey on Obedience to the Present Leader

Name of the tribe	*No. of inter-viewed*	*No. of respo-dents*	*N.A.*	*Willing to obey the present leader*	
				Yes	*No*
Great Andam-anese	15	15	-	3	12
Onges	70	56	14	30	26

*Data of the Table collected by the researcher on the spot in between 1988-1990.

Similarly, among the Onges, a local group attitude prevails in respect of the selection of their leader. Apart from their traditional leader, they have at present two Rajas or leaders.

One is the ex-leader who is treated as a Raja by his supporters and others are Mr. Tambolai from South Bay and Mr. Nabekutte, ex-Raja from Dugong Creek. If a leader is choosen from Dugong Creek, the people of South Bay do not like to accept his leadership and vice versa.

Such group politics among the Onges was visible at the time of 9th Lok Sabha elections when the supporters of the sitting leader of the Onges cast their votes at the request of the present leader. The supporters of the ex-Raja and the ex-Raja himself abstained from casting their votes as requested by the present Raja. After a prolonged discussion between the two leaders later, the ex-Raja and his supporters agreed to cast their votes in favour of a common candidate.

Table 10 offers interesting details. It reveals that 12 Great Andamanese, that means majority of the respondents and 26 Onges out of 56 respondents informed that they were not willing to obey the present Raja or leaders.

Defects of the Procedure of selection of leaders

Under the new system, the Samiti has power to replace the leader of the Great Andamanese and select some one else by nomination. It nominates the leader of the Great Andamanese from amongst the old individuals without consulting the tribal people concerned. Similarly, it is the duty of the Samiti to select the fittest candidate from amongst the Onges for contesting the elections. No other individual has a right to contest in the election. Such arbitrary powers of the Samiti regarding selection of the community leaders have created complex problems among the two ethnic groups. The supporters of the ex-Raja in the Onge society expressed their discontentment on the replacement of their leader by the Samiti. They still believe that the Samiti removed their previous leader arbitrarily and unlawfully. They thought that he was the fittest leader. The supporters of the present leader or Raja said that the former leader had no leadership capacity, the power of command and controlling authority on relevant matters. Loss of the post of leadership of the Nabekutti (ex-Raja) made the ex-Raja jealous causing group feelings against the present leader. Therefore, the supporters of the Nabekutti could not have accepted the commands of the present leader wholeheartedly.

Further in the Great Andamanese Society, the present Raja or leader Mr. Kota was a successor of Late Mr. Loka (ex-Raja). Mr. Kota (Raja), was nominated as the oldest surviving person by the Samiti along with the previous Raja or leader. But most of the old and some of the young Great Andamanese are not satisfied with his selection. Mr. Nao (Sr.), a senior member, directly expressed his discontentment before the researcher on the nomination of the present Raja. He considered himself the fittest and best qualified person from amongst the old surviving members who could hold the leadership post. It supported by some individuals. They thought that the present leader had no ability to guide the society.

A gap has been created in the Onge society between two leaders with their two groups of supporters. The Onges have had a sort of primitive miniature democratic socio-political system. They have been drawn into the democratic political system that prevails in India now. The introduction of the formal democratic system had led to the dis-appearance of genuine traditional leadership and an artificial leadership has now been propped up by vested interests. The cohesiveness of the small ethnic community tends to be disrupted. The traditional Raja of the Onges lives at South Bay. Here most of the old persons of both settlements want to re-establish the rule of the traditional political leader. They still have faith on their primitive socio-political institutions. The elders of the society could exercise almost similar powers as the leaders do now. But under the present political institutions, the traditional leaders and the elders have been neglected. Therefore a climate of distrust and dissatisfaction has been growing within the two tribal societies. Some problems have cropped up dividing the traditional scene of political democracy and the modern form of political institutions. The latter has created a problem for developmental administration in the tribal areas. The traditional institutions of the tribals appear to be handicapped in meeting the present day problems of the tribal communities. At the same time the governmental institutions have not yet evolved suitable norms and standards which the tribals could have comprehended easily. The former, that is the traditional institutions lack inadequacy, legality and modern perspectives, while the latter, that means, the modern political institutions are almost alien to the tribals thinking and generally lack of effective applicability.[10] Therefore, a gap has been created between the two types of institutions. No serious attempt has been made to bring about a fusion between the merits of the two sets of institutions.

The present leadership among the Onges is mobilised by the younger section of the tribals compared to their past political line of mobilisation. The present representatives who are normally comparatively younger in age. The views expressed by them may not be always the views of others. This, in many cases, may cause resentment among the tribals in general and come as a hindrance to the implementation of development programmes.

Their tribal institutions were mostly informal, socio-cultural and these enjoyed unquestioned traditional loyality and obedience. Now, in most of of the cases, the leader himself takes decision with the approval of the Samiti. Later it creates a problem and heightens discontentment and group-ism among the tribesmen. The authorities often give weightage to the views of the leaders, who neglect the respect and position of the elders of the society.

The elders of the Onges and the people of the opposite camp of the present leaders of both the ethnic groups think that due to misuse of the powers of the Samiti regarding selection of the leaders, the whole social, cultural and political atmosphere is gradually turning unpleasant for the tribals. They feel that due to the weakness of the present tribal leadership some alien authority is damaging their rich traditional sociopolitical system. Their socio-cultural system is decaying slowly. The young Great Andamanese want a dynamic and upto date political system, where they could participate by electing their own leaders. Naturally, they often try to segregate themselves from this system. They even realise that the Samiti is the ultimate source of power to rule the society in the name of the new political and leadership system. Commensurately, they are known as the close associates of the present leader or 'Raja'. They are the blind supporters of the present leader and the system. They often accept and respect the advice of their leaders. Therefore, they want to continue this system as far as possible. This points out that the political organisation of the aboriginal tribes in India, are now much disturbed and partly superseded by the modern Indian Government, comprising a wide range of forms.

Dass (1988), reveals truly that the modernisation in the commonly accepted sense has done more harm than good to the tribals of Andaman and Nicobar Islands. This has resulted in detribalisation and in the process most of the tribals have lost the vigour and virtues of traditional tribal societies. In this context, it is high time that the Union Government should help the tribals of India including the tribesmen of the Onges and the Great Andamanese, to adjust themselves with the changing environs of the regions undergoing the, process of development through planning. This implies both a perspective and a motivation that could balance the best of the two trends in the Indian tribal context—Tradition and Modernity.

Comments

With the attainment of Indian independence, a wave was imported in Island politics in general and tribal political system in particular. For better administration and development of political consciousness among the Great Andamanese and the Onges, a new model of leadership and politics have been imparted by the government instead of the simple and informal democratic system which these tribals had for centuries. They have recently been given voting rights for democratisation and modernisation of their political life. The new political system, however, has divided the Great Andamanese and the Onge people into two opposite poles. Groupism has developed in their society in connection with the selection of the leaders of the society. The discontentment is raised among the young as well as among the old generation^ in connection with the present political system and its activities. The people of old generation are trying to perpetuate their old socio-political system, where the elders would have powers and prestiges.

So proper democratic norms are not being practised in connection with the selection, operation and perpetuation of the emerging community leadership. Powers has still been concentrated in the hands of the local authorities, which is ; executed through the Samiti. Though the tribals have been given democratic rights, they are not able to develop their sense or awareness of the significance of exercising votes, propagandas and other mass-media used in connection of the election and political activities. Due to lack of political education, the tribals have no ideas about election symbols and any general idea of the party-system and politics, that is, the pattern of the national mainstream. They have not obtained modern political education either from their community leaders or from the party leader outside. On the contrary, the Great Andamanese and the Onges seem to apprehend that in the name of encouraging modern politics and administration, the governmental authorities are exposing them to exotic influences which they do not like. The young individuals among the Great Andamanese want a political system and rights, where they can freely be exercised their democratic right through adult franchise.

REFERENCES

1. Nehru, Jawaharlal, "Opening speech on Conference of Tribes and Scheduled Area 1952". *Vanyajati,* (1964), vol. 12(3), pp. 129-31.
2. Man, E.H., *The aboriginal Inhabitants of the Andaman,* Royal Anthropological Institute/London, (1902), p. 40.
3. Chakraborty, D.K., *The Great Andamanese,* Seagull Books Calcutta, (1990), p.43.
4. Mann, R.S., *Bay Islanders,* Institute of Social Research and Applied Anthropology, Simla, p.91.
5. Shyamchaudhuri, N.K., *Territorial arrangement traditional and Village organisation in Car-Nicobar,* An.S.I., Calcutta, (1957), p. 10.
6. Das, Hari Hara & R.N. Rath, *The Land of the Coral Beds: Andaman and Nicobar Islands,* Behrampur, Orissa, (1988), p. 90.

7. Mathur, K. K., *Nicobar Islands*, National Book Trust, N. Delhi (1967), p. 206.
8. Das, Hari Hara and Rabindra Nath Rath, *The Land of the Coral Beds: Andaman and Nicobar Islands*, Behrampur, Orissa (1988), p. 101.
9. Austin, Justice, *The Nicobarese*, Seagull Book, Calcutta, (1990), p. 98.
10. National Institute of Community Developments, *Tribal Development and Administration*, Hyderabad, (1974), p. 92.
11. Fuchs, Stephen, *Aboriginal Tribes of India*, Macmillan Company, Delhi, (1957); p. 50.
12. Das, Hari Hara & R.N. Rath, *The Land of the Coral Beds: Andaman and Nicobar Islands*, Behrampur, Orissa, (1988); p. 115.

7

Present Eco-cultural Scenario

Human culture fully depends on the nature of environment, where man lives. Culture as a whole is the life pattern of the human being. It connects him or her with the group to which he immediately belongs. Forest dwellers, particularly, have close relations between their culture and the surrounding ecology. The forest forms a part of eco-cultural system of almost all tribal communities as do in the plains in respect of non-tribal communities. The relationship between the eco-sỳstem and human group is direct in case of primitive communities like the Great Andarnanese and the Onges of Andaman Islands, and indirect in case of modern non-tribal urban communities. The primitive tribes form a culture which grows out of their immediate environment. Their culture and material life define them as 'Primitive'. The primitive community, in the total eco-cultural system, can be said to be connected with environment through the 'rod continum' of its culture. They form a part of the immediate eco-system. So a change in the eco-system will naturally have a direct bearing on the primitive and small communities which depend on it. The eco-system and for that matter the eco-cultural system is not a static system, but in the normal course it is an equilibrium. That means both the cultural system and environment should change equally and simultanelously, otherwise a crisis may arise in the life of the community in question. Change in cultural system is expected to lead to a change in the socio-economic identity of a community. On the cultural side, various component factors must change on a priority basis. So any change of environment may create a eco-cultural crisis. Before the intrusion of the British rulers in the Andaman and Nicobar territory, the aborigines of the Andaman Islands were the sole authority over the area of 6408 sq. km. and its environment. They had a culture based on forests and the sea and were technologically backward. Their socio-economic activities were culturally conditioned. But after the British intrusion, the tribesmen were gradually uprooted from their natural habitat. Their subsistence economy, social system and other activities were thereby affected adversely. Formerly, they were supplied with foodstuffs and shelter by the forests and sea. Their ecology was balanced and remained static for centuries.

Table 1

The area of movements of the Andaman Tribals have been reduced at different periods of time as is shown in Table 1*

Name of the area of movements in 1858	*Expected area of movements in 1858(km²)*	*Name of the area of movements and name of the tribals in 1957*	*Area of movements in 1957 (km²) Reserve for tribals*	*Position of the same tribal area in 1984*	*Area of movements and position in 1984 (km²)*
Whole Great		-Jarawa Reserve area (Jarawa)	742	742	742
Andaman Islands which is extended from Landfall		-Little Andaman(Onges)	732	clearance & settlement for non tribal & tribal.	110
Island to		-Rutland 1	137	-do-	-
Brother		-Chinque 1	9.53	tourist spot	-do-

Island &	6408sq.km.	-North Sentinelese	59.67	59.67	59.67
Little		(Sentinelese)			
Andaman		-South Sentinelese	1.67	Wildlife sanctury	1.67
was the		-Passege 1	0.62	Unreported	-
Exclusive		-Sister Island(2)	0.36	-do-	-
authority of the		-Brother Island(2)	1.99	-do-	-
Andaman tribals		-Strait Island	-	3.11	3.11
to moves					
Year 1858	6408 sq.km.	year 1957	1685.89 sqkm	Year 1984	856.72 sq.km

*Whitaker, Romulus, "Endanger Andamans" in *Environmental Service Group*, World Wildlife Fund, India and MBA, Department of Environment, New Delhi, (1985), p. 6.

Since 1858, the year of the second penal settlement of the British rulers in the Andaman and Nicobar Islands, the environment, culture and area of activity of the Andaman tribes have been changing. The Table 1 shows that in 1957 on account of the Andaman and Nicobar "Aboriginal Protection Act of 1956", the areas of activities of the aborigines has been reduced from 6408 sq. krn. in 1858 to 1689 sq.km. in 1957. Between these times, a lot of changes have taken place in the environment of these tribes and they have lost their rights over the forests and the sea by 26%. Simultaneously, the Great Andamanese population have come down remarkably. After independence of India, under the rehabilitation scheme of the Indian refugees, the area of their activities has been reduced further and their environment has been altered. Again in 1984, 856.72 sq. km. of forest areas were fixed as Tribal Reserved Areas, which were reduced by 50% of land of previous (1957) times. Out of the total areas of 6408 sq. km. of Andaman Islands, the area of the movements of the Andaman tribals has been fixed by 852 sq. km. or 13% in 1984.

In 1970, the Great Andamanese were settled in an isolated island covering an area of 3.11 sq. km. with a new environment. Though an area of 668 sq. km. of land has been reserved for the Onges, the area of their activities have been restricted to two small settlements, because without proper demarcation of the tribal areas properly, the non-tribal settler of the Little Andaman Island and other Islands often use tribal lands to exploit the forest and sea resources of the island. The Onges are not in a position to compete with the non-tribals for exploiting the natural resources and nor can they establish their rights over their reserved areas. The Director of Tribal Welfare, was clear in his statement that 668 sq. km. in the Little Andaman Island constituted a Tribal Reserve. However, the Forest and Plantation Development Corporation records list this areas as Reserve Forest, while at the same time restricting the Tribal Reserve to only 52.296 hector. It would seem that by shifting the Onge at Dugong Creek and South Bay, the rest of the Island has been opened up for commercial exploitation[2].

The relationship of the tribals with forest is symbolic. Every culture, by and large is adopted to the ecology. The Islanders are supposed to belong to an old stone age civilisation. Their way of life, habits, their culture in general are seldom different from those of their paleolithic ancestors. The aborigines of these islands, set the unique example of original culture of human pre-civilisation. But the Great Andamanese and the Onges have failed to sustain their paleolithic cultural heritage like the hostile aborigines i.e. the Sentinelese and the Jarawas of these Islands. The new re-settlement policy of the authorities have forced them to modify their primitive culture and tradition.

Further, the de-forestation policies and new plantation, rehabilitation policies of the administration have adversely affected the ecology of the Islanders. Due to close proximity to the sea and being in the tropical rain forest zone, the habitat of the tribesmen is extremely hot. To avoid being exposed to heat, they always construct their huts in the midst of forest having large shady trees. Their huts are thatched with palm leaves. But while they have come in contact with alien culture and atmosphere, their tastes have undergone slow changes. Naturally, the Onges now expect that the local authorities should provide them with the same types of houses as have been built for others in the Hut Bay. These are constructed in a semi-circular layout with adequate arrangement for bathing place, cooking apartments, water and electric supply. Every individual has also demanded supply of mosquito nets.

All these new amenities have been provided by the administration as demanded. They never used such materials before and these are great changes in their out look on culture and environment. The old generation have not been able to adjust with the new styles of living in special types of accommodation like pucca huts with tin roofs. The settlements were made in places near the sea-shore cutting down all shady trees. Every family has been provided with a single two roomed pile-house. This style follows alien concepts and labour. Here their traditional socio-cultural behaviour has lost its grounds. Previously, they constructed two or three types of huts in response to their socio-cultural and economic needs. All former types of apartments were made by the locally available natural materials and the labour of the islanders. The communal huts were made by their joint efforts for living permanently and jointly. A simple art and craft work symbolised in the making of the old thatched huts. In these permanent communal huts, they performed various cultural and ritual functions like, marriages, puberty ceremony, funeral ceremony etc. by organising group dances and songs jointly. The temporary lean type hut, was erected formerly for subsistence pruposes by individual efforts for seasonal use. It was made platform type, used for burial the dead persons. Construction of such houses have been, discarded now. After the mourning period would be over, the rest of the people of the bereaved family re-occupied the settlement of the dead person. The permanent hut of a particular group of the family was decorated with human skull, sea shell ornaments, jaws and feather of the animals and the fishes.

Now the Onge and the Great Andamanese are sheltered in houses provided by the administration. These houses are of modern design and have modern facilities. In their new settlements, there are neither permanent bee-hive like communal huts nor lean type temporary huts. Moreover, all the shelter are permanent. There is no question of shifting from one place to another as a nomadic community usually does. Moreover, they do not have any scope to desert the hut after burying the bodies of their dead relatives under the houses. As the traditional facilities are now absent, the tribes are unable to follow their ancestor's cultural activities. There is no separate hut for delivery of babies, for ceremonies like marriages or puberty. Now, they are bound to bury dead bodies in the jungles. Delivery of the babies take place either at their individual houses or in the hospital. The Onges society in particular is divided into two groups on the basis of their socio-cultural background. The old tribals still prefer to sustain their old cultural tradition. Comparatively, the new ones try to accept the new socio-cultural atmosphere. Naturally, the old people still now live in their traditional bee-hive type huts made by themselves near the settlements. All the elder persons now live at their traditional hut and have abandoned the new quarter type houses. The surrounding hot atmosphere discourage the present generation to live in the modern accommodations. Therefore, Awardi (1989), says that the cultural modernisation process relating to the Onges is a classic instance of miscarriage as the development pace and process are unnatural. For example, the natural course should be to allow the maid to mature providing her with a cultural millieu through carefully planned acculturation and then try to select her mate[3]. Comparatively, the Great Andamanese have adjusted themselves under the new settlement patterns, in a greater degree, though the old generation in this community still prefer to live in their traditional huts. But they do not have any scope to make bee-hive type huts with individual efforts. Naturally, they have adapted themselves to the new system.

Tribal culture is largely based on the economic and material aspects of the culture of the tribe concerning its livlihood. The Great Andamanese and the Onges, as primitive tribesmen, tried to follow certain pursuits for serving their material need according to their environmental conditions. For food procurement, the forest dwellers often used hunting materials like bows, arrows, harpoons, knives etc. for digging and collection of wild roots and fruits they used adze, digging sticks, iron equipments etc. For storing water and honey, they used to make wooden pots, bamboo containers, buckets etc. For fishing in the sea, they used canoes, harpoons and small nets. That means all the materials they made for daily use were derived from bamboo, wood, leaves, iron or bark thread.

At the present moment the Great Andamanese and the Onges often use many things which were not directly related to their culture and environment. All the usable articles are now imported from outside, those are either purchased by themselves or gifted by the outsiders to them. These "foreign" articles are: plastic jars, tin, suit case, alluminium pots, glass ware. Here the main problem is that all the articles are market oriented. They have to buy them from the markets. But their present financial condition is not such that they can buy them readily. Nonetheless, they have no other alternative than seeking gifts from others. The Great Andamanese have forgotten to make such articles like bows and arrows, baskets, buckets, nets, harpoons and earthern pots which were the symbols of their primitive culture.

Likewise, the Onge society can now be divided into two classes the old and the new generations.

Table 2

Findings of field survey indicating the likeness of the people using old and new materials in 1990*

Name of the tribe	*No. of persons inter-viewed*	*No. of respo-ndents*	*N.A.*	*Opinion regarding using old materials*		*Opinion regarding making of old materials*	
				Yes	*No*	*Yes*	*No*
Great Anda-manese	15	15	-	-	15	3	12
Onges	70	60	5	30	35	30	35

* The data have been collected by the researcher during his field survey in between 1988 and 1990.

So far as using of old indigenous articles like bows, arrows, baskets, harpoons, adze, nets, for subsistence purposes is concerned. The Table 2 shows that the people of present generations of the Great Andamanese both old and new are not in a position to use such articles. All 15 respondents replied that they have no scope to use their indigenous articles. Moreover, due to change of their present daily economic activities, they do not have to use such materials.

It is a fact that 12 individuals, majority of them are youngs, do not like to use and do not know how to make these traditional materials. Here only 3 old Great Andamanese do know the making of indigenous materials to some extent. Further, the Table indicates that among the Onges, 5 of them abstained from answering the questions. The rest of them have given their answers. Of the 65 respondents, 30 often use old materials occasionally and irregularly, but rest 35 majority of them are youngs do not use the old articles.Thirty of them know and like the making and using these old articles, but the rest 35 respondents do not like to make and use these old articles. It is found that in the both societies, the young generation do not like to use the old^ indigenous materials like bows, arrows, backets, huts, canoes, nets, adze, harpoons etc. for livelihood and nor do to making of such articles. While majority of old Onge respondents like and know the making and using of the primitive art and crafts work as a partners; in a process of continuity as a part of their old culture.

Table 3

Opinion survey on traditional and modern garments*

Name of the tribe	*No. of person inter-viewed*	*No. of respon-dents*	*N.A.*	*Like traditional loin or tassel dress*		*Like Modern dress*		*Remarks on the use of modern garments*	
				Yes	*No*	*Yes*	*No*	*Comfor-table*	*Uncomf-ortable*
Great Andam-anese	15	15	-	-	15	15	-	15	-
Onges	70	58	12	16	42	42	16	22	36

* Field survey conducted by the researched on Great Andamanese and the Onges in between 1988 and 1990.

Both human culture and environment are correlated and interdependent on each other. "Culture", says James (1971), stems from the species. Here culture operates in relation to the environment in which man lives. James prefers to call the environment (the actual land and resources and climate) "the surrounding", reserving the term "environment" to apply to the special situation created by man interacting in cultural situations. In short, the human environment is made by man himself.[4]

The Great Andamanese and the Onges gradually came in contact with the people of other eco-culture. They are slowly giving up their traditional "tassel" or "loin" dress by adopting the modern garments which they previously called "strange". Usually, they uncovered most parts of their bodies to avoid the tropical hot and humid climate. Women often used indigenous "tassel" made of tender palm leaves to cover their genitals and men used "loin" clothes for years. It was the exclusive job of the womenfolk to make "tassel" by the palm leaves with a creative bent of mind. Now men use half-pants and shirts and women use petticoats, bras and blouse like under garments.

Data in the Table 3 indicate that all the Great Andamanese like and use the modern dress. They have given up their traditional "loin" clothes and "tassels" after coming in contact with the British rulers. Every female now uses petticoats, blouses, sarees and lungis. Men use pants, shirts, baniyans etc. A few Onge respondents replied that they like to wear loin clothes. Particularly, the male folk often prefer to uncover their bodies except the genitals. They feel uncomfortable to cover their bodies with clothes. Even old women often uncover the upper portion of their bodies to avoid the excessive hot weather, particularly while they stay at the settlements. It was found that 80% of the old Onge individuals do not know how to wear the modern dress. They do not know wash the clothes and often use torn and shabby clothes. Majority of the families of both the ethnic groups are unable to provide proper dress to the members of their families due to poor economic conditions. All the women of the Great Andamanese and the young women of the Onges have now almost forgotten the traditional tribal art of making of "tassels" with the tender palm leaves.

Changes of Cultural Habits

In their earlier cultural history it was reported that the Great Andamanese and the Onges used sea-shells, bark fabrics, coloured leaves and clay for decorating purposes. Surrounding natural materials often helped them to create an exceptional indigenous craft and cultural. But now the researcher found from field observation and data collection that none of the Great Andamanese out of 15 interviewed uses or likes to use traditional sea-shell ornaments. Except 1 woman, no individuals of either sex knows how to make sea-shell ornaments, head belts and armlets with bark fabrics and coloured leaves. Youngsters do not like to use their traditional decoration articles nor do they know the art of making ornaments through crafts. Only 20 old Onge individuals were found knowing the arts of making sea-shell ornaments and bark-fabrics for preparing decorating ornaments. Of the remaining 40 respondents, majority of whom being youngsters, do not like to wear and do not know how to make such traditional decorating ornaments. On rear occasions, they reported that they use and make these articles. Details are given in Table 4.

Table 4

Opinion survey on significance of traditional ornaments in the new atmosphere*

Name of the tribe	*No. of person inter-viewed*	*No. of respon-dents*	*N.A.*	*Know the uses of traditional decorating ornaments*		*Do know making of traditional ornaments*		*Willingness to use traditional ornaments*	
				Yes	*No*	*Yes*	*No*	*Like*	*Dislike*
Great Andam-anese	15	15	-	-	15	1	14	-	15
Onges	70	60	10	20	40	20	40	20	40

* Field survey conducted by the researched on Great Andamanese and the Onges in between 1988 and 1990.

Body decoration as well as house decoration is an indigenous art in the traditional tribal culture. The Great Andamanese and the Onges used white clay and red ochre for celebrating their social customs and rites. In their socio-cultural lives, they followed certain norms. During periods of mourning, they used red ochre on the forehead. Painting with white clay signified celebration of a joyful events like marriages, puberty ceremony, etc. Further painting of the whole body with white clay signified various socio-cultural activities. It was an exclusive job of the women to decorate their husbands and children carefully regularly.

Table 5

Opinion survey on Clay Paintir ¸ and Its Usefulness*

Name of the tribe	*No. of person inter-viewed*	*No. of respon-dents*	*N.A.*	*Know the art of clay painting*		*Like the use of clay painting*		*Use of clay painting*	
				Yes	*No*	*Yes*	*No*	*Regular*	*Irregular*
Great Anda-manese	15	14	1	-	14	-	14	-	-
Onges	70	58	12	16	42	16	42	-	58

*Field Survey conducted by the researcher on the spot in between 1988 and 1990.

Data of the Table 5 indicate a different cultural life of the tribesmen. Like other traditional craft culture, the present survivors among the Great Andamanese have forgotten the art of clay painting. The usefulness of clay in their socio-cultural life has been lost. At present, all the 14 respondents interviewed do not like and do not know the art of clay painting. Sixteen old Onges majority of them women, out of a total of 58 respondents interviewed know and like the clay painting, though now-a-days they use it on rare occasions. Of the remaining 42, most of them, young and belonging to both sexes, do not like and do not know the art of decorating the bodies with white clay on socio-cultural ceremonies. The causes behind the gradual decrease of the significance of the uses of clay painting are: irregular observation of social customs like marriage, puberty ceremony, renaming initiation and funeral rites etc. Secondly, the present young generation does not like to observe such ritual ceremonies and related arts and cultural activities. Thirdly, the new environment forces them to give up their traditional cultural pattern. These data have been collected from the opinions of the present old and young individuals of both the ethnic groups.

Table 6

Language Performance of the Individuals*

Name of the tribe	*No. of persons interviewed*	*No. of respondents*	*N.A.*	*Speak the mother tongue*	*Speak language other than the mother tongue*	*Understand but not speak fluently other language*	*Language spoken with family members*		
							Mother tongue	*Hindi*	*Other language*
Great Andamanese	15	15	-	4	15	-	4	11	-
Onges	70	66	4	66	26	40	66	-	-

*Field survey conducted by researcher on Great Andamanese and the Onges in between 1988 and 1990.

Present Cultural Activities

The song and dance are a part of the human culture. The singing rhythm and the dancing performance signify the importance of the tribal culture and activities. The dance reflects a condition of intense group euphoria, in which social activity is at its maximum and all the social sentiments are pleasurably and intensely excited.[5] Every community has its own style of performing songs and dances, which signify its separate cultural and ethnic identity. The songs and dances exist as expressions of the nature and environment. The joy and sorrow of individual human life are often projected through various types of songs and dances with different styles and rhythm. The Great Andamanese and the Onges are not any exception. They have their own styles of songs and dances, which represents their cultural and traditional individuality. Nehru, the first Prime Minister of the Indian Republic, said that the tribals of India celebrate a way of life which particularly makes them rejoice in songs and dances.[6] The tribals of the Andaman and Nicobar Islands celebrate group dances and songs, which they observe on account of every ritual ceremony. Govind Ballabh Pant, the first Home Minister of free India, said that India is a vast country with a rich variety of culture and topography and in this scene of diversity, the tribal people of India occupy a very important^ place. They have been truely described as an artistic creation of God passionately devoted to their own way of life. They express their joy of life through the colourful forms of their folk dances and the rhythms of their music.[7]

Language is an important way of expression, which helps to enrich and carry the human culture where the language of a group of individuals has lost its existence, the cultural link between the members of the groups becomes weak. Table 6 shows that only 4 out of 15 Great Andamanese respondents can speak their mother tongue. The other 11, all are young and cannot speak their mother tongue. These members even speak Hindi with their family members. However, 66 out of 70 Onge respondents know to speak their mother tongue and often use their mother tongue while conversing with their family members. Out of 66, 26 can speak only Hindi and the rest 40 can understand Hindi but cannot fluently speak Hindi language other than their mother tongue. Among the Onges, within the family, none of them uses Hindi or other language as medium of expression. They only use their mother tongue. A few old Great Andamanese have failed to sustain their original dialects. They now speak a modified language which is different from local group language.

It is quite natural that most of the Great Andamanese youngsters cannot sing their tribal song. The data of Table 7 indicate that among the Great Andarnanese respondents, all 11 youngsters cannot sing and do not like to sing their tribal songs on any cultural function. Though they know their tribal traditional group dances in a modified style along with their elders, but all 11 expressed the view that they do not like to perform their traditional dance. However, it is found that the 60 Onge out of 64 respondents know how to perform their traditional group dance and can sing their own traditional tribal songs. So far as likeness of traditional songs and dances is concerned, 30 young respondents out

Table 7

Opinion survey of Traditional Dancing and Singing Performance in the Present Society*

Name of the tribe	*No. of person inter-viewed*	*No. of respo-ndents*	*N.A.*	*Know Traditional dancing*	*Does not know tradi-tional*	*Like Tradi-tional dancing*		*Know tradi-tional singing*	*Does not know traditional*	*Like tradi-tional singing*	
						Yes	*No*			*Yes*	*No*
Great Andamanese	15	15	-	12	3	4	11	4	11	4	11
Onges	70	64	6	60	4	34	30	60	4	34	30

*Field Survey conducted by the researcher on Great Andamanese and the Onges in between 1988 and 1990.

of 64 do not feel any impetus to perform their group dances and songs. Moreover, it is found that only a few old individuals appear as the last instance of the Great Andamanese and the Onges singing and dancing in the traditional manners. Once group dances and songs were intimately related to the ways of life and culture of the tribals. Now among the Great Andamanese performance of traditional dances and songs has become rare in their cultural history. The number of traditional dancing and singing performances is comparatively large among the Onges. Details are given in Table 7.

Concepts on Modern Music and Songs

Those tribals who are frequently exposed to the mainstream culture are denied opportunity to sustain their traditional songs. It is found that the Great Andamanese young individuals prefer modern Hindi film songs and dances. Particularly they prefer fast-beating music which often characterise modern Hindi film songs and the colourful dancing which is shown on the silver screen. Similarly, among the Onges, those who are exposed to the mainstream, like movies and the video films in addition to film songs and dances without fully understanding the meaning of the songs. However, the old Onges do not like modern Hindi film songs and dances. Details are given in Table 8.

Table 8
Opinion Survey on Modern Film Songs and Dances*

Name of the tribe	*No. of person inter- viewed*	*No. of respo- ndents*	*N.A.*	*Like modern film songs and dances*		*Understand modern songs*	*Understand modern dances*
				Yes	*No*		
Great Andam- anese	15	15	-	12	3	10	10
Onges	70	64	6	40	24	10	6

*Field survey conducted by the researcher on Great Andamanese and the Onges during 1988-1990.

The data in Table 8 show that majority among the Onges like modern film songs and dances ; but a few of them understand modern songs and dances. It was found that they had 5 radio-sets and 3 tape-recorders and that there were 3 radio sets among the 15 Great Andamanese respondents and 70 Onges respectively. Here majority of them like modern film songs and dances and understand modern songs and dances.

Under the new environment and the dwindling of population, the Great Andamanese replaced their regular dancing and singing performances by a week long festival once in a year. This acculturation from the mainstream is called "Jurai", though for the last two years, such festival has been discontinued. For the last few decades, the tribesmen had been continuing these "Jurai" like festivals. During this festival, two families are the principal hosts of the dance in each night. The dance begins in the late evening after dinner and continues throughout the night with the accompaniment of chorus and clapping of hands by women and stamping of the "bomu" or the sounding board by a male. The "Bomu" is a Shield-shapped musical instrument made of *padak* (Pterocarpus) with which a dance rhythm is provided by an Andamanese stamping it with his foot. The host families prepare food and keep it in a plate on the respective burial mound of their with kith and kin in the late afternoon. No other musical instrument is used except the "bomu". Only Mr. Nao (Sr.) can make this "bomu". He has a sound-board "bomu". The bracelets, ornaments worn on the waist, calflets etc. are prepared by using the dentalium shells which produce peculiar sounds when dancing takes place. The women do not always use such traditional dancing ornaments. Under the new socio-environmental milieu, no group dance or group song is performed by the Onges. Only on any special occasion or at the request of the Samiti's authorities, they perform their group dances and songs before the V.I.P. delegates. They do not feel any enthusiasm on such cultural functions performed under compulsion. They do not use any instrument or sound board like drum; clapping of hands is the only accompaniment.

The young generation of both the ethnic group do not

like to continue their traditional cultural functions, because they do not feel any encouragement performing their rhythmless and musicless songs and dances. Naturally, they are trying to emulate an alien culture attracted by its colourful dress, music and rhythms. The old tribals are making conscious efforts to reinforce their own traditional socio-cultural system. Further, the old generation in the tribal society wants to maintain group solidarity and identity by preserving its traditional culture.

Religious Performance among the Present Generations

Like all other primitive tribesmen, the Great Andamanese and the Onges are animists. They believe in concept of nature worship. The Stone Age or Paleolithic people were the worshippers of stone, fire, tree, sea and wild animals. No religious activities were found in them. They believed in the myths and legends. The Great Andamanese and the Onges have their mythology, "Bilika" or "Puluga" who is supposed to be their originator. They fondly believe that "Puluga" or "Bilika" has created the world and all things seen and unseen. Yet they also believe in powers of good and evil in the phenomenal world and in a world beyond the grave. These prove that even these savages have traditions more or less approximating to the belief of modern people in the mystery of religion.[8]

But some old Great Andamanese are very orthodox as they still believe in "Bilika" as the Supreme Being. They do not like to worship any image of the Gods or Goddesses other than nature. But it is also found that a few families or individuals, all of which have youngsters, worship the non-tribal Gods and Goddesses. The acculturation process with the Burmese and other religious people through marriage ties and other relations, perhaps accounts for these "modernistic" religious beliefs of the few young tribals. A few of them now worship the "Pongi", the Burmese God. Some of them are worshipping the Hindu Gods and Goddesses. They have the photographs of Lord Krishna, Lord Budha, Lord Siva, Goddesses like Kali and Durga in their houses. They worship lighting candles, resin and agarbati. It is true that while they face any problem, they often pray to the Gods and even offering them "sweets" to save themselves. They have no intention to receive initiation in any other religion. Now majority of the Great Andamanese and all the Onges neither follow traditional nature worship nor do they pertain to non-tribal religious beliefs fully. They still believe in the power of nature. But their devotion to nature is getting less and less on account of their greater exposure before and interaction with the non-tribals.

Position of the Individuals under New Eco-cultural Situation

Ironically, the tribals, under the new atmosphere feel some sort of physical and socio-cultural problems. The perplexed tribals quite often become physically sick in the new environment, because here they have to take different food, have to develop a new type of body resistance process or immunity pattern. Old individuals of both sexes and children are the worst victims as they perpetually suffer from malt-nutrition. It is obvious that the new physico-psychological changes are for the better. But they also necessitate a new type of adjustment. The old generation could not perfectly adjust themselves. As they are simple, they become easy preys to unscrupulous elements. Particularly, the women face problems in the new environment. It is quite natural to expect that the socio-cultural life-style of the tribals steadily undergoes modifications as for the dictates of the new environment. It has, however, created various problems in the process as the simple tribals face problems of how to internalise in a complex culture that appears to them as quite sophisticated. Life in the new environment is fast, complex and individualistic. Under these circumstances, the Great Andarnanese and the Onges, particularly the old people of both the ethnic groups, feel themselves as groups of problem oriented and helpless individuals as the new stage of modernisation has set in.

Both the Great Andamanese and the Onges, along with other primitive tribes of these two groups of Islands have no scripts for communicating with others. Even they did not use any symbolic sign to express their views. No specific symbol is used to determine anything which is related to their culture and tradition. They have no concept of writing and reading culture. Due to absence of proper script for writing, they have preserved their traditional songs and social codified laws on an oral basis from generation to generation. The old individuals are the only sources of their traditional socio-cultural evidences and records. Without proper written documents and symbolic conceptions, the tribal cultural heritage is now about to be forgotten. Among the Great Andamanese, there are only two or three, old people who are the preservers of their traditional culture. They are also not fully able to memorise the details of their original cultural heritage in its oral forms as practised by their forefathers. Such selected old individuals of both the ethnic groups have expressed the view that the present young generation do not like to follow the advice of the old people about their socio-cultural past. These few old people should be encouraged by the government to explain these oral specimens for the benefit of posterity.

Regarding tribal cultural crisis of the Andaman and Nicobar Islands in general and the Great Andamanese and the Onges in particular, Das and Rath (1988), rightly said that their intermixing with different culturally advanced people has imbibed in them a sense of ego, prestige consciousness and formalities. They have lost their traditional simplicity. It has also been observed that the tribal people are gradually moving towards a state of blind initiation of modern ways of life. They further said that the tribal should not be deprived of their ancient heritage. It is the prime duties of us to protect their traditional cultural identity.[9]

Comments

Both human culture and environment are corelated and interdependent on each other. With the appearance of the outsiders, the eco-cultural atmosphere of the Great Andamanese and the Onges has altered slowly. They had a culture based on forests and sea. They are being constantly pushed out from their original areas of movement. The new environment is not only threatening their biological survival, but also forcing them to face cultural disintegration and even an identity crisis. They have been settled into small and isolated places permanently, which affected their nomadic life and culture. They have been delinked from their forest life and from their old culture and heritage. New accommodations and hutments have developed a strange atmosphere that is not helping them to continue to practise their age-old traditional cultural activities—rites, rituals, festivals, modes of livelihood, customs, behaviour, dances and songs. Even their using materials, that were related to their culture and heritage are changing. They are about to forget their traditional craftmanship concerning the making of earthern pots, baskets, buckets as containers, making of huts, bows, arrows, nets, harpoons, adze, canoes for using livelihood and making of sea-shell ornaments, bark-fabric ornaments, white and red ochres for decorating in connection with their cultural activities. These were the symbols of their indigenous cultural heritage.

The new generation among both the tribal communities seem to be averse to their traditional cultural activities due to the change of the cultural landscape. On the other hand, the people of the old generation are still unable to adjust themselves to the new environment and culture. Therefore, the new patterns of shelter, occupations, dress, religion, customs, mode of livelihood are not being gladly accepted by the old generation. The people of the new generation are forgetting their own tribal songs and dances and other cultural activities. The role of the mother tongue among the Great Andamanese is very weak. They have no sign of natural worshipping. No festival is performed on regular basis. Among the Great Andamanese few individuals caught by the Hindu and Buddhist cultural mores of the mainstream including the religion activities and festivals. They have been loosing their cultural identity due to changing of the environment and ecology.

REFERENCES

1. Awaradi, S.A., *Master Plan for Primitive Tribes (1990-2020)*, Director of Tribal Welfare, Port Blair, (1989), pp. 204-205 (cyclostyled paper).
2. Saldanha, Cecil J., *Andaman, Nicobar and Lakshadweep: An*

Environmental Impact Assessment, Oxford Publishing, New Delhi, (1989) p. 13.

3. Awardi, S.A., *Master Plan (1990-2020) for Primitive Tribes*, Directorate of Tribal Welfare, Port Blair, (1989), p. 508 (Cyclostyle-paper).
4. Downs, James F., *Culture in Crisis*, Glencoe Press, Beverly Hills, California, (1971); p. 107.
5. Radcliffe-Brown, A.R., *The Andaman Islanders*, Glencoe, Illoinis: Free Press, (1922); p. 248.
6. Elwin, Verrier, *A Philosophy for NEFA*, North Eastern Frontier Agency, Shilong, (1959), Introduction chapter.
7. *Ibid.*, 1959, p. 12.
8. Man, E.H., *The Aborigines of Andamans*, Royal Anthropological Institute, London, 1902; pp. 88-97.
9. Das, Hari Hara and Rabindra Nath Rath, *The Land of the Coral Beds: Andaman and Nicobar Islands*, Berhampur, Orissa (1988); p. 117.

8

Findings

Modernisation of the Great Andamanese and the Onges started with the provision of various welfare measures by the Government of India during various Five Year Plan periods after independence for the speedy and smooth development of the tribals. But it has been observed that many proposed measures have not yet been fully implemented. Among them are—culture of honey bee, poultry farming, provision of training in craftmanship, supply of raw materials to the tribesmen for running the craft centre, provision of an adult education centre for educating the tribals about the aspects of modern life, culture, health, sanitation and economy.

Some of the proposed schemes were implemented half-heartedly. As a result, either the scheme failed to reach the target or stopped soon after its implementation. For example - white piggery, milch cow schemes and the scheme for providing modern fishing techniques were withdrawn. The tribals do not still like to domesticate the animals like pigs with suitable techniques. They could not get benefits in the form of food and finance from some of these schemes. Fruit and vegetable cultivation also failed. The tribal people do not seem to be interested in improving the cultivation of coconut-cum-fruits-cum-vegetable gardening as means for cultivation of food and cash crops. Though the Onges like coconuts as food, the Great Andamanese do not. Due to disfunctions and negligence of the authorities, T.V. relay, power supply, transport and communications are not giving the tribals full and proper service. Due to the lack of imparting instructions on health and sanitation, majority of them are not interested in health care through Hospital. They live in unhygienic conditions having no ideas of sanitation and they badly need medical relief just for their bare survival. Adults are addicted to intoxicating liquor and consumption of harmful tobacco. Schools with trained teachers and teaching aids for educating the tribal children are not yet functioning properly. Supply of pure drinking water and the quota of foodstuffs as 'Doles' is not sufficient to meet their requirements. Free clothes are not regularly supplied. The failure of the major schemes gives the impression that the welfare measures for the tribesmen were formulated without proper planning by the authorities concerned and without the knowledge of tribal culture and tradition.

With the introduction of modern agriculture and horticulture, an effort has been made,to change the occupational and traditional subsistence economy of the two ethnic groups. They have of course changed their primitive hunting-gathering occupation structure into a modern cash crops and wage-based economy. Many tribals are involved in white collar jobs, skilled and unskilled workers. But majority of the able individuals of both sexes among the Great Andamanese and the Onges are still unemployed, having before them no scope to utilize their labour power. So it could not be ascertained yet whether the present generation could have adjusted themselves with alien occupations and economy. No income is ensured from their plantations due to lack of market and transport facilities. They have developed no sense of money matters and saving benefits. Majority of the families are living under poor conditions. The Great Andamanese are suffering under the trap of indebtedness. The causes of their extravagance are-excessive wastage of money on liquor, tobacco, video shows, luxurious goods etc.

The new modern economy made their unified classless society into a class-divided society on the basis of privilege, income and power. Those who earn well and socio-politically privileged have made themselves a new superior class.

The causes of the backwardness of the present economy of the two ethnic groups are - lack of education on modern economy, inadequate market facilities, the inactive role of their Co-operative Societies and absence of sense of money transaction among the tribals. People neither make themselves fullfledged agriculturists nor good labourers. The present free food supply system makes the tribesmen idle and crippled both physically and mentally. So the new 'spoon-feeding1 welfare measures have not been able to create any confidence among the people of these communities. They are not ready to engage themselves in any self-employment scheme to solve their unemployment problems. They have been removed from their traditional modes of subsistence without being replaced by any new type of food-producing economy.

The on-going developmental activities, sudden exposure to the outsiders, import of alien economy and technology and continuous depopulation along with disordered socio-cultural conditions are considered to be the factors which account for the present pattern of social organisation of the two tribal groups. Their places of settlement are remarkably isolated and congested and so even now the tribesmen are restricted to their nomadic character and tradition—band or group like social organisation. Continuous de-population has ruined these people for centuries due to various diseases. The size, structure and marital status of the respective tribal family have thus been affected. The present individual family system has further weakened their social and community feelings. Nobody bothers about maintaining any social or customary laws relating to marriage or divorce. Celibacy, dissimilar marriage and child marriage are increasing. Aged widows or barren females have to be married to young boys who marry for the first time and vice versa. The local administration often interferes with the social affairs of the Great Andamanese and the Onges in matters like marriage, divorce and marriage with outsiders. The respective tribal societies have been divided into haves and have-nots on the basis of income and political facilities. The tribesmen have now been able to own individual property rights. One man rule has been started in place of the traditional Elder Council. Elders have mostly lost their age-old social status and powers.

Women are feeling themselves somewhat helpless and they are often exploited, physically and mentally, by the unscrupulous outsiders. Financial misery has forced the women of the Great Andamanese tribal society to have sex-relations with outsiders which resulted in various deseases. Youths are not ready to render help to the old by providing them with food and protection. Once socially coherent and unified tribal people are now suffering from distrust and disintegration in their family as well as in their society. The new hierarchial system in the society exists on an evolving economic and socio-political infrastructure.

For better administration and development of political consciousness among the tribals, a new model of leadership and politics has been imparted by the government instead of the simple and informal democratic system which the tribals had for centuries. They have recently been given voting rights for democratisation and modernisation of their political life. The new political system, however, has divided the tribal people into two opposite poles. The people of the old camp are trying to perpetuate their old socio-political systems. Groupism has developed in their society in connection with the selection of the leaders of the society. So proper democratic norms are not being practised in connection with the selection, operation and perpetuation of the emerging community leadership. Power has still been centralised in the hands of the local administration. Though the.tribals have been given democratic rights, they are not able to develop their sense or awareness of the significance of exercising votes, eagerness to know the results of elections, participation in election propaganda, election meetings, election procession, slogans etc. The democratic role of the mass-media is not yet fully exposed to them. Moreover, they have no ideas about election symbols and any general idea of the Indian party system and politics, that is, the pattern of the national mainstream. They have not obtained modern political education either from their community leaders or from the party leaders outside. On the contrary, they seem to apprehend that in the name of encouraging modern politics and administration, the governmental authorities are exposing them to exotic influences which they do not like. They have often expressed their discontentment on the present political system that is evolving.

With the infiltration of the outsiders, the eco-cultural atmosphere of the two groups of tribesmen has altered slowly. They are being constantly pushed out from their original areas of movement. The new environment is not only threatening their biological survival, but also forcing them to face cultural disintegration and even an identity-crisis. They have been delinked from their forest life and from their old culture which was forest-based culture. New accommodations and hutments have developed an atmosphere that is not helping them to continue to practise their traditional cultural pursuits—rituals, rites, customs, festivals, group dances, songs and public gatherings. They are about to forget their traditional craftmanship concerning the making of huts, bows, arrows, sea-shell, products, bark-fabrics, ornaments, nets, harpoons, adze, baskets, buckets and canoes. These were the symbols of their indigenous cultural heritage.

Although the new generation in the Great Andamanese and the Onges seem to be averse to their traditional cultural activities due to the change of the cultural landscape, the old are still unable to adjust themselves to the new environment and culture. Moreover, it has been revealed that the new patterns of shelter, occupations, dress, religion, which appears to be alien to them, are not being gladly accepted by the new as well as old generations. Gradually, they are forgetting their own tribal songs and dances and other cultural activities. The role of the mother tongue among the Great Andamanese is very weak. They are caught by the Hindu and Buddhist cultural mores of the mainstream including the religious activities and festivals.

The Government should be cautious enough to understand that cultural planning of the Great Andamanese and the Onges, or of any ethnic group for that matter, must not make them lose what has been the best in the traditional folk culture of these people. These should be encouraged for sustenance even as the process of Modernisation to follow.

Bibliography

Andaman Adim Janjati Vikas Samiti (AAJVS), *Retrieval From Precipice,* Andaman and Nicobar Administration, Port Blair, 1977.

Andaman and Nicobar Administration, *Annual General Administrative Report,* Port Blair, 1973.

Andaman and Nicobar Administration, *The Andaman and Nicobar Information,* Port Blair, 1976.

Andaman and Nicobar Administration, *Basic Statistics 1985,* Statistical Bureau, Port Blair, 1985.

Andaman and Nicobar Administration, *Basic Statistics 1989,* Statistical Bureau, Port Blair, 1989.

Andaman and Nicobar Administration, *Tribal Sub-Plan;* Sixth Five Year Plan 1980-85, Port Blair, 1980.

Andaman and Nicobar Administration, *Tribal Sub-Plan; Seventh Five Year Plan 1985-90,* Port Blair, 1985

Appteker, Herbert, *The Nature of Democracy, Freedom and Revolution,* National Book Agency, Calcutta, 1974.

Aron, Raymond, *Main Currents in Sociological Thought,* Penguin Books, Harmondsworth, 1969.

Arya, Prem Chand, and Gireesh B. Mathur (ed), "Tribal Development Through Bharatiya Adimjati Sevak Sangh" in *Tribal Souvenir,* New Delhi.

Awaradi, S.A., *Master Plan (1990; 2020) For Welfare of Primitive tribes,* Directorate of Tribal Welfare, Port Blair (Cyclostyled paper) 1989.

Basu, Badal K., *The Onge* (ed.) by K.S. Singh, Seagull Books, Calcutta, 1990.

Cappieri, Mario, *Andamanese: Cultural Elements—Elements of Demongenetics Physical Anthropology and Raciology,* (ed.) by Henry Field, Miami, Field Research Projects, 1974.

Census of India 1901, *Andaman and Nicobar Islands,* 3 vol. Government Printing, Calcutta, India, 1903.

Census of India 1911, *Andaman and Nicobar Islands,* 2 vol. Government Printing, Calcutta, India, 1912.

Census of India 1921, *Andaman and Nicobar Islands.* 2 vol. Government Printing, Delhi, India, 1923.

Census of India 1931, *Andaman and Nicobar Islands,* 2 vol. Central Publication, Delhi, India, 1932.

Census of India 1941, *Andaman and Nicobar Islands,* Manager of Publication, Delhi, 1955.

Census of India 1951, *Andaman and Nicobar Islands,* Manager of Publications, Delhi, 1965.

Census of India 1961, *Andaman and Nicobar Islands,* Director of Census Operation, New Delhi, 1978.

Census of India 1971, *Andaman and Nicobar Islands,* Director of Census Operation, New Delhi, 1985.

Chakraborty, D.K., *The Great Andamanese* (ed.) by K.S. Singh, Seagull Books, Calcutta, 1990.

Chakraborty, D.K., *The Great Andamanese: A Study of Persistence of Culture in the face of Biological Extinction—A Preliminary Report.* (Unpublished), An.S.I., Port Blair, 1974.

Chakraborty, D.K., *The Great Andamanese of Strait Island,* An.S.I., Port Blair, 1975 (Unpublished).

Chanda, Sudhendu, "Economic structure of a Nicobarese Village: In Chowra Island", in *Indian Journal of Social Work,* vol. 32 (l), 1971.

Chanda, Sudhendu, "The Socio-economic and political structure of Car-NIcobar", in *Khadigramodyog*, vol. 16(9), 1970.

Chengappa, B.S., "(The) Andaman Forest and their Development", in Census of India 1951, *Andaman and Nicobar Islands* (ed.) by A.K. Ghosh, Manager Publication Delhi, 1955, Appendix C.

Chengappa, B.S., "On the Shompen of Great Nicobar", in Census of India 1951; *Andaman and Nicobar Islands*, (ed.) by A.K. Ghosh, Manager of Publication, Delhi, 1955, Appendix F.

Cipriani, Lidio, "On the Origin of the Andamanese", in Census of India 1951; *Andaman and Nicobar Islands*, (ed.) by A.K. Ghosh, Manager Publication, Delhi, 1955, Appendix E.

Cipriani, Lidio, *The Andaman Islanders*, Weidenfold and Nicolsòn, London, 1966.

Danda, G. Depali, "Little Andaman and The Onges", in *Human Science*, vol. 36 (1); 1987.

Danda, G. Depali, and Sumit Mukherji, "A Study on Onge Population", in *Journal of Indian Anthropological Society*, Vol. 24(I), Calcutta, 1989.

Das, Hari Hara and Rabindra Nath Rath, *The Land of the Coral Beds : Andaman and Nicobar Islands*, Berhampur, Orissa, 1988.

Das, Nityananda, "The Safeguards for Tribal: Past and Present", in *Adibasi*, Vol. 8(2), Tribal Research Bureau, Bhubaneswar, Orissa, 1966-67.

De, D.C., "A Demographic study of the Onges of Little Andaman" in *Bulletin of Department of Anthropology*, vol. 19(2), 1970.

Department of Social Welfare, *Report of the Study team on the Negrito Tribes of the Andaman*, An.S.I., Government of India, (unpublished), Port Blair, 1969.

Dhebar, U.N., *Scheduled Areas and Scheduled Tribes Commission Report, 1960-61*, Government of India, Ministry of Tribal Welfare, New Delhi, 1961.

Dobson, G.E., "On the Andaman and the Andamanese", in *Journal of the Anthropological Institute of Great Britain and Ireland,* Vol. 4(4), 1875.

Downs, James F., *Cultures in Crisis,* Glencoe Press: Beverly Hills, California, 1971.

Eisentadt, S.N., *Modernisation: Protest and Change,* Prentice-Hall of India Pvt. Ltd. New Delhi, 1969.

Eisentadt, S.N., *Tradition, Change and Modernity,* John Wiley and Sons, New York, 1973.

Elwin, Verrier, *A Philosophy for NEFA,* North Eastern Frontier Agency, Shillong, 1959.

Freud, Sigmond, *The Origins of Religion: Totem and Taboo Moses and Monotheism and Other Works,* Penguin Books, London, 1985.

Fuchs, Stephen, *Aboriginal Tribes of India,* Macmillan Company, Delhi, 1973.

Gupta, S.K., "The Andaman and Nicobar Islands", in Census of India, 1951, *Andaman and Nicobar Islands,* (ed.) by A.K. Ghosh, Manager Publication, Delhi, 1955.

Hobhouse, L.T., *Social Evolution and Political Theory,* Columbia University Press, New York, 1928.

India-Constitution, *The Constitution of India,* Ministry of Law and Justice, New Delhi, 1973.

Justin, Austice, *The Nicobarese* (ed.) by K.S. Singh, Seagull Books, Calcutta, 1990.

Kochar, V.K., "The Great Andamanese today", in *Man in India,* Vol.49(3). 1969.

Krishna, R. Shyamji, "Survival of the weakest, Symposium: Island Culture", on Post Plenary Session International Congress of Anthropological and Ethnological Science, Port Blair, 1978.

Krishnatry, S.M., "Report on the work done and achievements", in *Journal of Social Research,* vol. 19(2), 1976.

Lenin, V.I., *State and Revolution,* Burman Publishing House, Calcutta, 1917.

Majumder, Deptosh, "Arunachal Worried over disharmony among tribals" in *The Statesman,* Calcutta, March 20, 1991.

Majumder, R.C., *Penal Settlement in the Andaman,* Ministry of Education and Social Welfare, Delhi, 1975.

Man, E.H., *The Aboriginal Inhabitants of the Andaman,* Royal Anthropological Institute, London, 1902.

Man, R.S., *Bay Islanders,* Institute of Social Research and Applied Anthropology. Simla.

Marx, Karl and Frederick Engels, *Communist Manifesto* (ed.) by D. Razianoff, Burman Publishing House, Calcutta, 1944. (First Indian Edition).

Mathur, K.K., *Nicobar Islands,* National Book Trust, New Delhi 1967.

Mathur, L.P., *History of the Andaman and Nicobar Islands,* Sterling Publishers, New Delhi, 1968.

Mookerjea, Sobhanlal, *The Political Philosophy of John Stuart Mill,* S. Gupta & Brothers, Calcutta, 1966.

Mookerjea, Sobhanlal, "Synthesis: The Keynote to Tagorean Culture", in *Visvabharati Quarterly,* September-December 1961.

Mouat F.T. , *Adventures and Research Among the Andaman Islanders,* Hurst and Blackott, London, 1863.

Northrop, F.S.C., *Social Structure,* The Macmillan Company, New York, 1949.

National Institute of Community Development, *Tribal Development and Administration,* Hyderabad, 1974.

Nehru Jawaharlal, "Conference of Tribes and Scheduled Areas, 1952", in *Vanyajati,* Vol. 12(3), 1964.

Pandit, T.N, "On the plurality of Culture", in *American Sociological Review,* vol. 4, 1939.

Pandit, T.N., "Economy of the Onges", in *Economics of the Tribes and their Transformation* (ed.) by K.S. Singh, Concept Publication, New Delhi, 1982.

Pandit, T.N., "The Tribal and the Non-Tribal in Andaman Islands: A Historical Perspective", in *Journal of Indian*

Anthropological Society, Vol. 20(l), 1985, Calcutta.

Pandit, T.N., "The Original Inhabitants of the Andaman and Nicobar Islands", in *Yojana* (August), Planning Commission, New Delhi, 1976.

Pandit, T.N., *Tribal Policy in Andaman and Nicobar Impact on Nehru's Philosophy* (Unpublished), An.S.I., Port Blair, 1990.

Patnaik, N., "Reading on Tribal Development Administration", in Tribal Sub-Plan, 1978, New Delhi, 1982.

Radcliffe-Brown, A.R., *The Andaman Islanders,* Glencoe, Illionis: Free Press, 1922.

Robson, W.A., *Welfare State and Welfare Society: Illusion and Reality,* George Allen and Unwin, London, 1976.

Sachchidananda, "Social Structure, Status and Mobility Patterns: The Case of Tribal Women", in *Man in India,* vol. 58(l), 1978.

Saldanha, Cecil J., *Andaman, Nicobar and Lakshadweep: An Environmental Impact Assessment,* Oxford and IBH Publishing Co. Ltd., New Delhi, 1989.

Sarkar, S.S., "The Origin and Migration of the Negritos", in *Man in India,* Vol. 33(2), 1953.

Sen, P.K., *Land and Peoples of Andaman,* The Post Graduate Book Mart, Calcutta, 1962.

Service, Elman R., "The Andaman Islanders", in *Island Culture of India,* (ed.) by G. Prakash Reddy and V. Sudarshan, 1989.

Sharma, B.D., "An Approach to the Development of Onges of Little Andaman", in *Journal of Social Research,* Vol. 19(2) 1976.

Shyamchaudhuri, N.K., *Territorial Arrangement, Traditions and Village Organisation in Car Nicobar Islands,* An.S.I., Calcutta, 1957.

Singh, K.S. (ed.), "A note on the series", in quoted from the book, *The Great Andamanese* by, D.K. Chakraborty, Seagull Books, Calcutta, 1990.

Singh, Yogendra, *Essays on Modernization in India*, Manohar Book Service, New Delhi, 1978.

Sorokin, Pitirim, *Social and Cultural Dynamics, A Study of Change in Major Systems of Art, Truth, Ethnics, Law and Social Relationships*, (abridged in one volume), Peter Owen Ltd., London, 1959.

Spencer, Herbert, *Man Versus the State Principles of Social Static*, William and Norgate, London, 1885.

Srinivas, M.N., *Caste in Modern India and Other Essays*, Asia Publishing House, Calcutta, 1962.

Temple, R.C., Census of India 1901, *Andaman and Nicobar Islands*, Government Printing, Calcutta, 1903.

Titmuss, Richard Morris, *Essays on the Welfare State*, George Allen and Unwin, London, 1958.

Toynbee, Arnold Joseph, *Civilizations on Trial*, Oxford University Press, New york, 1948.

Venkatesan, D., "Innovations and their impact on The Onge of Little Andaman", in *Man in India*, vol. 68(4), 1988.

Verma, Ishwar C., "Health Problems of Tribal Communities in Andaman and Nicobar Islands", in *Journal of Social Research* vol. 19(2), 1976.

Verma, R.C., *Indian Tribals Through The Age*, Publication Divisions, Ministry of Information and Broadcasting, Government of India, New Delhi, 1990.

Vidyarathi, L.P., "Development plans of the Tribes of Andaman and Nicobar Islands: An Action Oriented Report", in *Journal of Social Research*, Vol. 19(2), 1976.

Vidyarathi, L.P. and B.K. Rai, *Tribal Culture of India*, Concept Publishing Company, Delhi, 1977.

Whitehead, G., *In the Nicobar Island*, Seelay Service and Co., London, 1924.

Whitakar, Ramulus, "Endangered Andamans", in Environmental Services Group World Wildlife Fund India and MBA, Deptt. of Environment, New Delhi, 1985.

Winick, Charles, *Dictionary of Anthropology*, Littlefield Adams and Co., Iowa, New Jersey, 1970.

PERSONS INTERVIEWED Arranged in alphabetical order

Awaradi, S.A. Executive Secretary, Andaman Adim Janjati Vikas Samiti, Port Blair, 1990.

Dutta, Amit: Medical Officer. Dispensary, Dugong Creek, Little Andaman, 1990.

(Md.) Hamid : Pharmacist, Dispensary, Strait Island, Andaman, 1990.

(Mr.) Kota: Raja or Chief of the Great Andamanese, Strait Island, 1990.

Lakra, Habil : Social Worker-cum-settlement-in-Charge, Strait Island, Andaman, 1990.

(Mr.) Mohan: Constable, Police Department, Andaman and Nicobar Islands, belongs to Onge Community, Dugong Creek, Little Andaman, 1990.

(Mr.) Nabekutti: Ex-Raja and ex-Member of Pradesh Council, Andaman and Nicobar Islands, 1990.

(Mr.) Nao (Sr.): Senior member, among the Great Andamanese, Strait Island, Andaman, 1990.

(Mrs.) Nau : Teacher, Balwadi Centre, Strait Island, Andaman, 1990.

Pillai, Jaganath : Social Worker-cum-plantation-in-Charge, South Bay, Little Andaman, 1990.

Mr. Ramesh : Helper, Marin Department, belongs to Onge community, Port Blair, 1990.

Sarkar, Deepak: Teacher, Education Department, Ex-in-charge of the Onges, Little Andaman, 1990.

Singh, Balvir: Plantation-in-Charge, Dugong Creek, Little Andaman, 1990.

(Mr.) Tambolai: Raja and Member of Pradesh Council, Andaman and Nicobar Islands, Onge Community, South Bay, Little Andaman, 1990.

Thomas, John : Engine Driver, Power House, Strait Island, Andaman, 1990.

Toppo, Kanchan: Social Worker-cum-settlement-in-Charge, Dugong Creek, Little Andaman, 1990.

Index